NEW STUDIES IN BIBLICAL THEOLOGY

PIERCING LEVIATHAN

NEW STUDIES IN BIBLICAL THEOLOGY 56

Series editor: D. A. Carson

PIERCING LEVIATHAN

God's defeat of evil in the book of Job

Eric Ortlund

APOLLOS

Academic
An imprint of InterVarsity Press
Downers Grove, Illinois

APOLLOS (an imprint of Inter-Varsity Press)
36 Causton Street
London SW1P 4ST, England
ivpbooks.com
ivp@ivpbooks.com

InterVarsity Press, USA
P.O. Box 1400
Downers Grove, IL 60515, USA
ivpress.com
email@ivpress.com

InterVarsity Press® is the book-publishing division of InterVarsity Christian Fellowship/USA®, a movement
of students and faculty active on campus at hundreds of universities, colleges, and schools of nursing in the
United States of America, and a member movement of the International Fellowship of Evangelical Students.
For information about local and regional activities, visit intervarsity.org.

Inter-Varsity Press, England, originated within the Inter-Varsity Fellowship, now the Universities and
Colleges Christian Fellowship, a student movement connecting Christian Unions in universities and colleges
throughout Great Britain, and a member movement of the International Fellowship of Evangelical Students.
That historic association is maintained, and all senior IVP staff and committee members subscribe to the
UCCF Basis of Faith. Website: www.uccf.org.uk.

First published 2021

Typeset in Great Britain by CRB Associates, Potterhanworth, Lincolnshire

USA ISBN 978-1-5140-0337-4 (print)
USA ISBN 978-1-5140-0338-1 (digital)
UK ISBN 978-1-78974-298-5 (print)
UK ISBN 978-1-78974-299-2 (digital)

Printed in the United States of America ∞

InterVarsity Press is committed to ecological stewardship and to the conservation of natural resources in all
our operations. This book was printed using sustainably sourced paper.

British Library Cataloguing-in-Publication Data

A catalogue record for this book is available from the British Library.

Library of Congress Cataloging-in-Publication Data

A catalog record for this book is available from the Library of Congress.

P	22	21	20	19	18	17	16	15	14	13	12	11	10	9	8	7	6	5	4	3	2
Y	39	38	37	36	35	34	33	32	31	30	29	28	27	26	25	24	23	22	21

This book is dedicated with profound gratitude to
my father, Ray Ortlund, Old Testament scholar
and faithful pastor, who has taught me
more than he knows and means more
to me than I can say

Contents

Series preface

New Studies in Biblical Theology is a series of monographs that address key issues in the discipline of biblical theology. Contributions to the series focus on one or more of three areas: (1) the nature and status of biblical theology, including its relations with other disciplines (e.g. historical theology, exegesis, systematic theology, historical criticism, narrative theology); (2) the articulation and exposition of the structure of thought of a particular biblical writer or corpus; and (3) the delineation of a biblical theme across all or part of the biblical corpora.

Above all, these monographs are creative attempts to help thinking Christians understand their Bibles better. The series aims simultaneously to instruct and to edify, to interact with the current literature and to point the way ahead. In God's universe mind and heart should not be divorced: in this series we will try not to separate what God has joined together. While the notes interact with the best of scholarly literature, the text is uncluttered with untransliterated Greek and Hebrew, and tries to avoid too much technical jargon. The volumes are written within the framework of confessional evangelicalism, but there is always an attempt at thoughtful engagement with the sweep of the relevant literature.

Recent years have witnessed a plethora of studies on Job, but none of them is quite like this one. Most make much of God's apparent refusal to address Job's questions directly: on this reading, God wants us to trust the One who cast Orion into the heavens, who controls the treasures of the snow, who made the crocodile. God is to be trusted because he is incomparably greater than we are. But Eric Ortlund argues that this interpretation of the book misreads too many passages. Probing carefully such features as the double speeches of God, the differences between Job's first and second responses to God's speeches, and the meaning of Leviathan, he argues persuasively that the book of Job is not as open-ended as many have thought, but offers a firm foundation for Job's ultimate response.

D. A. Carson
Trinity Evangelical Divinity School

Author's preface

When the Lord graciously opened a teaching position for me after I finished my doctorate, my exposure to wisdom literature was basically zero. My schedule at Briercrest College and Seminary had me teaching wisdom literature every year, however, and sometimes more than once. It was a bit of a scramble to familiarize myself with that part of the canon! I expected to enjoy it and did. What I did not expect was the profound pastoral relevance of Proverbs, Job and Ecclesiastes. I was especially struck by the way Proverbs relentlessly probes sins of the tongue and unwise speech (a terrible problem for the church in North America), and how Ecclesiastes disassociates the value of our work from visible results (which are all too soon erased), but affirms the value of our earthly lives as gifts from God.

Job, too, turned out to be deeply relevant, but for a sadder reason: Job's story is so common. There are many Christians for whom God allows some terrible suffering that seems to have nothing to do with any sin, past or present, nor anything to do with their growth in Christ. A sense of confusion only deepens the pain: Why is God doing this? Is he angry with me? Have I misunderstood something he wanted me to do? Or . . . was I wrong about God? Is he not the person I thought he was? As we will see, these are all Job's questions; but they inevitably occur to Christians suffering inexplicably, whether they have read the book or not.

A second discovery followed the first: the book of Job enjoys (in my opinion, and for the present moment, at least) fewer helpful and insightful commentaries than Proverbs and Ecclesiastes do. A preface is not the place for a long bibliography, but my sense is that Proverbs and Ecclesiastes have superb expositions at both scholarly and practical levels.[1] But while many modern commentaries on Job exist, there are fewer I feel comfortable recommending without qualification.[2] Some are simply

---

[1] For Proverbs, pride of place goes to Waltke 2004, 2005 and Fox 2000, 2009; for Ecclesiastes, Fox 1999 and Seow 1997 are superb. Gibson 2016 is easily the best practical Christian exposition of Ecclesiastes I have ever read.

[2] Ash (2014) and Hartley (1988) distinguish themselves as especially worth reading, however.

unconvincing; some even heretical. Modern interpretation of YHWH's speeches to Job is all over the map in an especially unhelpful way. This book is humbly offered as an attempt to help fill this gap. It aims at an exegetically responsible and theologically orthodox reading of the book, constantly remembering those readers who, like Job, want to remain faithful to the Lord Jesus in suffering, if only they knew where they could find him (Job 23:3).

This book had its genesis in an upper-level seminar on Job taught at Briercrest in the autumn of 2012. I am deeply grateful to the hard-working and sincere students who journeyed with me through the book – especially as the class was held from 4 pm to 6 pm, the only time my schedule would allow. (Imagine having to tackle Job on an empty stomach!) I am also indebted to many students and colleagues, both at Briercrest and at Oak Hill (where I teach), for helping me understand Job better. There are too many to mention them all, but I am grateful for each one. I am also extremely grateful to Don Carson for accepting this into the NSBT series and for his insights and encouragement along the way. Philip Duce deserves thanks for his help and encouragement as he worked with me on the manuscript. Sincerest thanks are also due to my copy editor (and, I trust, new friend), Eldo Barkhuizen, whose tireless and cheerful efforts in getting the manuscript ready to publish are deeply appreciated. Finally, I am deeply grateful to my dear wife, Erin, who proofread the manuscript and saved me from many embarrassing mistakes: thank you, dear one.

May God use this book to nourish joyful courage and patient endurance in suffering until the Lord Jesus returns, and, like Job, all of God's saints can say, 'Now our eye sees you.'

Eric Ortlund

Abbreviations

AB	Anchor Bible
ALASPM	Abhandlungen zur Literatur Alt-Syrien-Palästinas und Mesopotamiens
ANE	Ancient Near East(ern)
ANEP	James Pritchard, *The Ancient Near East: An Anthology of Texts and Pictures*, Princeton: Princeton University Press, 1969
ANET	*Ancient Near Eastern Texts Relating to the Old Testament*, ed. James Pritchard, 3rd edn, Princeton: Princeton University Press, 1969
ATANT	Abhandlungen zur Theologie des Alten und Neuen Testaments
BCOTWP	Baker Commentary on the Old Testament Wisdom and Psalms
BDB	Francis Brown, S. R. Driver and Charles Briggs, *A Hebrew and English Lexicon of the Old Testament*, Peabody: Hendrickson, 1996
BETL	Bibliotheca ephemeridum theologicarum lovaniensium
BHS	*Biblia Hebraica Stuttgartensia*, ed. K. Elliger and W. Rudolph, Stuttgart: Deutsche Bibelgesellschaft, 1983
Bib	*Biblica*
BibInt	*Biblical Interpretation*
BSac	*Bibliotheca sacra*
BZAW	Beihefte zur Zeitschrift für die alttestamentliche Wissenschaft
CAT	Commentaire de l'Ancien Testament
CBQ	*Catholic Biblical Quarterly*
ConBNT	Coniectanea biblica: New Testament Series
COS	*The Context of Scripture: Canonical Compositions, Monumental Inscriptions and Archival Documents from the Biblical World*, ed. William Hallo and K. Lawson Younger, Leiden: Brill, 2003

DOTWPW	*Dictionary of Old Testament: Wisdom, Poetry and Writings*, ed. Tremper Longman and Peter Enns, Downers Grove: IVP Academic, 2008
ESV	English Standard Version
ExAud	*Ex auditu*
GKC	Wilhelm Gesenius and E. Kautzsch, *Gesenius' Hebrew Grammar*, Oxford: Clarendon, 1910
GUS	Gorgias Ugaritic Studies
HALOT	Ludwig Koehler and Walter Baumgartner, *The Hebrew and Aramaic Lexicon of the Old Testament*, Leiden: Brill, 2001
HBT	*Horizons in Biblical Theology*
Int	*Interpretation*
JAOS	*Journal of the American Oriental Society*
JBL	*Journal of Biblical Literature*
J-M	Paul Joüon and Takamitsu Muraoka, *A Grammar of Biblical Hebrew*, 2nd edn, SubBi 27, Rome: Pontifical Biblical Institute, 2013
JNSL	*Journal of Northwest Semitic Languages*
JSOT	*Journal for the Study of the Old Testament*
JSOTSup	Journal for the Study of the Old Testament: Supplement Series
JTI	*Journal of Theological Interpretation*
km	kilometres
KTU	*Keilalphabetische Texte aus Ugarit*, ed. Manfried Dietrich, Oswald Loretz and Joaquin Sanmartin, Münster: Ugarit-Verlag, 1995
LXX	Septuagint
mi	miles
MT	Masoretic Text
NABC	New American Bible Commentary
NAC	New American Commentary
NCB	New Century Bible
NDBT	*New Dictionary of Biblical Theology*, ed. T. Desmond Alexander et al., Leicester: Inter-Varsity Press; Downers Grove: InterVarsity Press, 2000
NIB	*The New Interpreter's Bible*, ed. L. Keck, 10 vols., Nashville: Abingdon, 1996

Abbreviations

NICOT	New International Commentary on the Old Testament
NIDOTTE	*New International Dictionary of Old Testament Theology and Exegesis*, ed. Willem VanGemeren, 5 vols., Grand Rapids: Zondervan, 1996
NIV	New International Version
NIVAC	New International Version Application Commentary
NSBT	New Studies in Biblical Theology
NT	New Testament
OT	Old Testament
OTL	Old Testament Literature
PRSt	*Perspectives in Religious Studies*
RB	*Revue biblique*
SBL	Studies in Biblical Literature
SHBC	Smyth & Helwys Bible Commentary
SOTBT	Studies in Old Testament Biblical Theology
SubBi	Subsidia biblica
THC	Two Horizons Commentary
Them	*Themelios*
ThTo	*Theology Today*
TJ	*Trinity Journal*
TOTC	Tyndale Old Testament Commentary
tr.	translation, translated
TynBul	*Tyndale Bulletin*
VT	*Vetus Testamentum*
WBC	Word Biblical Commentary
WMANT	Wissenschaftliche Monographien zum Alten and Neuen Testament
WOC	Bruce Waltke and Michael O'Connor, *An Introduction to Biblical Hebrew Syntax*, Winona Lake: Eisenbrauns, 1990
WTJ	*Westminster Theological Journal*
ZAW	*Zeitschrift für die alttestamentliche Wissenschaft*

1

Introduction and statement of the problem

How one understands the book of Job as a whole essentially depends on how one understands God's speech(es).[1]

The significance of the Leviathan pericope can scarcely be overstated. It is both the climax and the epitome of what God has to say to Job.[2]

The whirlwind speeches, more than any other section of the book, appear in the diverse literature written about them like a readerly Rorschach test.[3]

The problems of the book of Job

Job easily qualifies as one of the most difficult books in the entire canon of Scripture, but the difficulties the book generates are of different kinds. It can be morally troubling for some readers, for instance, to watch YHWH allow the death of Job's children in the opening chapters of the book to test whether Job loves God or only the gifts God gives (see 1:9). Some cynically question whether the death of Job's children is a price worth paying for the Almighty to win a bet with the devil. A different problem meets the reader in the debate between Job and his friends in chapters 3–37, for the simple and straightforward style of the narrative changes to poetry that is very complex and frequently difficult to understand.

---

[1] Rendtorff 1986: 252.
[2] Newsom 2003: 250.
[3] Greenstein 1999: 302.

Fortunately, the basic trajectory of the debate is clear: while the friends consistently preserve God's justice by insisting that Job deserves to suffer as punishment for unconfessed sin, Job accuses God of injustice because God has punished him as a sinner when God knows Job is innocent; at the same time, however, Job refuses to curse God and longs to reconcile with him. Despite this clarity about the general outline of the debate, however, these chapters contain many thorny exegetical, textual and philological questions, and a number of short passages are difficult to make sense of at all.

When YHWH speaks to Job in chapters 38–41, the reader breathes a sigh of relief: finally, after a repetitive and seemingly interminable debate, God himself will settle the matter. But YHWH's two speeches in 38:1 – 40:2 and 40:6 – 41:34 do not obviously directly address the question animating the debate between Job and the friends. In the first speech, God takes Job on a tour of creation and its different animal inhabitants – but does not say anything explicit about Job's suffering or his protest against the God who allowed it. And why do Behemoth and Leviathan take up so much space in the second speech? If these two creatures are, as commonly understood, a hippopotamus and a crocodile, in what possible sense is this a satisfying answer to Job? Bernard Shaw was being sarcastic, but it is hard not to agree with him when he writes, 'If I complain that I am suffering unjustly, it is no answer to say, "Can you make a hippopotamus?"'[4] But one's perplexity only deepens when we read of Job's response to YHWH's second speech and realize how different it is from his reaction to God's first speech: while Job's first response in 40:3–5 is submissive, it seems somewhat cold and formal in comparison to his unrestrained worship as Job despises himself and says, 'Now my eye sees you!'[5] It is also confusing that YHWH says almost nothing directly about himself in chapters 38–41, but Job responds by claiming better insight, not into Behemoth and Leviathan, but into God himself. What inferences has Job drawn from the complex poetry of chapters 38–41 that prompt such a change? What breakthrough into YHWH's character and action has Job gained that transforms his unrelenting criticism of God into awestruck worship? Other questions follow from these: If Behemoth and Leviathan are just two more ordinary

---

[4] Quoted in Walton 2012: 397.
[5] Translations are taken from the ESV unless otherwise noted. The exact meaning of Job's speech in ch. 42, especially with regard to v. 6, is debated. What is said above anticipates the interpretation argued for at the beginning of the fifth chapter of this book.

animals, how is YHWH's second speech any different from the first, which already described many of the animals in God's world? And how does describing the physical characteristics of a hippo and crocodile satisfy the initial statement of the theme of the second speech as having to do with God's justice (40:8)? It is difficult for modern Western readers to avoid a sense of anticlimax in reading the book of Job, just when we most expect a satisfying resolution.

The difficulties of the ending of the book of Job have significant repercussions for understanding the book as a whole and, in turn, can significantly influence how we think about God's rule over all things in the Old Testament and the continuing presence of suffering and evil. Some scholars go so far as to interpret Job as an 'anti-theodicy' in the sense that they understand the book of Job not merely as an ambiguous or unsatisfying answer to the problem of evil, but as demonstrating that God is unjust.[6] If this is the case, of course, the most dramatic and pointed discussion of inexplicable suffering in the Bible turns out to have nothing helpful to say about the problem of evil – the book demonstrates rather that there is no answer to the problem. If true, this would have some very sinister implications for how we think about God.

This book will not address all the difficulties of the book of Job summarized above, or the many other questions readers have had over the years (Is Elihu's counsel helpful to Job or not? Why is Job's wife not mentioned at the end of the story? etc.). With regard to the difficult poetry of chapters 3–37, a number of commentaries give helpful guidance on technical text-critical, philological and exegetical problems in the poetry of Job.[7] Furthermore, although chapters 1–2 remain uncomfortable to read, we quickly learn in those chapters why God occasionally allows his saints to experience horrendous suffering: it is the only way to prove the reality of the relationship, to prove that Job really loves God for God's sake, and is not merely deceptively flattering God in order to have a nice life. In an important sense, Job 1 – 2 is about the all-surpassing worth of knowing YHWH, a worth surpassing even the value of knowing one's children. In contrast to this, however, the problem of the interpretation

---

[6] James Crenshaw and Edward Greenstein argue most strongly for this conclusion; their various works will be discussed at multiple points in this book.

[7] Seow 2013 and Clines 1989, 2011 deserve pride of place on this score.

of YHWH's speeches is one that has continued to bedevil modern commentators and forms the focus of this book. Many commentaries follow the course of the debate in chapters 3–37 in generally the same way (regardless of those very difficult passages), but when it comes to YHWH's two speeches, widely differing and incompatible interpretations are given, most of which are exegetically and theologically unsatisfying because they cannot explain how the descriptions of Behemoth and Leviathan count as a defence of God's justice (40:8), nor how this defence moves Job from defiant criticism to abject worship. The present volume attempts to address this interpretative impasse by arguing that Behemoth and Leviathan are symbols of cosmic chaos and evil. It will be argued that YHWH is speaking to Job within Job's cultural framework, drawing upon symbols common in the ANE and the Old Testament, both in order to assure Job that God is more intimately acquainted with the magnitude and malignity of the evil at work in his world than Job ever could be, and to promise him that God will one day defeat it (41:7–8). Without explaining to Job why he allowed Job's ordeal and without offering an apology, God implicitly asks Job through the Leviathan speech to trust him in his way of running the world, allowing evil some real but limited agency – but not for ever. In this way, God defends the justice of his administration of creation (40:8), an administration that sometimes allows terrible suffering. And in response, Job worships.

In my opinion, the interpretation of Behemoth and Leviathan as symbols of cosmic evil has very significant exegetical and pastoral pay-offs, giving a satisfying resolution to the urgent issues raised in the book of Job and providing compelling reasons for joyful hope in the midst of unexplained suffering. This position is, however, mostly in the minority. Many commentaries and popular works, whether written from a confessional perspective or not, tend to assume the most natural and obvious way to understand the two creatures YHWH describes to Job at such length is as a hippopotamus and crocodile. Within this larger interpretative context, the present volume will present a 'minority report' on Behemoth and Leviathan according to the following plan. I begin with a chapter summarizing the larger background to Job's suffering in chapters 1–2 (of which Job is, in a tragic irony, totally unaware), as well as the debate between Job and his friends in chapters 3–37. This summary is necessary because YHWH's answer in chapters 38–41 is not a general or timeless defence of the policies by which he administers creation, but a specific response to the charges brought against him by Job in the debate. A third and fourth chapter will explore YHWH's first and second responses, respectively. Although God's speech in 38:1 – 40:2 is generally better understood than the second, it has generated some significantly diverse interpretations (some of which draw sinister conclusions about God) that will need to be explored. The fourth chapter will focus on YHWH's second speech in 40:6 – 41:34 and the varying interpretations of Behemoth and Leviathan, arguing for their status as symbols of supernatural chaos and evil. A fifth and final chapter will consider the significance of Job's response in 42:1–6 and his restoration in 42:7–17. Job 42 comes after the Leviathan speech, of course, and that speech is the main focus of this book. But it is in chapter 42 that the question of theodicy takes on especially sharp focus. As mentioned above, the book of Job is, for some commentators, not just an ambiguous answer to the problem of evil, but a negative one, in that it demonstrates that God is uncaring about unjust suffering. The divine speeches play an important role in these interpretations, of course, but a careful reading of Job's response to the divine speeches is especially significant for them as well. It will thus be necessary to engage with them in relation to Job 42 in order to appreciate fully what the book has to say about suffering, evil and faith in a God who allows them. This engagement will show that sceptical, 'anti-theodicy' readings of Job 42 fail exegetically at numerous points. This does not mean, however, that the book of Job should be reinstated as the Bible's prime example of theodicy. If theodicy is defined as a justification of God's tolerance and/or guidance of evil for his own purposes, or an explanation of what role evil and suffering have in God's good purposes, the book of Job counts as a theodicy only in a limited and somewhat ironic way. Only in the larger theatre of Job's ordeal in the divine council revealed in chapters 1–2 is the reader given an explanation of why God allows such unimaginable pain to overwhelm those who seem to deserve it least. Otherwise, God offers no explanation to Job about why his sufferings were allowed, nor does he seek to justify his decision to allow this pain to Job. As a result, even if it is impossible to read Job as an 'anti-theodicy', it is difficult to classify the book of Job as a theodicy in a straightforward way.

This may seem like a discouraging conclusion, and readers may worry at this early stage that the one book in the Bible most obviously addressing the problem of evil has little to say to God's people who want to remain faithful in the midst of pain. Surprising as it may sound, however, I believe the book of Job presents its readers with immense resources for cheerful and courageous endurance in the midst of unexplained suffering *without* counting as a theodicy in the strict sense. In fact, my sense is that if the book were to qualify more neatly as a theodicy in the sense of justifying or explaining God's ways to us, this would hamper the way in which it nurtures joy and courage in its readers. It will furthermore be argued that the way the book of Job goes about this is unique in the canon. Job does not in any way contradict other perspectives on suffering found elsewhere in the Bible, of course. But the book of Job does say something unique about them, and uniquely encouraging. The aim of this book is thus to explore this unique perspective with exegetical precision and with an eye to its rich pastoral implications. But we will have to work our way through the book methodically and slowly in order to gain this perspective. This is no easy task, for the book seems almost intentionally designed to tire and frustrate the reader. There is, however, no other way to access the joy and comfort Job receives at the end of his ordeal except to journey with him through each of the book's long chapters.

A word on myth

One does not have to read much in the literature on Job before one comes across the word 'myth'. As we explore the significance of the monsters Behemoth and Leviathan, it will be impossible to avoid this subject. In fact, the issue of mythic language meets us before reading about those creatures, for the poetry of the book often describes cosmic realities in symbolic language in ways that might suitably be called 'mythic'. One example of this is the way in which the wisdom poem of chapter 28 imaginatively reaches for the outermost reaches of reality (vv. 20–23); the more-than-natural darkness Job calls down on creation in his opening curse is another example (3:1–8). The problem is that the English terms 'myth' or 'mythical' often mean something obviously false or even silly. This makes them problematic to use in the study of an inspired biblical book. For this reason, I will avoid the term as much as possible. But because this book touches on subjects often described as 'mythic', a brief word or two about myth and its relation to the Bible is appropriate.

The most important thing to emphasize at the outset is that myth, in the best and most subtle meaning of the word, refers to symbolic narratives that address cosmic realities of chaos and order. In the ancient world, myth has to do with those deep, foundational realities and archetypal relations between heaven and earth that order human existence but are difficult to state directly and so are usually invoked in symbols.[8] According to this definition, the primeval garden in Eden, where the Man and the Woman walked with God and shared his immortality, which we lost because of our sin, and which God's covenant and temple in the Old Testament intend partially to reinstate, are 'mythic' not in the sense that they are unbelievable fictions, but because they pertain to those most basic and primal issues of human life and death, sin and atonement, alienation and homecoming, issues that evoke those deep longings only God can answer. In offering this best possible definition of myth, it should immediately be emphasized that ancient Semites did not think of mythic and historical reality as excluding each other, as modern English speakers tend to do. On the contrary, from an ancient Semitic perspective, the intervention of the gods and matters of cosmic chaos and order were thought to impinge on and affect real life and datable historical events. Any division between 'myth' and 'history' is a modern idea that would have been foreign to ancient writers – but just such a division used to be common in biblical studies, such that the literature of the ANE was placed firmly in the category of myth and the Old Testament described in contrast as history. There are, however, so many examples from ancient Mesopotamia and Egypt of historical events being described in mythic ways that this distinction is untenable and has largely been abandoned.[9] Ancient Semites simply did not think of myth and history in dichotomous ways. Furthermore, there are enough connections between the Old Testament and the literature of the surrounding cultures that it is reasonable to assume that biblical authors would not have made a strong disjunction between what we might dismiss as 'mythic' and what is real – 'mythic' here referring to cosmic

---

[8] A great deal more discussion could be offered here about myth in the ancient world and its presence in the Bible, how it is precisely to be defined and interpreted, and the history of scholarship on these questions; but since it would not greatly affect the interpretation of Behemoth and Leviathan in the book of Job to do so, the interested reader is referred to Ortlund 2010: 5–63 for more discussion, as well as the works cited below in n. 10.

[9] Albrektson 1967 is a classic text here, which occasioned a significant change in biblical studies in how the OT was positioned in relation to its cultural and religious environment.

action on God's part to establish order and beat back chaos and darkness, uncleanness and death.

All of this is to say that scholarly literature on myth uses the word in a very different sense from its meaning in colloquial English. Any number of studies show that 'myth' is a helpful category not for describing ideas or stories that are childish or impossible to believe, but for describing the way in which ancient peoples thought of and symbolically narrated the archetypal relations between heaven and earth – how the present order of things came about and how it is preserved and defended when threatened.[10] According to this definition, some aspects of the book of Job count as 'mythic', and not at all in the sense of being unhistorical, childish or ridiculous. As a result, describing parts of Job or the Old Testament as 'mythic' in no way casts any doubt on the absolute truthfulness and historical validity of God's Word.

To register these nuances about the term 'myth' is in no way to reduce the Bible to one more human religious production from the ANE or to imply it is no different from ancient pagan myths or idolatrous texts. In fact, study of the literature of the ANE reveals as many differences between it and the Old Testament as it does similarities. For example, although YHWH thunders in the heavens (Ps. 18:13) and makes the storm clouds his chariot (Ps. 104:3) just as Baal does, he also far transcends Baal's limitations, even defeating death (Isa. 25:6–9) – something Baal never accomplished.[11] Maarten Paul helpfully articulates a way in which to appreciate both the similarities and the differences between the Old Testament and ANE myths when he writes that

[w]hile in the OT monotheism is incompatible with the belief that the dragon and the sea were gods, it is compatible with the view

---

[10] The best scholarly discussions of myth and its relation to the Bible are found in Doty 1986, Forsyth 1987, Fishbane 2003 and Csapo 2005. It is not necessary for the present argument to go into more depth on this subject, except to state that I will use the terms 'chaos' and 'evil' in roughly synonymous ways even though they are technically distinct, e.g. the darkness and water in Gen. 1:2 are not bad, but are just unorganized and unfruitful (chaotic). Equating chaos and evil in a discussion of the book of Job is appropriate and helpful, however, for the unjust suffering Job undergoes and the God he thinks caused it are often described in chaotic ways (e.g. 7:12; 9:5–10). In other words, the book of Job frequently associates moral evil and cosmic chaos.

[11] In the fifth and sixth tablets of the Baal Epic, Baal and Mot (Death) fight to a stalemate until Sapsh (the sun god) intervenes and convinces Mot to yield under threat of the loss of his kingdom. Baal the storm god, who brings life, never decisively defeats death – in stark contrast to YHWH. See COS 1.86, pp. 265–273, for translation of this part of the Baal Epic.

that they represent demonic forces, which often appear portrayed in animal form in the ancient world.[12]

This is a point worth remembering.

But this discussion, although perhaps conceptually useful, may pose some danger of presenting as lifeless and abstract what ancient Israelites would have found deeply moving. When our biblical forebears heard of YHWH's roaring (roaring!) from Zion, so that the very heavens and earth shake (Joel 3:16), or when they read of their covenant God setting out for battle on their behalf with a splendour that covers the heavens (Hab. 3:3), so that the mountains writhe in agony and the sun and moon are arrested in their course as he crushes the nations and tramples on the surge of mighty waters (vv. 10–15) – is it too much to imagine the hair standing on the back of their necks? A chill running down the spine? These texts are meant both to instruct and invoke awe before the transcendent God who intervenes to save but cannot be fully comprehended, but only symbolized. By way of analogy, remember how it felt to read about Narnia for the first time: although one never forgets the books are pure fiction, products only of the imagination of a pious Cambridge don, surely I am not the only one who had a sense that some great truth was being given to me through those books, something almost beautiful beyond words, something 'more gold than gold'.[13] But where Narnia is only a made-up story, the biblical texts that speak of God's warfare in such thrilling ways are inspired Scripture and thus reveal God's reality to us. This means that when we read poetic descriptions of God's storming against the raging waters, we do them justice by holding together both the intellectual and the imaginative, by remembering the way these texts are meant both to instruct and amaze. This is especially relevant to our study of Job, a book that ends with the longest recorded encounter between a mortal and the Almighty in which God speaks to his wounded servant from the storm (38:1). Even while being careful to exegete the significance of the storm within an Old Testament framework in a responsible way, we must not forget the evocative power the storm has in Old Testament

---

[12] Paul 1997: 779. John Walton presents another helpful distinction when he writes that although the cosmology of the OT is often similar or apparently identical to that found in the ANE, the kind of God the OT describes is consistently different from the deities in the ANE (see Walton 2009).

[13] Lewis 1946: 22. The phrase is from the ancient Greek poetess Sappho.

poetry, nor the greatness of the cosmos YHWH describes from the storm, or those lurking, sinister powers he allows to live there – but only for a time.

2
Job's tragedy (chs. 1–2) and the failure of the debate with his friends (chs. 3–37)

In order to appreciate the meaning and beauty of YHWH's response to Job, we need to understand Job's initial tragedy in its full dimensions (chs. 1–2) and the complete failure of Job and his friends to interpret what Job's suffering means (chs. 3–37). As stated above, YHWH's two speeches are not a general defence of his policies, but specifically respond to Job's protest of divine injustice and (implicitly) the simplistic theology of the friends. As a result, it is only with the context of the entire book of Job in mind that we can fully appreciate what YHWH has to say to Job and to later readers of the book.

Job's integrity, the Accuser's question and Job's costly worship (Job 1 – 2)

After the location of his home and name, the first thing we learn about Job is his spiritual qualities: Job is a man 'blameless and upright, one who feared God and turned away from evil' (1:1). Since Job later says he confessed sin openly when necessary (31:33–34), this does not denote perfect sinlessness, but rather a wholehearted obedience. There are no areas of Job's life closed off to God, where sin is the dominant pattern. He is a saint 'in complete armour', 'whole' and not partial in his loyalty to God. In the wisdom literature of which the book of Job is a part, 'fearing God' is shorthand for a good relationship with him (Prov. 1:7; 2:5; 14:27; Eccl. 12:13; in Deut. 10:12–16, fearing God is tied to loving, serving and obeying him). As Christopher Ash aptly puts it, Job is the same on the inside as he is on the outside.[1] Job shows every quality needed for a wonderful relationship with God.

As a result, Job is blessed (vv. 2–3) with everything Old Testament wisdom literature promises: a vibrant family (cf. Ps. 128:1–4),[2] as well as great wealth and honour (cf. Prov. 8:18). We learn as well that his family life is wonderful, consisting of a series of happy family reunions (v. 4). Not only that, but Job is an extremely conscientious parent, availing himself of the means God has provided to keep his children safe from the danger of possible sin by sacrificing for them. Job understands there is something dark in the human heart that can curse God even in the midst of blessing and only sacrifice can expunge sin,[3] but 'the godly parent making doubly sure that all is well' is '[t]he finishing touch to this happy scene'.[4] The retribution principle, so clearly taught in books such as Deuteronomy and Proverbs, is clearly evident in the way verses 2–5 follow verse 1.[5] Job is reaping what he has sown (Gal. 6:7). God responds to Job's faithfulness and love not only by giving a spiritual intimacy with himself (see Job 29:2–3), but also by being extremely generous in earthly and secondary gifts.

Unbeknownst to Job, however, his profound piety and subsequent blessing have drawn attention to him in high places. We are next shown

---

[1] Ash 2014: 31.

[2] The numbers of Job's children – seven and three – suggest not just the size of his family but its quality, seven (and, to a lesser extent, three and ten) in the OT connoting completeness and perfection.

[3] Ash 2014: 35.

[4] Andersen 1976: 80.

[5] Job was, of course, not an Israelite: his name is not Israelite and his homeland Uz is apparently in or near Edom (see Jer. 25:20; Lam. 4:21). There are also hints that Job lived very early in the redemptive history: in the patriarchal age, before Deuteronomy and Proverbs were written; e.g. his long life of 140 years (42:16), his offering of sacrifice without a priest (1:5), his use of the archaic name Shaddai for God (with the exception of the text-critically suspect 12:9, the characters of the book never invoke the covenant name YHWH); see Waltke 2004: 927, n. 1, for other evidence that Job lived very early in redemptive history. This creates some dissonance when discussing Job in relation to Deuteronomy and Proverbs, for they had not been written when Job lived – and even if they had been, would a non-Israelite like Job have had access to them? The way in which Job's story connects with other OT theological themes may simply be an example of God's treating fairly everyone who seeks him (cf. Acts 17:27; Rom. 2:6–11; remember that Job had forsaken all idolatry [Job 31:24–28]). Alternatively, there are examples in extra-biblical texts of Deuteronomic ideas, where disobedience leads to punishment and exile, and contrition leads to restoration and blessing (for examples, see Kitchen 2003: 310–312). Perhaps Job did not need the biblical books written later than he lived to understand this principle at some level, even as he forsook the false gods of his contemporaries.

God's heavenly servants making their regular report to the divine king (v. 6). The Accuser also is among them (the wording of v. 6 implies that the Accuser is on an equal level with God's other supernatural courtiers, but somewhat set apart – with them but not of them).[6] He, too, makes a report to the divine king, albeit a somewhat vague one (v. 7). YHWH then takes the initiative to call attention to his exemplary servant, Job (v. 8). Surely, if anyone can survive accusation it is Job.

Three points should be clarified here. First, the conversation between YHWH and the Accuser in verses 6–12 is no incidental or insignificant interchange. The narrator is portraying for us the divine throne room, known from other passages such as 1 Kings 22, Isaiah 6 and Revelation 4 – 5. This is YHWH's royal assembly, the place where he announces and enacts his policy decisions for how he will govern the world. Patrick Miller perceptively points out that since 'the maintenance of world order . . . is a responsibility of the divine assembly', it is not surprising that a book exploring undeserved suffering begins with two important scenes in the divine council.[7] Unbeknownst to Job, the whole future course of his life is about to be determined, in a way that reflects God's policies for how he administers all of creation. Job's suffering has a significance far beyond himself as an individual. The canvas on which Job's drama will play out is as large as can be.

Second, we must not miss how YHWH repeats the narrator's sterling endorsement of Job from verse 1, but adds the phrase 'there is none like him on the earth' (v. 8). This is very striking because the phrase is more

---

[6] I speak above of the 'Accuser' instead of Satan because it better captures the nuance the Hebrew word had for ancient Israelite audiences. The definite noun *haśāṭān* describes a role, not a proper name: names do not take the definite article in biblical Hebrew, and the verb *śṭn* elsewhere speaks of ordinary human accusations (Pss 38:20; 109:4) and is even used in Num. 22:22, 32 to describe how the angel of YHWH opposes Balaam. This is not to deny, however, that we meet the character known as Satan in the NT in the early chapters of Job (cf. Rev. 12:9). But we must try to appreciate how the book's first hearers would have received *haśāṭān*. Some Christian commentators unwisely deny any connection between the Accuser of Job 1 – 2 and Satan. John Walton, for instance, sees nothing sinister about the Accuser's questions, understanding them only as 'intended to promote the general good by putting potentially questionable policies and decisions under scrutiny' (2012: 66; Walton prefers to speak of the 'Challenger' here instead of the 'Accuser'). But this has the effect of multiplying entities beyond necessity, for it gives us two heavenly beings, both with the same title, both of whom accuse God's saints, one malicious and the other apparently not so. Furthermore, the fact that the Accuser has to be told not to kill Job (2:6) and says nothing at all about Job's passing the first test so beautifully (2:2) hints at the Accuser's malicious motives and speaks against seeing the Accuser as someone who promotes 'the general good'.

[7] Miller 2000: 439.

commonly applied to God than it is to human beings.[8] This is high praise indeed! Furthermore, calling Job 'my servant' puts him in the privileged company of Abraham (Gen. 26:24), Moses (Exod. 14:31) and David (2 Sam. 7:5).[9] Yhwh's very high regard for Job is important to remember when we come to the debate of chapters 3–37, for both Job and his friends assume (wrongly but understandably) that Job is under the wrath of God, if for different reasons – the friends because Job has sinned, and Job because God is an irrational tyrant. The narrator is clarifying for us from the beginning that this is definitely not the case, and that God is incredibly proud of Job. John Walton astutely points out in this connection that while Job imagines himself as standing falsely accused by God and bringing a lawsuit against the Almighty, there is an important sense in which God and his policies for creation stand accused, with Job as the unwitting key witness for the defence.[10]

Third, it is difficult not to wonder if all the agony of the book of Job would have happened without this question from God – after all, Satan never accuses Job until yhwh brings him to the Accuser's attention. Is there a hint, in God's volunteering of Job, of his sovereign guiding of all of Job's suffering, to his own good ends?

Whatever the case, Satan's earlier terseness breaks into a damning accusation in verse 9: 'Does Job fear God for no reason?' (or 'for nothing?'). The implied answer is obviously 'no': Job is (according to Satan) enduring a relationship with a God he secretly despises, mouthing pious lies only in order to hold on to the picture-perfect life he enjoys. Job loves the gifts but hates the Giver. Take away Job's only motive for being in the relationship, the Accuser implies, and his real feelings about God will surface and he will irrevocably break his relationship with God. For the curse which the Accuser predicts Job will make (1:11) does not mean just to utter obscene speech, but to abhor someone or something, to assign a person or thing to the rubbish heap of the universe, to treat someone or something as worthy only of disgust and scorn. Take away the secondary blessings, Satan says, and Job will quickly give up on God.

---

[8] See e.g. 1 Kgs 8:23; Pss 35:10; 71:19; 86:8–9; Jer. 10:6–7; Mic. 7:18. The only humans to be described this way are Saul (1 Sam. 10:24; but this appears to describe Saul's physical characteristics, not his moral integrity), Solomon (1 Kgs 3:12), Hezekiah (2 Kgs 18:5) and Josiah (2 Kgs 23:35).

[9] Habel 1985: 90.

[10] Walton 2008: 340.

This accusation is, of course, unfair. It would be bizarre for God to respond to faithful love from his creatures with anything else other than blessing. (What else should God do? Remain silent and indifferent? Or return loyalty with pain?) And were God to pursue so strange a course, doubtless Satan would turn that into an accusation. Note as well that when Satan cannot find any fault in Job's integrity, he manages to turn Job's integrity itself into a problem.[11] As Michael Fox points out, however, the principle of retribution, while fair in itself, can be used against God: perhaps Job and God are just 'colluding in a game of bribery and payoffs'.[12] Paradoxically, the only way to prove the honesty of the relationship is to allow 'a local suspension of justice'[13] in which Job is treated as an unrepentant sinner, even though he clearly is not. God temporarily 'breaches his own justice' to make unconditional loyalty possible. 'Inexplicable suffering has a role in the divine economy, for it makes true piety possible.'[14]

We are only nine verses into this long and complex book, but already we are near its heart. Do God's people love and fear him for his sake, as an end in himself? Or is God used a means to some other earthly end, such as having enjoyable lives? Will we enter into a relationship with God in which all we ultimately gain is God? Can we keep the secondary blessings we accrue in that relationship truly secondary and dispensable? Or are we too selfish? The question is a very great one, for a relationship with God for God's sake only is surely the only kind of relationship that will save us. '[I]f we love God for something less than himself, we cherish a desire that can fail us. We run the risk of hating Him if we do not get what we hope for.'[15] Even more frightening is the possibility that Christians will insult God by treating a person of infinite worth as a means to some other end – all without realizing it. After all, even if we do not benefit in the same way Old Testament saints did, surely each Christian benefits from his or her faith in ways other than and secondary to the forgiveness of sins and eternal life. But who can be absolutely certain of the true state of one's heart with regard to those blessings and the God who has

---

[11] Murphy 1996: 36.
[12] Fox 2005: 360.
[13] Ibid.
[14] Ibid. 362–363. This is a very helpful and pithy way of expressing a central issue in the book of Job and is a quotation to which we will return.
[15] Merton 1983: 18.

given them? How can we be certain we have not become overly attached to the wrong thing? It is not until we receive the dreaded phone call from the doctor, or one of our children is in the hospital, that we learn the true quality of our love for God. Job is not an everyman, of course: there is something extreme about both his piety and his suffering. But Christopher Ash rightly says we have no reason to expect God will treat his new-covenant children any differently from the way he treated Job, even if our suffering is not as extreme as Job's.[16]

C. S. Lewis powerfully expresses the shock of realizing the true state of one's own heart before God after he suffered the loss of his wife. Although he apparently did not have the book of Job in mind, he gets to the heart of the significance of the Accuser's question in 1:9 when he writes:

> Of course it is different when the thing happens to oneself, not to others, and in reality, not imagination. Yes; but should it . . . make quite such a difference as this? No. And it wouldn't for a man whose faith had been real faith and whose concern for other people's sorrows had been real concern. The case is too plain. If my house has collapsed at one blow, that is because it was a house of cards. The faith which 'took things into account' was not faith but imagination . . . It has been an imaginary faith playing with innocuous counters labelled 'Illness,' 'Pain,' 'Death,' and 'Loneliness.' I thought I trusted the rope until it mattered to me whether it would bear me. Now that it matters, I find it didn't.
>
> Bridge-players tell me that there must be some money on the game, 'or else people won't take it seriously.' Apparently it's like that . . . [Y]ou will never discover how serious it was until the stakes are raised horribly high; until you find that you are playing not for counters or for sixpences but for every penny you have in the world. Nothing less will shake a man – or at any rate a man like me – out of his merely verbal thinking and his merely notional beliefs. He has to be knocked silly before he comes to his senses. Only torture will bring out the truth. Only under torture does he discover it himself.[17]

---

[16] Ash 2014: 21, 426.
[17] Lewis 1976: 42–43.

One supposes it is possible that YHWH, who knows all things, could simply rebuke Satan at this point, as happens in Zechariah 3:1. After all, the stricture against taking Job's life implies the Accuser's insincerity: he is not genuinely interested in testing his accusation but only in destroying Job. But YHWH gives permission for an ordeal to proceed in which Job will be given every earthly reason to give up on God (v. 12). One hopes the reader is beginning to see why. Just as declarations of love between romantic partners, no matter how sincere, are not sealed until the couple pledge themselves before God in sickness and health, for better and for worse, so God sometimes pushes us beyond easier affirmations of love and faithfulness made to him in health and safety to affirm the same when he allows us to suffer some profound loss. Some affirmations cannot remain theoretical for ever.

There is a deeper reason why God allows Job to lose everything. The costly affirmations made in terrible pain do more than show the quality of our love for God that exists hidden inside us – they seal and bind us in a relationship with God where God is proven as being of all-exclusive worth. In the same way that the relationship between an engaged couple is externally different after the swearing of vows in marriage, so Christians' relationship with God takes on profound authenticity when they engage in tear-stained worship of God for his own sake, regardless of what secondary blessings he may take from us. How else will we ever grow up out of our merely theoretical faith into reality with God? If God never pushes us beyond hypothetical statements of the all-surpassing worth of knowing him, how will our souls be saved? How else will God prepare us for eternity, which will chiefly consist in enjoying God himself, for his own sake? Joblike suffering is, contrary to all appearances, a preparation for heaven, when all secondary blessings have fallen away. As Christopher Ash writes:

> the Satan, for all his malice, is doing something necessary to the glory of God. In some deep way it is necessary for it to be publicly seen by the whole universe that God is worthy of the worship of a man and that God's worship is in no way dependent on God's gifts.[18]

---

[18] Ash 2014: 44.

From this perspective, YHWH 'uses mortals to validate truths about himself' in a way that confers 'awful dignity' on us.[19]

Job's 'awful dignity' is given to him quickly. The Accuser leaves the presence of YHWH (v. 12) and, like clockwork, Job's wealth (vv. 14–16), servants (v. 17) and children (vv. 18–19) are all destroyed – everything listed in verses 2–3. We see the Accuser at work through both human intermediaries (the Sabeans of v. 15) and directly ('fire of God' in v. 16, a fire others could understandably but wrongly assume came directly from God himself[20]). It is crucial to emphasize at this juncture that within the theological framework of the Old Testament, the losses of verses 14–19 would have looked like God's cursing Job for sin (Deut. 28; Prov. 3:33), punishing Job for secret and terrible transgressions, even though the reader has already been assured that the reasons for Job's tragedy are entirely different.

Job's response is as poignant as it is noble. Without suppressing his grief (v. 20), Job worships in a way that shows he unambiguously passes the Accuser's test (v. 21): every blessing Job received in life was only a gift ('the LORD gave') that he knew he would not enjoy past the grave. Furthermore, God is to be praised no less when he takes away than when he gives – no less. Clearly, Job's love and loyalty to God are in no way tied to ancillary blessings: every secondary blessing from God remains secondary for Job, pure gift and subordinate to God himself. Although the narrator does not draw attention to it, it is worth noting that the opposite of what Satan predicted has happened: instead of God's suffering the humiliation of one of his favourite servants openly hating him, Job is blessing God more deeply as a result of his suffering. Instead of God being cursed, he is being blessed in a costly, painful and deeply beautiful way. In God's sovereign guidance, the Accuser's hostility and the evil he inflicts has the opposite effect of what it intended. The trauma intended to pry Job away from God has driven him deeper into worship.

We should also note, in anticipation of a later discussion, that Job's worship in 1:21 reveals a crucial difference between Job's theology and that of his friends: while Job thinks of blessing as pure gift, the friends tend to speak of divine blessing as reward for services rendered. This will be explored further below.

---

[19] Waltke 2007: 932.

[20] Cf. the 'fire from heaven' as judgment on Elijah's enemies in 2 Kgs 1:10–14, or as a fire-consuming sacrifice in 2 Chr. 7:1.

The chapter's final verse briefly clarifies that when Job attributes the ultimate source of his tragedy to God, he does not say anything inappropriate, even though it was not God who directly struck Job (v. 22; the narrator will make the same attribution in 42:11). The presentation of divine providence in this chapter is subtle: God's rule is supreme and uncontested, such that even the Accuser must await and obey instructions; but God is not the only power at work in his world. On the one hand, God does take responsibility for everything that happens in his world; after all, when he appears to Job in chapter 38, YHWH does not shift responsibility by blaming the Accuser for Job's suffering. On the other hand, God is not the direct efficient cause of every evil. '[T]he relationship between God and mortals is not closed. Other spiritual personalities are at work.'[21]

Turning to chapter 2, we see another debriefing session in the divine courtroom (v. 1). Strangely, the Accuser says nothing about Job's costly worship (v. 2) until YHWH points to Job's extraordinary integrity even in the midst of unthinkable loss (v. 3).[22] Instead of admitting his wrong, however, the Accuser attacks Job more subtly, claiming that the first test did not probe deeply enough: Job still hates God and is lying about it, only to keep his own life (vv. 4–5). God responds by continuing to guide Job's sufferings for his own purposes, allowing the Accuser to bring Job as close to the grave as possible (v. 6). Since the book of Job does not have a

---

[21] Waltke 2007: 932.

[22] YHWH's statement that the Accuser 'incited' him 'to destroy Job without reason' can be troubling: Is God admitting he was manipulated into making a mistake? Two considerations suggest otherwise. First, the verb 'incited' (*sût*) can be used for enticing someone to do something wrong or unwise (e.g. Deut. 13:7; 2 Kgs 18:32; Jer. 43:3), but is also used more neutrally for urging someone towards some action (Josh. 15:18/Judg. 1:14) and once for enticing someone away from sin (Job 36:16). As a result, translating the verb as 'urge' is exegetically justifiable and avoids any sense of God's being tricked or manipulated. Second, the different senses of the adverb 'without reason' (*ḥinnām*, repeated from 1:9) suggest a more positive intention behind God's statement in this verse. The word can mean 'without compensation' (e.g. Num. 11:5), 'in vain' (Prov. 1:17) or 'without cause, undeservedly' (Ps. 35:7, 19; see *HALOT* 334). Its use in 1:9 falls within the first definition, while the adverb's use in 2:3 falls in the third (Rowley 1983: 31, 34). YHWH is, in other words, defending his servant as being entirely innocent of Satan's accusation – it was completely undeserved. God is also stating that it is his wish to bless his servants, not destroy them (Fox 2005: 359) and that the test, from Satan's perspective, failed because Job did not curse God. '[T]he test proved that the Satan's accusations against Job were "without cause" or had no inherent worth, and that Job feared God "without cause" – Job trusted God with a pure heart filled with love for God, not for the benefits God had bestowed upon him' (Hartley 1988: 80). But this need not imply that Job's suffering happens for no reason in an absolute sense – Satan's accusation was without value, but there are deeper reasons why God allowed it (Shields 2010: 268–269). The last word of v. 3 thus has an ironic twist.

well-developed eschatology, Job cannot die: the test must be resolved within this life. At the same time, in order to prove Satan's accusations baseless, Job must be as close to death as possible. The reader should notice that, at this point, there is nothing else to take from Job; no third test is possible without Job's dying.[23]

As was the case in chapter 1, this second wave of suffering would have been interpreted by Job and his friends not just as misfortune, but as punishment for sin. This is the case because the word for the boils on Job's skin (*šĕḥîn*, v. 7) is relatively rare, but is found in Deuteronomy 28:27, 35 for the sicknesses faithless Israelites will suffer.[24] Job's sickness is thus, from his perspective and that of his friends, evidence of divine anger. In fact, from their perspective it probably looked as if God was about to take Job's life. It is unclear whether Job's scraping himself with a potsherd (v. 8) is an ancient medical practice or an act of grief or both, but sitting on the ash heap does represent a place of humiliation and anguish (2 Sam. 13:19; Esth. 4:1; Ps. 102:10; Isa. 61:3). Tragically, just when Job is at his lowest, his wife betrays him by asking why he maintains integrity with God when it is costing him everything (v. 9). Why keep loving God, she asks, if he keeps hurting you? The echo in verse 9 to 2:3 – Job still 'holds fast' his integrity – shows the opposite intent behind the same phrase: while YHWH commends Job for holding on to his integrity, Job's wife criticizes him for the same reason. She stumbles over the test Job has already passed.

In stark contrast, Job passes this second test with the same poignant clarity he showed in the first chapter. Although he could have responded to his wife with anger, he tells her only that she is speaking foolishly about God – both disaster and blessing are to be accepted from God in equal measure (v. 10). Job's reason for not cursing God when God allows disaster is virtually identical to that given in 1:21. No matter how deep the test goes, Job will not betray his integrity with God.

The last thing we are told in these stylistically simple but theologically profound chapters is the approach of Job's friends (vv. 11–13). Their motives are entirely admirable (v. 11), but the friends seem to underestimate the tragedy of which they heard – they cannot even recognize their friend, and they weep openly and remain silent for an entire week (vv. 12–13). There is 'something painfully strange about . . . the emptiness in [Job's] eyes, the

---

23 Ash 2014: 53.
24 Only elsewhere in Exod. 9:9–11; Lev. 13:18–20, 23; 2 Kgs 20:7/Isa. 38:21.

lines in his face, the brokenness in his demeanor'.[25] Their silence – which surely must have become uncomfortable after a while[26] – is due to Job's obvious, but thus far unspoken, pain (v. 13). It is a little surprising to read this after Job's apparently serene submission to the loss of his family and health: Job seems entirely at peace with his losses in 1:21 and 2:10, so what is the source of this other pain? As we read further into the book, however, and listen as Job obsessively talks about God, without ever asking for the return of the blessings of chapters 1–2, we infer that while Job is resigned to the loss of his blessed life, the God who (from Job's perspective) caused this tragedy for no reason has become problematic. Job is at peace with his losses, but not with the God who is (apparently) punishing him without just cause. This 'very great pain' will dominate Job's speeches.

The debate between Job and his friends: round one (chs. 4–14)

Job's curse on creation (ch. 3)

Just as the Accuser does not initiate his attacks on Job but twice responds to God's prompting (1:8; 2:3), so the friends do not initiate their well-intentioned but deeply harmful assault on Job until after Job himself speaks. For reasons we will explore below, the friends were probably shocked by what Job initially says in chapter 3; they probably expected a confession of the sin that had caused God's anger and Job's suffering, while Job instead responds to (what looks like) God's curse with a curse of his own. A sense of shock at Job's curse is, however, appropriate, if for reasons other than the friends' misguided expectations. This is because Job seems to overreact in this chapter. Instead of wishing only for death, Job wishes he had never been born in the first place – and even implies he wishes there had never been any light or space for any human life at all. This raises questions about Job's motives for speaking, which will be important to keep in mind as we consider the chapter.

It is also important to remember that the word 'wish' is probably too weak, for curses and blessings in the Old Testament express not just

---

[25] Ash 2014: 60–61.

[26] Ash points out that although silence doubtless would have been wise at first, seven whole days of nothing but silence would not have been a comfort to Job (ibid. 62).

wishes but count as ritually effective speech, helping to bring about what they describe. Although Job perhaps did not literally expect creation to dissolve into chaos around him as he spoke, his first poem does count as a verbal assault on God's world. To appreciate the gravity and magnitude of this curse, it should be remembered that an ancient Semite like Job would have viewed creation significantly differently from modern Westerners. Job is verbally assaulting not just impersonal matter obeying scientific laws, but that beautiful, complex, dependent environment God made for us for the sake of significant relationship and satisfying work (Gen. 1; Ps. 104). But the goodness and grandeur of God's world in no way restrains Job's pain (2:13). Job's curse encompasses not just himself, but all of existence.

Job begins by cursing not just the day of his birth, but even the night it was announced he was conceived (v. 3). Let that day be darkness, Job says; let it simply fall out of existence (v. 4). The first clause of verse 4 echoes God's initial calling into existence of light in Genesis 1:3[27] – the first hint that Job is restricting his curse not merely to his own existence, but to the whole world. A second hint comes in the next verse, when Job calls on the 'shadow of death' (my tr.) to claim the day he was born (cf. Ps. 23:4). This is no natural darkness Job is summoning to seize, to dwell on, to terrify his birthday; he hopes spiritual darkness will 'win back [its] demonic rights' over creation.[28] Unusually, verses 4–6 each have three clauses, as if the vigour and viciousness of Job's curse cannot be contained within the normal two-part structure of a poetic line.

Leviathan himself is mentioned in verse 8, where Job cheers on those magicians skilled to rouse the chaos monster that would overwhelm creation. Ancient Egyptians imagined that a giant serpent, Apep, would try to swallow the sun (Ra) each night as it travelled through the under-world on a ship, and their priests had extensive magic rituals that would help to repel that chaos so that the normal order of sunrise could continue each day.[29] Job here poetically calls on these religious specialists to reverse their normal procedure and help chaos win – but, of course, if Leviathan is aroused, the 'fleeing serpent' (see Job 26:12–13) will do far more than

---

[27] See Hartley 1988: 102 and Fishbane 1971: 154 for more echoes between Job 3 and Gen. 1.
[28] Ash 2014: 71.
[29] Religious specialists termed *apkalli* seem to have had a similar function in Mesopotamia, reciting spells to maintain cosmic order. For further discussion and references to ANE texts, see Seow 2013: 324–325 and Walton 2012: 122.

just swallow Job's day. All light and life will be endangered. The next verse ends Job's curse in a moving way as we watch the stars at twilight wink out and the 'eyelids' of morning wake to nothing (v. 9).

The reason for Job's curse occupies the rest of the chapter, stated in two plaintive questions (vv. 11, 20). Why is Job alive at all (vv. 11–12), when he could have been resting in Sheol as a stillborn (v. 13)? The four successive verbs in verse 13 imply an eagerness on Job's part, but his euphemism is chilling, because elsewhere Sheol is a place to be avoided at all costs (Pss 6:6; 30:4; 116:3; Prov. 5:5; 9:18; Isa. 14:9, 11, 15). Job can, however, think of no other path to peace (vv. 14–19): as he imaginatively surveys both great and small there, from kings to prisoners, he portrays all their earthly accomplishments as being of no significance – whatever kings built has now crumbled (v. 14), and there the wicked cease from turmoil (v. 17). Although the implication remains unstated, Job appears to be longing for a place where his own life would be reduced to nothing as well, and all the agony of chapters 1–2 would be of no significance and no longer trouble him. This is the only redemption poor Job can hope for.[30] Verse 17 repeats 'there' twice, as if he cannot turn his mind away from death as his only hope. Poor Job!

Job asks the same question from a different perspective in verse 20, implicitly probing why God would punish him so severely only to stop just before his death (vv. 20–22). Since death is the final punishment for sin, if Job is being punished, why is he not granted this release? Why is Job's way hidden from God's care (v. 23a), while God 'hedges' Job in in hostility (23b)? When considering Job's limited perspective on his situation, one sympathizes with his question. At the same time, it is impossible to miss how verse 23 repeats the rare verb *sûk* (to hedge), first used in 1:10 (found elsewhere in the OT only in Job 38:8; 40:22; Hos. 2:8). The first time this verb is used, it expresses how God hedged Job about in blessing, not pain. The repetition of the unusual word is not accidental. The narrator is implying (and not for the last time) that Job is eerily close to the truth of his situation without being able to understand it fully. Job will later learn that God does 'hedge in', but in a much happier sense than Job thinks (38:8).

---

[30] This thought is anticipated in v. 5, which begins with the verb *g'l*, often fairly translated as 'claim', but meaning 'to redeem'. As Seow points out, while God in Hos. 13:14 redeems Israel from Sheol and death, here Job calls for the opposite (2013: 321). The only 'redemption' Job can imagine from God's apparent anger and the suffering it brings comes from cosmic darkness and the grave.

Job finishes his opening lament by saying there is no reason for him to continue with life. He cannot participate in normal life (symbolized in v. 24 by eating) and finds no resolution or closure anywhere (v. 26; the triple negative is especially affecting).[31] The last word of the verse, usually translated 'trouble' or 'turmoil', is more troubling than either, for it often refers to the waters of chaos (Exod. 15:10; Pss 29:3; 93:4; Isa. 17:12–13; Hab. 3:2, 16). Chaos has entered Job, and he has entered a world of chaos, for no reason he can think of. Why is he still alive?

Job 3 is a powerful poem. The poet will not let us keep a safe distance from Job's agony, but involves us in it as Job's imagery and urgency linger in our minds. 'The poetry catches the wild cries . . . Translators spoil the art by making it smooth.'[32] Christopher Ash appropriately writes that we 'need to learn to be shocked and shocked again by this story and never to let familiarity dull the sharpness of the pain'.[33] While letting this shock linger, however, we can return to the question that opened our discussion of this chapter. Why does Job go beyond wishing to die? Why imply that he wishes he never enjoyed a single day of the picture-perfect existence of 1:1–5? And why call on forces that would ensure no-one would have a chance to enjoy life? Has Job's bitterness distorted his perspective? Is malice towards everyone the only way he can articulate his pain?

Fortunately, when we take into account Job's probable perspective on the events of chapters 1–2, these questions become unnecessary. From his vantage point Job has lost God's favour and come under God's fiercest wrath, for no reason Job can think of. His curse on creation is tantamount to affirming that if he cannot live under God's favour and within his friendship, Job sees no point ever to having lived in the first place. In other words, the blessed life of chapter 1 means nothing to him without God and God's friendship – in fact, without God's smile, Job cannot think of a reason for anything in creation to exist. In the light of this, we see that, for all its vociferousness, Job's curse is something like the photographic

---

[31] Although it is left unstated, the perfect verbs of v. 25 may suggest that some fear from Job's past has now overtaken him without specifying further what this fear was. Although it is not certain, it is difficult not to think of his sacrifices for his children in 1:5. Was a lingering fear that God might visit him in anger part of the reason for Job's sacrifice? A half-conscious unease that disaster might strike, which also suggests some uneasiness in his relationship with God?

[32] Andersen 1976: 101.

[33] Ash 2014: 49. Ash reflects on the devotional implications of this chapter in a particularly helpful way (ibid. 49, 66, 132).

negative of his worship from 1:21. It expresses the same high view of God, albeit in a negative way. Job would not curse so terribly if he did not value God so deeply.

Eliphaz's hideous gentleness (chs. 4–5)

What was Eliphaz thinking as he listened to Job's curse? We quickly learn that the friends do not have any room for innocent suffering – their interpretation of the retribution principle is naive and mechanical, such that everyone suffers quickly and exactly proportionately for every sin. So when Job first opened his mouth, Eliphaz probably expected a confession of some dark misdeed that would explain Job's tragedy. Although the narrator does not say so, the real reason Job's friends come (2:11–13) is to help Job through his repentance. The only 'comfort' they have to give is blame. (This is not the last time the narrator will present Job's friends in a superficially attractive way, only to undermine them and their theology later.)

In the light of this, Eliphaz is probably shocked and mystified by Job's cry that creation would come undone. Why would Job needlessly confuse so simple (if painful) a case? Eliphaz will express this shock later (see 15:11–14), but for now begins very delicately, asking Job if he may say something (v. 2a) – because, after all, something has to be said (2b). Job has helped other stumbling sinners towards repentance and restoration in the past (cf. the image of v. 4 to Prov. 4:10–19). Now, however, 'it' comes upon Job and, strangely, Job is completely undone (v. 5). Eliphaz is too polite to say so, but the 'it' of verse 5 is clearly the calamity of chapters 1–2. Since Job has already helped sinners suffering for their stupidity, the way forward for Job should be perfectly obvious (according to Eliphaz). Because innocent people never perish (v. 7 – remember that Job is close to death), repentance and a return to integrity with God is the way to regain God's favour and the blessings this brings (v. 6). After all, all reap what they sow (v. 8) – especially evildoers, who, though powerful as lions, are put to death quickly (vv. 9–11). Eliphaz has personally seen this happen (v. 8).

Eliphaz's pastoral counselling is superficially plausible and even attractive, and without chapters 1–2 the reader would surely side with him against what look like the hysterics of Job. But when the attentive reader notices how the 'fear' (of God) and the 'integrity' Eliphaz recommends in verse 6 recall Job's spiritual qualities in 1:1, Eliphaz is immediately discredited: it is not because Job lacks these qualities that he is suffering, but precisely because he shows them so deeply. For all his good intentions, Eliphaz has read Job's situation exactly wrongly.

Eliphaz further unintentionally discredits himself by recounting a spiritual experience he had in the middle of the night (4:12–21). While dreams and visions are valid modes of revelation in the Old Testament, none is ever so harrowing or frightening as this – and none brings a message like this, in which God is the great fault-finder, who accepts no-one as clean or right in his eyes (vv. 17–18). This contradicts much of the Old Testament, which details God's reasonable and achievable standards to enter into his favour (e.g. Prov. 3:1–6).[34] Even more worrisome is the claim this spirit makes that God puts no trust in his servants. This is neatly contradicted by God's naming Job his servant in 1:8 and, in some sense, entrusting his reputation to Job. Even within the book of Job itself, we can see it is untrue that God puts no trust in his servants! Although it is not explicit, it is hard not to conclude that the same Accuser who condemned Job in chapters 1–2 has found another way to attack him, with Eliphaz as his unwitting mouthpiece. Eliphaz should have been more suspicious of the source of his vision (cf. 1 Cor. 12:10; 1 Thess. 5:20–21). Just when it seems Job cannot suffer any more, he feels another twist of the knife, this time in the well-meaning condemnation from a former friend.

The spirit's message ends with the questionable inference that frail mortals are even guiltier before God than his heavenly servants, and are thus quickly crushed (vv. 19–21). Although the Old Testament nowhere else supports any connection between human smallness and infirmity and moral fault, it is one to which the friends will return. Eliphaz then waxes eloquent on the judgment of the wicked (5:1–7). Resentment of God's judgment will only hurt Job (v. 2), so (it is implied) Job should stop these needless curses and accept divine punishment. But God is good, Eliphaz assures Job, and restores the humble who mourn for their sin (v. 11); as a result, Job should seek God (v. 8–16). All of this is a warm invitation for Job to return to the God he has abandoned. Eliphaz intends to make it as easy as possible to repent, finishing his first speech with an idyllic picture of restoration (vv. 19–26), all of which can be Job's if he only owns up to whatever he did to provoke God's anger. How could Job refuse such reasonable terms? (Multiple commentators point out, of course, that the

---

[34] Habel (1985: 123) rightly calls this account a parody of a revelatory dream.

friends' depiction of restoration does come true for Job, but not at all in way they anticipate.)

What are we to make of Eliphaz's first attempt at pastoral counselling? It is impossible to miss how 5:17 is almost identical in thought to Proverbs 3:11–12. This echo lends a superficial plausibility to Eliphaz's speech – but I would argue that this echo simultaneously subverts Eliphaz's theology, for, unlike the immature son of Proverbs 1 – 9, Job needs no correction from God, as the reader well knows from 1:8.[35] All of Eliphaz's talk of repentance and promises of restoration thus entirely miss the mark. (It is important to keep in mind God's warm approval of Job in chs. 1–2 and his preference for Job's speeches above that of the friends in 42:7.) For his part, Eliphaz probably expected that his counsel would be received, that Job would repent and be restored, thanking Eliphaz for his help, and that life would continue as normal. The reader, however, is a good deal more suspicious. The more one thinks about the implications of Eliphaz's speech, the more horrifying they become: according to him, the death of Job's children is a balanced and reasonable correction for sin (5:4), which Job should gratefully accept as a warning and wake-up call to repent. It is difficult to avoid the sense that the narrator is warning us against our good intentions towards suffering friends – warning us that our best intentions and our application of doctrines we have good reason to think are true (4:8; 5:27), and even have some biblical support (5:17), can deeply damage someone of whom God thinks very highly. One even wonders how coherent Eliphaz's theology is: If God restores penitents (5:17) but everyone is guilty (4:17–21; 5:6–7), how can anyone avoid punishment? The only way is to attribute incredible power to human repentance – as if sinners can clean themselves up before God. We will return to this thought below.

This is as good a place as any to emphasize that Eliphaz and his friends are not engaging in careful reasoning with Job, but in a form of speech known as contest literature. The goal of this kind of speech is to demolish an opposing position not through logic, but by powerful rhetoric.[36] In this context, Eliphaz is trying to demolish what he thinks is Job's irrational attempt to hold on to some unrepented sin, as well as Job's perverse desire

[35] A number of other verses in ch. 5 find superficial resonance with other parts of the OT; e.g. v. 9 with Ps. 40:5, v. 10 with Ps. 65:9–10, v. 11 with 1 Sam. 2:7–8 and Ps. 113:7–8. None of the larger contexts of these other passages, however, comports with Eliphaz's narrow view of God's judgment.
[36] Waltke cites Judg. 9, 2 Sam. 17 and 1 Esdras 3 – 4 as other examples (2007: 928).

that creation stop before Job lets go of the sin provoking God's wrath. Eliphaz is attempting to win from Job a confession by vividly presenting the terrible fate of rebels at God's hands and the wonderful future God has for any who repent.

Job's first lament (chs. 6–7)

Job, for his part, responds to Eliphaz's first speech with a sharp contest speech of his own, mixing lament over himself (6:1–13) and criticism of his friends (6:14–30) with a lament directed against God (7:1–10) and criticism of God (7:11–21). Numerous commentators have pointed out how Job deploys lament in a way different from its use elsewhere in the Old Testament: while laments in the Psalms are expressions of trust in God that attempt to move him to intervene, Job twists this form of speech in order to criticize God. This is especially seen in the way in which Job omits in his laments the expected concluding statement of trust or confidence in God (see e.g. Pss 3:6; 4:8; 6:8–10).[37] Although it is true that Job will elsewhere express remarkable trust in God, when he laments he distorts a familiar genre to put it to a darker purpose. His second speech is the first example of this.

Picking up Eliphaz's warning against vexation in 5:2, Job retorts that his own vexation would be immeasurable if it could be truly known (6:2–3).[38] Apparently, not even the cosmic dimensions of chapter 3 are sufficient to express Job's agony! Job does not identify the source of his pain as the death of his children in chapters 1–2, however, but direct terrorization from God (v. 4). Horrifying as chapters 1–2 are, those agonies pale in comparison to Job's sense of being under divine attack. As a result, if he speaks rashly (3b), Job has good reason (vv. 5–7; the disgusting food is either his suffering or Eliphaz's false comforts). Job's hope (v. 8) is not a return to integrity (4:6) but that God will end his life (vv. 8–9; cf. 3:11). Even here, however, Job has not compromised his integrity by transgressing or ignoring any of God's words (v. 10);[39] but this is small comfort, for Job

---

[37] See further Dell 1991: 116; Parsons 1992: 36–37; Timmer 2009b: 290.

[38] Habel 1985: 141 understands the first half of ch. 6 to respond point by point to much of Eliphaz's first speech, such that 6:2–7 counteracts 5:2–7 (God is not judging Job for sin, but terrorizing him for no reason) and 6:8–13 responds to 4:2–6 (Job's hope is not a return to his past piety, but that God will finish the job and kill Job).

[39] See Clines (1989: 174), who takes the phrase 'words of the Holy One' as a subjective genitive. Alternatively, the phrase may be an objective genitive, 'words about the Holy One', in which case Job may be saying he has not denied words about the Holy One in the sense that

is overwhelmed with his suffering (vv. 11–13). He cannot keep a stiff upper lip and wait for life to rebalance itself; no possible change to his fortunes will ever grant resolution or closure in the face of his new terrifying reality with God. Since Job thinks he has lost the friendship of God, death is the only thing he can look forward to.

Job is bereft of all internal resources (vv. 1–13) – but even worse, he finds no help from others (vv. 14–30).[40] Job looks for the life-giving waters of healing speech from his friends, but is betrayed (vv. 15–20; cf. the same image in Prov. 10:11; 13:14). He never asked for their help in the first place (vv. 22–23) and intuits Eliphaz spoke out of fear over Job's calamity (v. 21), a significant insight Job will develop later. But no arrogance drives Job's criticism of his friends: if they have hard evidence of wrongdoing on his part, Job will happily submit himself to their correction (v. 24). How troubling, how burdensome Eliphaz's words have been (v. 25); but when Job's own speech is counted as nothing ('wind'), why does Eliphaz think he will be convincing to Job (vv. 25–26)? When Eliphaz dismisses Job's words, why should Job take Eliphaz's words seriously? Job is experiencing the worst of both worlds: counsel that is painful and pointless. Whatever his intentions, speaking as Eliphaz has done is tantamount to 'selling out' a friend to make a profit: his theology is a betrayal of Job so that Eliphaz can benefit (v. 27). 'Job feels like property over which the friends argue.'[41] In counselling Job to repent, Eliphaz is really trying to meet his own needs and comfort himself. But no evasiveness is provoking this criticism from Job: he wants a real and sincere encounter with his friends (vv. 28–30). Job promises utmost sincerity and honesty on his part (v. 30) and wants the same from Eliphaz (v. 29).

---

he has never covered up valid criticisms about God (see Seow 2013: 574). This fits better with the piel of *kḥd*, which always elsewhere means 'hide' (*HALOT* 469); at the same time, since most of Job's direct criticisms of God come later (esp. in chs. 9–10), it is strange to hear him saying at this early stage of the debate that he has not avoided criticizing God. Since Job does, in fact, hold on to his integrity through his ordeal – whatever misguided things he says about God, he never uses his suffering as an excuse to break God's law and indulge in sin – I understand Job to be making a claim to personal integrity in v. 10. His one comfort in death is that he has not broken faith with God.

[40] Seow 2013: 461. In v. 14, Job is speaking of the loving-kindness he should be receiving from his friends but is not, and criticizing this failure in human relationships as constituting a break in the proper fear of God: 'He who withholds kindness from a friend forsakes the fear of the Almighty.' For discussion of the text-critical issue in this verse and another reading (which does not much affect the present discussion), see Seow 2013: 476.

[41] Habel 1985: 150.

But the friends, of course, are not what is really troubling Job. In chapter 7, Job turns to the God who he thinks is oppressing him so terribly. Although he is not mentioned, the one putting humans to hard service on earth (7:1) is implicitly the same God who orchestrated chapters 1–2 (this is not the last time Job will generalize from his experience to that of all humankind). Job's description of the life God has left for him is heavy with weariness as Job pants like a slave just to take a breather in the shade (v. 2), is denied the oblivion of sleep (v. 4; see vv. 13–14) and limps through months of nothing but futility (v. 3). Soon, so soon, he will simply be gone (vv. 7–10), and it will be as if he never existed (v. 10) – a state Job says he finds preferable (v. 15).

God is spoken of only indirectly in 7:1–10, but Job abandons this strategy in the second half of the chapter (vv. 11–21). After all, what does he have to lose by speaking his mind – what else can God do to him (v. 11)? God is treating Job as if he were some supernatural monster (v. 12), unleashing the full arsenal of heaven against him. All the proportions of just retribution in chapters 4–5 are here denied: Job is definitely not reaping what he has sown (4:8). And this in turn raises a troubling question: Why did God 'overreact' in this way? It cannot be because of anything in Job himself, for he is not nearly a big enough threat to God to provoke such an overwhelming attack (v. 17). And if, for argument's sake, there were some sin in Job that provoked God's anger, why was God provoked beyond all measure (v. 20)? And why not forgive this hypothetical sin (v. 21) – especially since Job has been forgiven before (see 31:32–34)? What sort of person would treat Job in this way? Job is at the very crux of his dilemma as he finishes his second speech with these questions. So far as he knows, only he and God were involved in the horror of chapters 1–2, and Job cannot explain the depth of his tragedy in relation to himself. His only recourse is (as it were, unwillingly) to draw some terrifying new conclusions about the God he thought he knew. These new conclusions will dominate chapters 9–10 and 16, but are rising to the surface at the end of chapter 7.

Bildad's bluntness (ch. 8)

It was mentioned above how Eliphaz, even if he finally fails, at least tried to be delicate in his address to Job (4:2–6). Bildad does not even try: since God never fails to do what is right (8:3), if Job's children died prematurely, then they got exactly what they deserved (v. 4). But God is so good that as soon as Job repents of whatever caused his suffering, his life will be even better than before (vv. 5–7). This truth has been tested for generations, so Job is simply not allowed to disagree (vv. 8–10). Two analogies with plants that can sprout up without water but wither just as quickly (vv. 11–12, 16–19) confirm the certainty of the judgment of the wicked (vv. 13–15). This is almost a point-by-point refutation of Job's second speech, made by repeating key words from chapters 6–7 with opposite intent: while Job accused his friends of treating his words like wind (6:26), Bildad fires back that Job's words are a mighty wind, too dangerous and destructive to go unanswered (v. 2);[42] while Job complains God will soon seek (šāḥar) Job but not find him, Bildad says Job should be the one seeking God (šāḥar, v. 5); while Job says he has no hope (7:6), Bildad points to the perishing hope of the godless (8:13); when Job rejects the life left to him (7:16), Bildad encourages Job that God rejects no-one with integrity (8:20). Despite all of Bildad's attempts to destroy Job's argument against God, a final echo to an earlier chapter undermines all of Bildad's confident assurances: when he refers to the integrity Job must regain in 8:20, Bildad echoes one of the spiritual qualities Job displayed in 1:1 that drew the Accuser's attention in the first place. As with Eliphaz, Bildad has completely misread Job's situation; it is not a lack of integrity that has prompted Job's suffering but just the opposite. His predictions are not worth much more, either, for his final promise that those hating Job will be clothed with shame (v. 22) does happen – but very much not in the way Bildad expects, for in 42:7–9 it is Bildad who is rebuked and demoted by God.

'He destroys both the blameless and the wicked': Job's nadir (chs. 9–10)

'How terrible are forceful words!' Job first voiced this in response to Eliphaz (6:25), but it is especially appropriate for Bildad's dogmatic harshness. But Job does not linger on any criticism of his friends in his next speech in chapters 9–10, focusing solely instead on his agony over the God who has become so strange to him. His first question in verse 2, about how someone could be right with God, is somewhat ironic, since Bildad has already clearly answered this (8:5–6); but it quickly becomes clear that Job has something else in mind when he asks this. Job is not thinking of a restoration to God's favour, but how he may win a legal case against God

---

[42] Seow 2013: 515.

for God's treatment of him in chapters 1–2. This is the 'rightness' Job is seeking in chapter 9. But although Job is certain he has been wronged by God, proving this is no simple matter for him. As one proceeds through the chapter, it becomes clear that Job finds himself faced with a bizarre dilemma as he develops the idea of a legal case against God. On the one hand, Job knows that the punishment of chapters 1–2 – or rather, what he mistakenly but understandably perceives as punishment – cannot be explained by any sin in him and so is unjust. Although Job is the first to admit he is not flawless, there is no secret pattern of disobedience that can explain his losses (1:1). Job thus finds himself driven to the unthinkable possibility that if he can somehow find an impartial court and somehow serve the Almighty with a court summons, that court will find in Job's favour so Job will win. But no sooner does this thought occur to Job than his mind recoils; he has such an exalted view of God, it is inconceivable to him that anyone can sue YHWH for damages and win. How on earth could it be possible for the Almighty to bow to humans and admit they were right and he was wrong? But, contrariwise, Job did not deserve what happened to him in the book's opening – God mistreated him. But this is God whom Job is arguing against! How can Job win an argument with the Almighty?

Job will twist in the contradiction between his sense of mistreatment by God and his fear and trembling before the Sovereign of the universe throughout chapters 9–10, see-sawing between the horns of this dilemma in a way that is sometimes difficult to follow.[43] These chapters are also difficult because Job will hit his lowest point in the debate, making claims that can be described only as blasphemous – claims of which Job will later be heartily ashamed (42:1–6). Nevertheless, there is some progress. Job has already cursed creation (ch. 3) and lamented his own existence under an inscrutably hostile God (chs. 6–7). Now, for the first time, vindication before God comes to the forefront. Even if this vindication is stated in a way that means God loses, he will later express the same idea in terms of reconciliation with his long-lost friend, without any idea of God's needing to be in the wrong (19:26; 23:3–7).

---

[43] Hartley writes how Job 'tends to state a position boldly, then abandon it when he sees its difficulty and jump to another idea, which is also quickly abandoned. Other times he reverts to despair … His jumping about reflects his frustration at the lack of any insight into the reasons for his plight' (1988: 165).

Job begins chapter 9 with the second horn of the dilemma mentioned above: the impossibility of winning a case against God. Job knows there is no way he can survive a cross-examination from the Almighty (vv. 3–4) – especially from one who can so powerfully destroy (vv. 5–7) everything he has made (vv. 8–10; that God's destructive activity comes first hints at Job's dark new view of God's character). Verse 10 is an exact quote from Eliphaz's speech in 5:9, but with opposite intent: instead of God's working out his moral rule in creation, the 'wonders' Job refers to are God's angry destruction of what he has made. Job is projecting on to the entire cosmos his own (understandable but misguided) interpretation of his suffering as baseless divine attack. God has become the Cosmic Destroyer.

Job then applies the vast ruin of verses 5–10 to God's treatment of himself (vv. 11–13). God has become a threatening, ghostly presence Job can sense but not see (v. 11), who pounces on his victims out of nowhere – and no-one can stand up to God, not even the powers of chaos (vv. 12–13).[44] In the light of this, even if Job prepared his case beforehand perfectly, even if he knew his case to be airtight, Job would not be able to utter a single word during his argument and would have to beg for mercy from his divine opponent (vv. 14–15).[45] He would be terrified his own mouth would trip him up (v. 20). And how can Job even believe God hears one so insignificant as himself (v. 16), especially when God is bearing down on Job so violently Job cannot even take a full breath (v. 18)? After all, God is multiplying Job's wounds for no reason ('without cause', v. 17) – but we are brought up short here as we remember the same word being used in 1:9 about Job's integrity. Job's suffering is 'for no reason', but not in the way he thinks; while Job thinks God is treating him as a sinner without sufficient cause, Job's suffering is because he loves God without ulterior motive. Job is eerily close to the truth of his situation without being able to penetrate it.

Verses 22–24 summarize Job's hypothetical case against God and show the way he is extrapolating from his own tragedy to make sweeping generalizations about God's character and activity in the world. It is all one, Job says: God treats people of opposite moral character exactly the

---

[44] 'Rahab' is another biblical name for Leviathan (see Job 26:12; Ps. 89:11; Isa. 51:9). More than once in the OT, such monsters are imagined at the head of a larger army; this is the meaning of the reference to Rahab's helpers in this verse (cf. Job 41:34).

[45] Coming after the negative clause of v. 13, the *'ap kî* beginning v. 14 means, 'how much less' (*HALOT* 76): in the light of vv. 11–13, how much less could Job answer God!

same – by destroying both (v. 22). Not only that, but God does so happily, laughing at innocent people when their lives fall apart (v. 23). The most evil people run the world, while God himself blindfolds those able and authorized to address injustices: '[I]f it is not he, who then is it?' (v. 24). Because of his limited perspective on the tragedy of chapters 1–2, Job can think of no-one else who stands behind the world's injustices.

These three verses are extremely difficult to read. Job has entered a Kafkaesque world in which, because he does not believe God is really good, all of God's other attributes take on a sinister aspect. After all, Job never denies God's omnipotence or irresistible ability to administer creation exactly according to his sovereign will – but these attributes only deepen Job's terror at what God can do to mortals.[46] There is, however, just a sliver of hope at this juncture in the argument, for despite Job's twisted theological vision, he has not yet cursed God. This is more hopeful than one might think. However slight the difference is between saying, 'God is an amoral tyrant who takes delight in destroying lives,' and saying, 'I hate God and want nothing more to do with him,' Job will affirm the former but not go so far as the latter. Of course, if the former is true, it is hard to imagine why one would continue in loyalty to such an untrust-worthy person. If 9:22–24 is in fact correct, as Job believes, then he has good reason to curse God! And yet, strangely but hopefully, despite the evidence Job presents that God is unworthy of faithfulness and devotion, Job will refuse to cut off his relationship with God. Even when Job receives (from his perspective) nothing but curses from God, he will not curse back. 'Job may be wrong in his perception of God and of the reality of his situation, but he is deeply right in his heart and the direction of his turning and yearning.'[47]

The second half of this speech (9:25 – 10:22) shows Job engaging in a long lament over the impossibility of ever getting a fair trial with God. Job has no reason to keep arguing in favour of his own innocence (v. 29; this is the 'labour' [ESV] or 'struggle' [NIV] of which he speaks). There is no possible restoration of his loss Job imagines he may be able to look forward to (vv. 25–26). After all, even if Job returned to the picture-perfect life of chapter 1, how could he ever let himself relax and enjoy it, knowing what

---

[46] No-one being able to deliver out of God's hand (10:7) is normally spoken as a comfort to Israel (Deut. 32:39; Isa. 43:13), but this same affirmation is anything but comforting to Job.
[47] Ash 2014: 151.

he now (thinks he) knows about God? At the same time, he is not able to suppress his pain and stoically soldier on – it is overwhelming (vv. 27–28). Most fearful to Job is the way in which his pain implies a guilty verdict from God ('you will not hold me innocent', v. 28) together with the sense of uncleanness this verdict produces in Job, a dirtiness so intense even Job's clothes abhor him (vv. 30–31). The same Job who can meet the death of his children with grief-stricken but amazingly faithful resignation to God's will (1:20–21) is terrified and utterly overwhelmed by the thought of God's disapproval.[48] If only there were some arbiter who could intervene between the two of them – for God is simply so great, Job does not know how to speak to him (v. 32). But since no such arbiter apparently exists, all Job can ask is that God ease up on his punishment so that Job can make his case without being completely intimidated (9:34 – 10:3). Why is God so angry with Job (10:2)? What possible reason can explain the punishment meted out in chapters 1–2? Was there some deep sin on Job's part that God needed to bring to the surface (10:4–7)? But no, God's perception is not limited like that of a human being (vv. 4–5), so God does not have to torture the truth out of him (v. 6). God can already see there is no sin in Job needing to be exposed (v. 7) – and Job is painfully aware that he will in any case not get away with secret sin (v. 14). But if Job's pain cannot be explained in relation to himself, it cannot be explained in relation to God's normal patterns of behaviour either: Why did God take such care to create Job (vv. 8–12) when his whole plan all along was to destroy him (v. 13)?

Considering these questions and unable to answer them, Job finds himself forced back to the conclusion of 9:22–24: it does not matter whether he is righteous or wicked, for God will punish him either way (v. 15). So why does he exist at all (vv. 18–19)? All he can ask is that the divine bully will leave him alone, so he can make the best of his miserable lot (v. 20) before he takes his final journey into that ultimate darkness (vv. 21–22). As his third speech ends, Job has regressed to the gloom and despair of chapter 3.[49]

As stated above, chapters 9–10 are the low point in Job's speeches. However, just as Job's refusal to curse God, even when Job gives himself

---

[48] Although typological connections between the book of Job and the NT do not fall within the main argument of this book, it is impossible not to notice how innocent Job's agony over what he thinks is God's condemnation whispers of a later Israelite who, completely undeserving of divine wrath, nevertheless suffered it. But if Job's agony was profound, Christ's was even greater.

[49] Ash 2014: 151.

good reason to do so, gives the reader a glimmer of hope, so some of the strange things he says in this speech provide some hope, however faint, that he will not stay for ever in his vision of a world ruled by an unjust and uncaring tyrant. Surprising as it may sound, one of these is the way Job internalizes what he perceives to be a divine verdict of guilt in his suffering (9:29). The beginning of this verse is somewhat obscured in translation, usually rendered along the lines of Job's expectation that he will be condemned or found guilty (e.g. NIV, ESV). But Job uses the qal of *rš'* to begin verse 29, normally translated as 'to be wicked'; the hiphil would be used to describe the act of condemnation.[50] This is strange because we expect Job to use the hiphil of this verb in his complaint that God is wrongly condemning him. But when Job uses the qal, it is better to translate his question as, 'I am wicked, why then do I labour in vain?' This is, of course, untrue, as Job well knows. But doubling the surprise of this verse is the repetition of the same verb with the same form in 10:15, where Job claims God knows he is not wicked (qal *rš'*). Why would Job contradict himself in this way? The only possible explanation is the incredibly exalted view Job has of God as a moral authority – one so exalted that Job finds it impossible to resist the conclusions of that authority, even when those conclusions directly contradict what Job knows with certainty to be true. Job *knows* he has done nothing to deserve the punishment of chapters 1–2. But if God disagrees, how can Job resist? He cannot help but put himself in the 'wicked' category, contradicting everything he knows. This is related to a significant ambiguity in 9:21, where Job says *lō' 'ēda' napšî*, suitably rendered as, 'I regard not myself' (ESV; NIV has 'I have no concern for myself'). This translation fits perfectly with the next clause ('I loathe my life') and fits within the normal range of *yd'*, 'know'.[51] But Job may also be saying more literally that he does not know who he is any more. His

---

[50] Outside Job 9 – 10, qal *rš'* is infrequent, occurring only in 2 Sam. 22:22 (= Ps. 18:22); 1 Kgs 8:47 (= 2 Chr. 6:37); Eccl. 7:17; Dan. 9:15. *HALOT* 1294 defines both the qal and hiphil along the lines of guilt (the qal for becoming guilty and the hiphil for being pronounced as such), but BDB 957 separates the qal of the verb for acting wickedly and the hiphil for the condemnation of such behaviour, as do Eugene Carpenter and Michael Grisanti (1997: 1201). Drawing a sharper distinction between the qal and hiphil of this verb probably fits the evidence better: while 1 Kgs 8:47/2 Chr. 6:37 and Dan. 9:15 could possibly have the sense of 'we have done wrong and become guilty', 2 Sam. 22:22/Ps. 18:22 and Eccl. 7:17 seem more unambiguously to address wicked behaviour itself, not the moral or legal consequences of it. This suggests a translation of 'to be wicked' for qal *rš'*.

[51] This verb in Exod. 23:9, Ps. 31:8 and Prov. 12:10 has the sense of acknowledging something or someone, or having regard for it.

view of God is so high and his sense of self so rooted in God that Job's most basic certainties about himself have less weight than how God views him. (The thought is strikingly similar to that expressed in 1 Cor. 8:2–3.) Job may know he has integrity with God (9:21) and the narrator may agree (1:1), but without God's approval all this is set at risk. Because Job feels God is condemning him, this exalted sense of God is expressed negatively – but even if Job's conclusion is wrong, his sense of the frailty of human certainty and human claims to righteousness outside God's approval is commendable and distinctly different from how the friends think of human righteousness. Even when Job protests, his theology is remarkably good; and we can hope that the God who spoke so highly of Job in the book's first chapter (1:8) will not leave his favoured servant in the dark valley through which Job is presently wandering. It is moving to wonder, in the light of Job's exalted view of God, at the relief and comfort that fill Job when God vindicates him at the end of his ordeal (42:7–9).

Zophar on the deep things of God (ch. 11)

Zophar, of course, will have none of this, as he quickly shows in the next speech (ch. 11). All Zophar can hear in Job's desire for a trial against God is a long-winded attempt to avoid Job's obvious need for repentance. Talk of defeating God legally is not the way for a human being to be justified (v. 2); this amounts to mocking God (v. 3). Zophar will not let Job get away with this and takes upon himself the burden of shaming Job into silence (v. 3). Any trial with God will unfold very differently from how Job imagines: the transcendent God (vv. 7–9) will quickly shut Job up by showing him that he is even worse than Job realizes (vv. 5–6). According to Zophar, God should have punished Job even more severely! So if God imprisons defendants before bringing them to court because he sees their evil (vv. 11–12; contradicting 10:4, 7), who is Job to argue? The implication is that when God imprisons someone for no apparent reason, he has reasons of his own (human sinfulness).[52] Thus is Job's suffering and God's apparent silence to be explained. But God's terms are very reasonable, Zophar says: if Job abandons the agonized complexities of chapters 9–10 and prays (v. 13) in repentance (v. 14), then all his suffering will be gone like a bad dream (v. 16) and, instead of darkness (10:21–22), a more-than-natural light will shine on Job – God's favour and blessing (vv. 17–19).

---

[52] Nam 2003: 52.

This is Zophar's first chance to speak, but he hardly acquits himself well. Zophar invokes the deep things of God (v. 7), mysteries higher than the heavens and deeper than the grave (v. 8), only to tell Job that Job deserved everything he got (vv. 6, 14). The anticlimax is palpable. It does not occur to Zophar to reflect on how God's greatness (vv. 7–9) might disrupt his own simplistic theology; he uses his theology only as a way to bludgeon Job.[53] Ironically, of course, Job will be led through the 'deep things of God' in chapters 38–39, but not at all in the way Zophar expects. Verse 12 applies to himself more than Zophar realizes.

Job's dawning desire for reconciliation (chs. 12–14)

Job closes the first round of the debate in a way that crystallizes his complaint against God while showing incremental progress in his desire to meet with his long-lost divine friend and possibly reconcile. He begins with sharp criticism of his friends (12:1–6). All Job can hear in his friends' advice is mockery of his predicament, a just man suffering unjustly (v. 4).[54] It is easy to hold suffering as insignificant when your own life is peaceful (v. 5). But Job's complete lack of peace has given him a new insight into the true nature of the world: there is no justice in how God orders and administers creation (v. 6). Retribution never obtains. All creation reflects this truth (vv. 7–9), as does the bitter wisdom Job has gained in his old age (vv. 11–12).[55] Job then launches into an 'anti-doxology'[56] in verses 13–25 in order to demonstrate the truth of God's injustice from verse 6. Most of the description shows God directly upending social structures and roles meant to create and protect order and shalom in society: according to Job,

---

[53] Ash 2014: 156; Fyall 2002: 41.

[54] That God has answered Job when Job called (v. 4) is strange, since Job has already complained God is not present to him or relating to him in a way Job can understand (9:11). Job is probably saying this in response to his friends' advice that he should seek God (8:5; 11:13), implying that he has already engaged in the pattern of calling out to God and receiving answers – yet his life still collapsed under God's baseless anger. The friends' advice is thus useless. Some translate this line to have Job 'calling on God that God might answer'; i.e. Job is crying out to God but God is silent (Hartley 1988: 206; Clines 1989: 275). But this is unlikely, for the combination of participle with consecutive imperfect which Job uses does not normally express a hypothetical (WOC 33.3.5; normally a perfect verb with a particle is reserved for this [WOC 30.5.4]).

[55] Job appears not to be literally imaging other sages agreeing with his new anti-theology, but backing up the claim of v. 6 by referring to his own ability as a discerning thinker (v. 11) and his status as a respected sage (v. 12); see Seow 2013: 625.

[56] Ibid. 626.

God 'de-royalizes' kings by stripping them of royal robes (v. 18), and priests lose their ministries (v. 19), as do wise elders (v. 20). All the leaders of the world wander, lost (v. 24). Job's frustration is palpable as he repeatedly puts God's action at the front of almost every line in verses 13–25: God directly and intentionally thwarts human desire for a just and moral world (or so Job claims). Even more upsetting is how Job begins his 'anti-doxology' with an invocation of divine attributes that, in almost any other context, would be comforting: God's wisdom and power, his complete understanding of every situation and limitless ability to achieve his purposes (v. 13).[57] But God's wisdom and power are no comfort to Job. They mean only that God is extremely effective at ruining innocent lives (9:22–24).

Job naturally expects that his friends will quickly dismiss his new theology, so he finishes his 'anti-doxology' with an assertion of his certainty about it (13:1–2). Because Job has personally experienced divine injustice (v. 1), his interpretation of creation should not be dismissed as inferior to that of the friends (v. 2) – especially friends who lie on God's behalf and make excuses for him (vv. 4–12).[58] Because God was not working out just punishment for sin in Job's suffering in chapters 1–2, the friends' insistence on this very point makes them (by definition) false witnesses and bad healers (v. 4). In other words, when the friends insist on something untrue and for which they have inadequate evidence, the friends break covenant with God, who loves truth-telling.[59] As will become clear, their counsel is a self-seeking piety more interested in its own theology than in God himself.[60]

In the midst of this criticism, Job says he is more interested in talking with God (v. 3). This is very striking. Although this desire does not show any lessening of Job's certainty that God is an unjust tyrant, he expresses it here in a more positive way than he did in chapter 9: instead of a zero-sum game, where God is proved wrong and Job is vindicated at God's

---

[57] The same divine attributes are enlisted to comfort Israel in 1 Chr. 29:10–12; 2 Chr. 20:6; Ps. 21:14; Isa. 40:12–31 (Nam 2003: 93).

[58] There may be a happy inconsistency on Job's part here, for if God is really as unconcerned about rewarding right behaviour as Job claims, who cares if one tells the truth about him? Certainly, elsewhere in Job's speeches such a hopeful inconsistency becomes apparent, as we will soon see with regard to v. 16 of this present chapter. However, it may also be that Job has the amoral bully of ch. 12 in mind as he criticizes his friends in this verse, implying to them that if they try to ingratiate themselves to this God through flattery, they will receive no better treatment than anyone else.

[59] Waltke 2007: 934.

[60] Clines 1989: 304.

expense, Job here leaves open the possibility of reconciliation.[61] Indeed, Job wants this so much he will speak in full recognition of the danger of arguing with a God who can cause such horrible suffering (v. 13).

> This longing to speak with the God who is responsible for all Job's loss and misery (of this Job has no doubt) is very remarkable. It is a sign of faith that Job in his heart of hearts so loves this God that he must speak with him.[62]

And this is a faith so strong that Job will continue to hope in God even if God treats him worse than he already has by enacting that final punishment and killing Job (v. 15).[63] Job's only hope in such a nerve-wracking encounter is that his total lack of hypocrisy will guarantee him a hearing (v. 16). (In a happy inconsistency, Job insists that God does not care about justice to those deserving it [9:22–24; 12:6, 13–25], yet also thinks that God cares enough about personal integrity to listen to and acquit him [23:7].) Indeed, Job's integrity is such that if anyone can produce concrete evidence against him, he will abandon his protest, be silent, submit to God's punishment and let his soon-approaching death take him (vv. 17–19). Job asks only that God not overwhelm him with terror (vv. 20–21) – and then God can summon Job and let him speak, or Job can speak and the Almighty can answer (v. 22). The equanimity in verse 22 is very touching. Job seems no longer concerned to win an argument about his bad treatment at God's expense; he wants only to reconnect with his long-lost friend.[64]

---

[61] The phrasing Job uses in the second half of v. 3 hints at this softening (but not abandoning) of his case against God. This is the only verse in the OT combining *ykḥ* (to rebuke) with the preposition *'el*; normally, the verb is used with the *b-* prefix to denote rebuking or refuting another party in the wrong (Prov. 30:6; Isa. 37:4), with *'al* denoting the grieved party on behalf of which a rebuke is made (e.g. Ps. 105:14), and with *l-* used to show a settlement in someone's favour (e.g. Isa. 2:4; 11:4). Job's unique phrasing in this verse seems best expressed by 'argue with', but not in a vindictive sense. Job does not appear here to be imagining his vindication coming at God's expense (see Clines 1989: 305).

[62] Ash 2014: 168.

[63] Assuming that we are to read v. 15 according to the Qere (supported by Aquila, Syriac, Vulgate, Targum [Seow 2013: 659]) and not according to the Kethiv, 'Behold, he will slay me, I have no hope; but my ways I will argue to his face.' The difference in the Hebrew is very slight and either reading makes sense in context; but if one takes the more negative reading, it is difficult to see why Job would say v. 16. But even if the Kethiv is correct, Job does enact a faith in God that clings to him even in the face of death; i.e. even if the reading given above is not the original, Job nevertheless does show the kind of faith implied by it.

[64] Brown 2014: 103.

But why, why is that long-lost friend treating Job like an enemy (v. 24)? If something in Job broke the friendship (v. 23), Job honestly wants to know what it is, doubtless so he can repent. But with no answer from God forthcoming, the brief spark of hope in verses 13–22 disappears and Job sinks into darkness. God's terrifying anger is too much for him (vv. 25–27). Job, along with all humanity, is fading and unravelling under such harsh treatment (v. 28; note again how Job generalizes from his own predicament to that of every human being). The next chapter is dominated by the image of 13:28: since God has inexplicably made life 'few of days and full of trouble', the best Job can hope for is that the divine tyrant ignore him (14:1–6). Job's brief hope from chapter 13 seems entirely gone; while other parts of nature may enjoy renewal (vv. 7–9), God will not allow this for humans (vv. 10–12). The best possible outcome Job can imagine is that God will somehow grant him asylum in the underworld until God's irrational anger blows itself out (v. 13); then, hypothetically speaking, God will not guard Job's sins so neurotically (v. 16), but forgive them (v. 17) in a change of heart towards Job (v. 15; even in his gloomiest moments, the deepest desire of Job's heart is to be right with God). But this impossible hypothetical will never obtain: God sends humanity in anger to Sheol, never to return or see its posterity (vv. 18–22). The vigour of the images impresses upon us Job's hopelessness: a falling mountain withers like a plant (v. 18), water rubs stones smooth and rain washes away soil (v. 19); everything is dissolving, losing consistency, dying. Job thus ends the first round of the debate on the same note on which all his speeches end: unbroken darkness and despair (3:26; 7:21; 10:21–22; 14:20–22).

Reflections on the first round of the debate (chs. 4–14)

John Walton helpfully writes that the debate between Job and his friends concerns three major truths: (1) God is just; (2) Job is righteous; (3) the retribution principle is true. From their perspective, not all three can be true at the same time, so Job will forfeit the first claim, and the friends the second. When God enters the debate, however, he will nuance, but not reject, the third claim.[65]

---

[65] Walton 2012: 340–341. See pp. 107, 181–189 of his commentary for some astute reflections on the first round of the debate.

To spell this out, we can summarize the friends' position as one that sees suffering as a contradiction in terms.[66] They turn a general principle of cause and effect into an ironclad rule in which the effect always and only shows the cause. But herein lies their mistake, for while it is true that we sow what we reap, it is not true that we reap only what we sow. Sin always causes suffering, but not all suffering is caused by sin. The friends thus unintentionally 'deny' God's freedom 'by not allowing God the freedom to use evil to accomplish his sovereign purposes'.[67]

In contrast to his friends, Job knows he has not committed any secret sin that can explain what looks like the punishment of chapters 1–2; as a result, he can only conclude that God is punishing him when God should not be, and is thus mishandling how he runs the world. God is not the person Job thought he was. As we have seen above, Job holds on to all of his theology except his belief in God's goodness; but without goodness, God's absolute sovereignty and power become monstrous and terrifying. Strangely but happily, however, Job moves from longing for death (ch. 3) to wanting to settle things with God and possibly reconcile with him (ch. 13). Although it is strictly inconsistent to believe that one could find a fair hearing or be vindicated by the kind of judge described in 9:22–24, Job nevertheless persists in this inconsistency. His desire to reconcile will only grow stronger as the book continues.

Round two of the debate (chs. 15–21)

Eliphaz on God's 'gentle comforts' (ch. 15)

If Job speaks better as the book progresses, the friends do not. As we enter the second round of the debate, we quickly see that the friends have nothing to add to their original contribution. Eliphaz's next speech is split between a rebuke to Job (vv. 2–16) and a statement on the principle of retribution (vv. 17–35). He says almost nothing new in his second speech, and whatever is new in this chapter serves only to cast further suspicion on him and unintentionally undermine his theology. His description of God's justice, for instance, unrealistically portrays wickedness as being

---

[66] Viberg 2000: 202.
[67] Waltke 2007: 933. For a perceptive study of differing nuances within a general agreement in the friends' approach to Job, see Baldwin 2018.

punished quickly and in obvious ways (e.g. the wicked is in anguish 'all his days' [v. 20] and is paid back 'before his time' [v. 32]). Each line of poetry in verses 17–35 is a miniature narrative that quickly dispatches the wicked, like dominoes falling in perfect order. But in addition to the lack of realism in Eliphaz's theology, it is very strange how God is not mentioned once in verses 17–35. One begins to get the impression that, for Eliphaz, God exists only distantly, and only to uphold the retribution principle itself, which is the centre of his theology.[68]

This raises the question of how much Eliphaz values God himself. Eliphaz makes a significant blunder in verse 4 that clarifies this question in an unfortunate way. This verse shows Eliphaz accusing Job of doing away with real spirituality and discipleship; if Job's new anti-theology takes hold, in which God does not reward good service with blessing, Eliphaz worries that people will abandon the fear of God. The unstated assumption is that no-one has a reason for piety except the blessing granted to it as a reward. But this is exactly the point at issue in the ordeal of chapter 1, where we learn that real piety fears, loves and is loyal to God even when secondary blessings are taken away. It looks very much as if Eliphaz would not have passed the Accuser's test from 1:9; as with the other friends, he gives no evidence of loving God for his own sake, outside the rewards the principle of retribution promises. In other words, all of Eliphaz's religion is 'for nothing' in the very unfortunate sense that he does not love God 'for nothing'. This means that an innocent Job is a huge threat to his theology, for if Job does not deserve the torment of chapter 1, then there is nothing to stop the same from happening to Eliphaz. Because Eliphaz loves the gifts more than the giver, it secretly terrifies him to think he may lose the blessings of obedience for some inscrutable reason even if he stays perfectly well behaved. As a result, he must insist that Job is getting what he deserves, and so smears Job as a terrible sinner (remember Job's intuition in 6:21 that Eliphaz speaks from fear; cf. his question in 16:3).

This deeper mistake twists everything in Eliphaz's speech. He cannot allow that Job is, with many missteps, genuinely trying to meet with God; as far as Eliphaz is concerned, all Job's talk about a court date with the Almighty is a ridiculous attempt to hold on to whatever secret sins prompted Job's punishment in the first place (vv. 5–6). Horrifyingly, this leads Eliphaz to describe the death of Job's children as a tender mercy and

---

[68] Viberg 2000: 201.

a gentle word spoken to Job that he should repent (v. 11). And Eliphaz sincerely thinks he is helping Job with pastoral advice of this kind! What could possibly have possessed Job, Eliphaz wonders, when Job's evil is so clear and God's terms for restoration so reasonable, so generous, that Job would rail against God and accuse him of wrongdoing (vv. 12–13)? Human beings are so sinful that no-one can complain when suffering comes – all of it must be deserved (vv. 14–16). From Eliphaz's perspective, all of creation is ugly, impure, abominable, even in its supernatural dimensions (v. 15) – an entirely unbiblical perspective, one contradicted by the unified Old Testament witness to the goodness of creation and supported by God's speech in chapter 38. But Eliphaz's wild claims, strange as they are, reveal the ugliness and narrowness of the world view God's people can sometimes have, as well as the profound degree to which such a world view is unsettled by innocent suffering: You mean all this might happen to me? Does all my good behaviour count for so little? It also reveals the nearly Pelagian power Eliphaz must attribute to human repentance. For in order to be consistent, Eliphaz must grant to human beings the power to reform their own lives and make themselves clean before God, thus satisfying the conditions of verse 14 and allowing God to bless them. All this runs contrary to the rest of the Old Testament.

Job first speaks of his heavenly witness (chs. 16–17)

As Eliphaz destroys his own credibility, however, Job uses his next speech to show his hope growing stronger, even if his criticism of God remains unchecked. A sense of dizzying violence pervades Job's description of God's unprovoked attack on him in 16:7–17: God has torn Job open in hatred, glaring at him with 'sharpened' eyes (v. 9); God broke the unsuspecting Job, seized him by the neck and shattered him (v. 12), slashed open his kidneys (v. 13), ran at him like a soldier and broke Job breach upon breach (v. 14). G. M. Hopkins seemed to have this passage in mind when he wrote his terrible and faith-filled poem, 'Carrion Comfort':

> But ah, but O thou terrible, why wouldst thou rude on me
> Thy wring-world right foot rock? lay a lionlimb against me? scan
> With darksome devouring eyes my bruised bones? and fan,
> O in turns of tempest, me heaped there; me frantic to avoid thee
> and flee?

Poor Job does not know, of course, that God's heart towards him is very different (remember 1:8). It certainly was not God who ruined Job's life so effectively; but however disturbing Job's mistake is, it is understandable. He does not know as much about his true situation as the reader does from chapter 1. If it is not God persecuting Job, who else can it be (9:24)?

As if all this is not enough, Job's false friends use God's attack as a reason to gang up on Job and insult him (v. 10). All Job's suffering counts as a witness against him in their eyes, demonstrating his guilt and how much he deserves his misery, when it should be evidence that God is in the wrong (v. 8). All Job can do in response is weep (vv. 15–16), especially because he gave his divine attacker no reason to do such violence to him (v. 17).

Then, seemingly from nowhere, hope surfaces in verses 18–22, and much more strongly than in 13:20–24. Job expects to die soon (v. 22), but does not want the injustice done to him forgotten (v. 18; Job's blood in this verse is a synecdoche for the violence committed against him [cf. Gen. 4:10; Isa. 26:21]). But in contrast to his scornful friends (v. 20), Job's witness is arguing in heaven on his behalf (vv. 19, 21). This is no mere wish on Job's part – this witness speaks 'even now' (v. 19). This witness will do what Job cannot as he makes the case with the Almighty that Job was treated unjustly and thus bridges the terrible distance and silence between Job and God. Furthermore, it is no mere human being making Job's case, for the witness is 'in heaven', a place no mortal can reach (14:20–22), and one able to argue with God in the same way one human argues with a neighbour (v. 21), which Job knows he himself cannot do (9:15–16). Even more encouraging is the way Job suggests in verse 21 that he expects the witness's activity on his behalf to be successful, so that God and Job will be able to be friends again. However despairing Job is at different points, a simultaneous and contradictory hope is flourishing within him that someone is working for him to resolve this dispute. Ironically, of course, Job speaks here better than he knows, since God is a witness for Job against Satan – but Job, in his ignorance, puts God in the role of accuser.[69]

Many questions arise at this point, of course: Who exactly is this witness? How can Job be so sure of this heavenly friend? But even if it is

---

[69] Fyall 2002: 43. This is not to identify the witness of v. 19 with God himself, for Job speaks of the former as a party separate from God; it is to point out only that v. 19 is truer than Job knows.

difficult to answer such questions specifically, it is amazing to see someone who has suffered so much maintain a hope and certainty for a reunion with God.

If Job's hope is expressed more strongly here than in chapter 13, it lasts hardly any longer. The last verse of chapter 16 sets the tone for all of chapter 17 as Job laments his condition, physically and socially. Job regresses here to the absolute darkness that has overshadowed his earlier laments, so no further comment will be offered here,[70] except to draw attention to the slightly positive note in verses 15–16, where Job says his hope will not let him rest in Sheol. This exactly reverses his hopelessness from 14:13. Even if Job thinks he will soon die, even if he still thinks God is implacably hostile, the fact that his hope will not let him rest in Sheol (contrast 3:11–19) is still a remarkable change.

Bildad on the terrors of hell (ch. 18)

As one would expect, all this is lost on Bildad. Deeply offended by Job's burgeoning hope (v. 3), he can ask only why Job insists on hurting himself (v. 4a) and unravelling the moral order of God's universe (4b) just so an exception can be granted him and Job can hold on to whatever unconfessed sin is causing his suffering. A long description of retribution follows in verses 5–21, from which God is almost entirely absent (he appears only in the last verse). The poetry of the speech is vigorous and vivid as Bildad describes the spiritual terrors of the wicked, but the whole of it is as unconvincing and unhelpful as that given by Eliphaz in chapter 15.

Job's great redeemer (ch. 19)

Job will have none of this. He finally names his false friends' tortures in his next speech (19:2) and insists the suffering they invoke as a witness to his wickedness instead casts doubt on God's character (v. 6). Job is hemmed in and humiliated (vv. 8–9), both torn down and uprooted (v. 10); everything a sinner and rebel should experience has somehow fallen on him (vv. 11–12). As a result, he is completely isolated, a stranger and a nobody to everyone else (vv. 13–19; the root for 'stranger' [zûr] repeats in vv. 13, 15, 17). Adding to the agony of the loss of his children, Job has

---

[70] In the especially difficult vv. 8–9, Job apparently imagines how people should act in the light of his suffering: instead of shaming him (v. 6), the morally upright should be shocked and act to defend him (v. 8) in such a way that they will be blessed (v. 9). See further Hartley 1988: 269–270 and Seow 2013: 756–757 for differing readings and more discussion.

become faceless, a ghost, a non-entity in relation to others. In the light of this, can Job's friends not treat him better (v. 21)? Can they not see their shaming and criticism is a kind of destruction of his character and person – a kind of feasting on him (v. 22)? Have they no fear their attacks will bring judgment on themselves (vv. 28–29)?

Then, as unexpectedly as in 16:18–22, hope reappears in verses 23–27. As in that earlier passage, Job expects to die very soon, and so wants a permanent record of his protest of the injustice done him (vv. 23–24). His reason for wanting this permanent record is the action of his redeemer (gô'ēl, v. 25). The implication is that this redeemer will work as a legal advocate on Job's behalf. This fits perfectly with the role of the kinsman-redeemer elsewhere in the Old Testament, for one of the many ways the gô'ēl could defend the defenceless was to engage in legal argument (rîb, the word Job uses for his own argument in 10:2) on behalf of an accused person (see Ps. 119:154; Prov. 23:11; Jer. 50:34; Lam. 3:58–59; all tying rîb with the gô'ēl). Only because Job has this advocate in heaven does he hope his case will always be remembered (v. 24).

Job is, however, doing more than repeating his hope from 16:19, 21 for an advocate. A variety of hints strongly suggest he expects not just legal representation, but a cosmic act of redemption from his heavenly gô'ēl. This is most clearly seen in that Job hopes for his redeemer to 'rise above' or 'triumph over' (qûm) the 'dust' ('āpār). To express Job's hope this way, of course, goes against the familiar rendering in most English translations that the gô'ēl will 'stand on the earth'. This translation of the Hebrew is possible. Although the normal verb for standing ('āmad) is not used in this verse, the verb Job uses can be found in legal contexts describing the action of a witness (Deut. 19:15–16; Job 16:8; Pss 27:12; 35:11).[71] Furthermore, the 'dust' to which Job refers not infrequently stands as part-for-whole for the soil or for the earth (e.g. Job 4:19; 28:2). That Job thus expects his redeemer to 'stand on the earth' in the sense of being a witness on his behalf thus fits both the Hebrew of the verse and with Job's expectation of a heavenly witness.

At the same time, the words Job uses in this verse suggest a different translation is at least as likely. Together with the preposition 'al, the verb *qûm* usually means 'to rise over' or 'rise above', such as when a new leader rises in place of another (e.g. Exod. 1:8; Deut. 28:36; Jer. 6:17), someone rises against an enemy (e.g. Judg. 9:18; Deut. 19:11; 28:7; Pss 54:5; 124:2; Isa. 31:2), or a person or thing is physically lifted higher than something else (Josh. 7:26; 2 Sam. 12:17). It is also significant that the verb frequently speaks of God's action of self-exaltation on behalf of his people, especially in the Psalms (see Pss 3:8; 7:7; 9:22; 10:12; 12:6; 44:27; 68:2; 74:22; 76:10; 82:8; as well as Job 31:14 and Isa. 2:19, 21; 33:10). As a result, 'triumph over' or 'be exalted over' is equally justifiable as a translation.

Similarly, while 'dust' can stand for the world, it is often used symbolically of the grave (just within the book of Job, see 7:21; 17:16; 20:11, 26; 34:15; 40:13). It is also significant that a number of these references to the dust of death in the book of Job speak of lying down in death (*šākab*); that is, the opposite of 'rising' (7:21; 14:12; 20:11; 21:26). In line with this is how the verb *qûm* is negated in Job 14:12 as Job expresses his gloomy certainty that humans will not rise from the grave. Additionally, Isaiah 26:19 uses the same verb to express exactly the hope of the resurrection that Job denies in chapter 14. But it seems Job's earlier denial is breaking into belief in 19:25: although the legal action of Job's redeemer is not eclipsed in this verse, his phrasing suggests that Job has new hope that his champion will triumph over death, even though Job will soon succumb to it. In other words, I read the verse to express a double entendre by which Job simultaneously expresses his hope for legal representation and cosmic redemption from the grave. This gives added weight to the redeemer being 'alive' – this saviour is not just present and active, but possessed of an indestructible life not even the 'dust' can destroy.

How Job benefits from the redeemer's 'rising above the dust' is detailed in verses 26–27: after Job's death, Job will be utterly reconciled with God. Although this is not the language he uses, several factors favour this interpretation. First, 'skin' is used as a synecdoche for one's whole body elsewhere in Job (2:4; 7:5); its being 'struck off' (my tr.) thus implies Job's physical death. This means that Job looks for the benefits of his redeemer's work both 'now' (16:19) and after Job is in the grave. Second, Job uses a verb for 'seeing' God that often denotes prophetic visions of the divine: while *ḥāzah* can mean to look at something intently (Prov. 24:32; Mic. 4:11), it is easy to find examples of its denoting visions of God (Exod. 24:11; Num. 24:4, 16; Pss 11:7; 17:15; 27:4; 63:3; Isa. 30:10). Job's sight of God is not some casual glance: it stands for that intimacy and joy and worship for which Moses and David longed. This is confirmed when Job specifies that he will see God, 'and not another' (literally, 'and not a stranger'; v. 27). This vision will reverse the alienation Job suffers (vv. 13, 15, 17). God will not be alienated from Job any more, but, because of the triumph of Job's redeemer, God and Job will be reunited in friendship. That Job sees God with his own eyes (v. 27), from within his flesh,[72] further implies a physical resurrection as one part of that ultimate reconciliation to God.[73]

In other words, because Job's redeemer triumphs over the dust, Job will be raised to new life and favour in God's presence after Job sleeps in the dust. To whatever extent Job's soon-approaching death is the final curse and punishment from God, the inevitable end of God's attack on him, Job is nevertheless certain that his redeemer's work will rescue him from all of God's anger. Little wonder Job's heart faints within him at the thought (v. 27)! Although Job has not retracted his brutal criticisms of God's indifference to justice, he amazingly (and contradictorily) also looks to a reconciliation with God after death because of the work of his redeemer. For all his dark thoughts of God, Job's deepest desire is still to be reconciled; he says nothing anywhere in the debate about wanting to return to his blessed life, but always obsesses over what God is doing and how he might speak with him.[74] Furthermore, as elsewhere in these chapters, Job is eerily close to the truth of his situation without knowing it. There is a heavenly being treating Job like an enemy, and Job does have a heavenly redeemer – but Job has mistaken the identity of both.[75] His future is far more hopeful than he realizes.

Zophar and Job lock horns (chs. 20–21)

The rest of round two of the debate in no way prolongs the triumph that ends chapter 19. Zophar predictably insists on an unrealistically quick and

---

[72] Although the *min* prefixed to 'flesh' in v. 26 could be taken as privative ('without' or 'outside' Job's body, he will see God), the reference to Job's own eyes suggests it is from within Job's body that he will see God after death (i.e. a physical resurrection). Both senses fall within the normal range of the preposition (WOC 11.2.11).

[73] For two careful readings of this passage which argue that it refers to a this-worldly vindication of Job, see Williamson 2017: 80 and Johnston 2002: 209–214. Both authors make astute observations about the text; my comments above do not so much disagree with them as try to tease out the multiple meanings Job invokes through his choice of words.

[74] Robert Polzin points out that Job will 'steadfastly resist' any suggestion from his tormentors that if he just confesses something, he will be restored (1977: 103). Polzin also points out that although Job longs for death, he never speaks of suicide, being seemingly unwilling to die without God's sanction (ibid. 104).

[75] Fyall 2002: 50.

neat version of the retribution principle in the next chapter in order to prove that Job must deserve his suffering (ch. 20). This, of course, is completely untrue; but Job's response in chapter 21 is unfortunately not much better. Apparently goaded into arguing on Zophar's own terms, Job spends an entire chapter insisting that retribution never happens at all; but his description of the perfect blessings of wicked lives (see vv. 7–13) is as unbelievable as the ironclad, mechanical system of sin and punishment envisaged by Zophar in chapter 20. One wishes Job had stuck to his desire to meet with God and his hope in a redeemer rather than trying to beat Zophar at his own game.

Round three of the debate (chs. 22–27)

Since the purpose of this chapter is to provide an appropriate context for God's response to Job's complaint, and since not much new is offered in its third round of the debate between Job and his tormentors, we will move more quickly through the book's middle chapters.

The dominant impression of these chapters is that the debate is breaking down: Bildad's speech is unusually short (ch. 25) and Zophar does not speak in the third round at all.[76] The human participants of the debate seem to be running out of things to say while the point at issue – the moral coherence of God's universe – remains unresolved. When Eliphaz does speak (ch. 22), the only part of his speech that is not repetitive serves to discredit him even further. Eliphaz invents an entire catalogue of heinous sins Job has committed (vv. 5–11), in complete contradiction of the narrator's (1:1) and the Almighty's (1:8) assessment of Job. The possibility that a righteous person might not be blessed for good behaviour is so deeply threatening to Eliphaz's theology that it drives him to make wildly outrageous claims.[77] Christopher Ash shockingly but rightly calls chapter 22 'the pastoral equivalent of rape' because 'to call on a penitent

---

[76] The second volume of D. J. A. Clines's massive commentary on Job (2006) reconstructs these chapters to make them resemble the first two rounds of the debate; e.g. expanding Bildad's speech to include ch. 26 and cobbling together parts of chs. 24 and 27 to give Zophar a third speech. But this is speculative and mutes the (in my opinion, intentional) impression that the debate is coming to a standstill. And if the third round originally mirrored the first two, how did it ever become so confused?

[77] Westermann (1981: 27) takes the fact that Job never responds to these accusations in ch. 22 as an indication that Job is refusing to debate with the friends any more – another indication that the debate has derailed.

believer to repent of sins he is not aware of is to pressure him to compromise his integrity'.[78]

For his part, Bildad uses his turn to speak in chapter 25 only to repeat that everything in creation is dirty (see 15:14–16), the implication being that all suffering is deserved. As above, this is both false and irrelevant to Job.

Job, in contrast, continues to mix harsh criticism of God's injustice with laudable confessions of faith in that same God. He begins superbly in chapter 23 by expressing his desire to meet with God and imagining a positive outcome to such a meeting (23:1–7). The reader is again reminded that although Job does think God is in the wrong, the deeper desire driving Job's criticisms is a desire to be right with God and receive vindication from him (v. 7), which is very admirable. But this is soon spoiled by Job's frustration over God's elusiveness (vv. 8–9) and his terror at how God destroyed his life in full knowledge that Job had done nothing to deserve it (vv. 10–17). This leads to another generalization from his experience as Job spends chapter 24 describing how God's failure as judge (vv. 1, 12c) produces moral and social chaos (vv. 1–17). Because judgment never comes, Job says, everyone does what is right in his or her own eyes (see esp. vv. 2–4). The chapter's final section (vv. 18–25) is confusing because of its description of the judgment of the wicked, something Job has just denied; it is usually taken either as an unmarked quotation of Job's friends (see ESV) or as Job's curse on the wicked.[79]

But just as Job cannot seem to maintain his confidence in God for long, so his hope (17:15–16) continually disrupts his complaint. This is nowhere more evident than in chapter 26. Bildad has just spoken, weakly and haltingly, about majesty and fear in high places (25:2). Job takes up the same theme and far outdoes him, describing God's victory against cosmic chaos and supernatural evil in truly impressive fashion. Part of the chapter's difficulty, however, is that Job describes the stages of this victory out of chronological order: the naked trembling of the underworld in verses 5–6 is best taken as a result of YHWH's warfare described at the chapter's end (vv. 11–13; cosmic shaking is elsewhere the result of God's warfare against chaos, not an anticipation [e.g. Joel 3:16; Hab. 3:3–6]). Job thus shows us God's creation of all things (vv. 7–10), his defeat of the

---

[78] Ash 2014: 237, 244.
[79] Hartley 1988: 352–353.

supernatural chaos that threatens his creation (vv. 11–13), and the totality and permanence of this defeat – Abaddon will never again resist God but remains trembling and vulnerable in submission (vv. 5–6). The results of the battle are, however, described first, in order to assure us of its certainty and allow us to enjoy this victory even before battle is joined.

The description of the battle itself is quite lovely: the serpent does nothing but flee (is there even a fight?), and the heavens are made fair as a result (v. 13). After the storm, the sun shines again. Truly nothing can stand before this God, not even the most securely founded parts of creation (v. 11). The implications Job draws from this victory are even more striking. The first is found as the chapter opens (vv. 2–4), where Job dismisses mere religious theorizing, however eloquent and superficially impressive it may be, if it cannot help someone in deep pain who is sincerely seeking God. Job articulates this dismissal by asking Bildad in verse 2 whether he has 'saved' (hiphil of *yš'*) the 'arm' (*zĕrôa'*) without strength. Although these two words are not repeated in verses 11–13, they elsewhere describe God's divine warfare against chaos and evil, which is described in the chapter's final passage (see Pss 44:4; 98:1; Isa. 51:5; 59:16; 63:5). The implication is that God's victory over evil and the peace it gives to creation (vv. 11–13) should be reflected in human wisdom (vv. 2–4) and should have the same effect: it should save people who have no other help. Because Bildad's wisdom has neither, it is worthless. According to Job, God's cosmic victory over chaos is reflected in wise pastoral counselling – a very striking connection!

Job reflects on the implications of God's victory in a different but equally significant way in the chapter's final verse (v. 14), where he claims that God's victory against chaos is but the outskirts of his ways, only the very edge – 'how small a whisper do we hear of him' (v. 14)! This is surprising because God's battle against the raging waters and the monsters in it is often touted in the Old Testament as a central victory for all creation and his people (cf. Pss 18; 65; 74; 89; 93; 144; Isa. 51; Hab. 3; etc.). But Job's view of God is so exalted, his theological imagination so capacious, that he sees an action of God hailed as central to God's whole programme in the Old Testament as only the beginning. How profoundly God must outstrip all our thoughts of him!

It has been mentioned above how Job occasionally says something that ironically illuminates his true situation before God far better than Job himself realizes. This is nowhere more apparent than in chapter 26, for there really is a serpentine power God will defeat, and this great victory can make a huge difference in wise counsel to those suffering. But Job does not apply the truths he has confessed in this chapter to his own predicament. Instead of comforting himself that God, far from being the great Destroyer (9:5–7), will one day root out all evil from his creation, and the suffering it brings, Job moves on to criticize his friends in chapter 27 (see vv. 7–23; 'my enemy' in verse 7 refers to his three tormentors). Given the inexcusable things they have said, this is understandable. But while foolish speech like that of the friends is a serious matter in Old Testament wisdom literature (see e.g. Prov. 10:8, 31; 12:19; 19:5, 9), one cannot help but notice that God, despite his anger at the three friends, treats them much better than Job predicts in chapter 27: God's ultimate intention is to restore even them (42:8–9). However plausible the pattern of Job's thought in chapters 26–27 might be, one cannot help but wish that Job had taken the next chapter to apply his vision of God's greatness from chapter 26 to himself instead of letting his justifiable anger at his tormentors dominate his speech. Job believes God is a victorious warrior, but cannot affirm that God is fighting on his own behalf.[80]

Wisdom's inaccessibility (ch. 28) and Job's final assertion of innocence (chs. 29–31)

The debate between Job and his friends about God's governance of the world and Job's character appears to grind to a halt after chapter 27. Job has nothing more to say to them: we read a poem about wisdom's inaccessibility in chapter 28 and then Job's final declaration of innocence against all charges in chapters 29–31, after which he stops speaking (31:40). No forward progress is made: Job binds himself formally and legally only to his original claim he did nothing to justify (what appears to be) the punishment of chapters 1–2.

The wisdom poem of chapter 28 does not advance the debate between Job and his friends either, as much as comment on what has already been said. In fact, it is not even clear that Job is the speaker in this chapter. Although no new speaker is introduced, chapter 28 is noticeably different

---

[80] Angel 2014: 65. When Job asks the question 'The thunder of his power who can understand?', Angel discerns confusion on Job's part – God is thundering in the heavens, but Job cannot understand why he is not benefiting from it.

from the surrounding argument both in its placid tone and in its claims about wisdom's inaccessibility. In contrast, both Job and his friends have made strong claims about the moral order (or lack thereof) of creation under God's rule, and claimed that wisdom supports their contradictory conclusions (e.g. 11:6; 12:6–12; 15:7–9). As a result, it is difficult to imagine either party making an extended argument that no humans have access to wisdom on their own. Furthermore, Job has portrayed creation as a moral chaos – a very different picture from the ordered world of chapter 28. It looks as if the intention of chapter 28 is not to take either side of the argument, but to comment on it from the outside.[81]

In order to discern what comment this chapter makes on the debate, it is important to follow the basic argument of the poem: human beings show amazing ingenuity in finding all kinds of precious, hidden materials from the earth (vv. 1–11), but wisdom – that understanding of the complexities of creation and how to live well in the light of them – simply escapes us (vv. 12–19). We do not even know where to begin looking (vv. 12–13), and none of the normal methods by which humans acquire precious things from the earth can gain that most precious jewel of all (vv. 15–19). Only God has wisdom (vv. 20–28); only he sees that orderliness in creation that humans need in order to live successfully (v. 27). In this chapter, wisdom is not so much one 'place' within creation as much as a characteristic of the whole, and only God has the comprehensive view of all reality necessary to gain that insight into the nature of wisdom.[82]

Strikingly, however, the poem ends not with our creator giving us direction about where to find wisdom in creation, but by turning our attention back to God himself (v. 28). This chapter does not push us to renew our search in the world for insight into it, instead presenting the only route to wisdom for finite and fallible creatures in the fear of YHWH. In other words, only when human beings turn away from self-constructed ideas about reality and how to live blessedly within it and bow before God does creation properly come into focus and we see clearly how to live wisely in God's world. Although not explicit, this is surely a critique of the

---

[81] Most commentators understand ch. 28 in this way (see e.g. Habel 1985: 391–392, and the citations listed there). Ash leaves the question open but does point out that the *kî* beginning ch. 28 could plausibly be understood to tie chs. 27–28 together, such that the judgment of the wicked friends leads into a meditation on the impossibility of humans finding wisdom on their own outside the fear of YHWH (2014: 277–278).

[82] Walton 2012: 290.

friends' theology, who insist that the inner workings of the world can be explained without much explicit reference to God at all. It is surely also an implicit commendation of Job who, in the midst of many false claims about God that will deeply pain him later, nevertheless continues to seek God. As long as Job continues this course, things turn out well for him – or so it is implied.

When Job takes up his discourse again (29:1), it is to make one final speech in which he surveys the blessed life he lost (ch. 29) and his present misery (ch. 30), and makes a solemn oath that he has done nothing to deserve the tragic change from the one to the other (ch. 31). This is Job's final protest, a final assertion that his punishment from God is undeserved; nothing remains to be said after this (31:40). Since chapter 31 is an ancient Semitic way of saying, 'God damn me if I committed this sin,' the assumption in this last speech is that 'silence implies consent'; if God did nothing in response to Job's self-imprecation, it would be assumed that Job was in fact innocent and God was wrong to punish him.[83] Job is thus forcing the issue of God's apparent silence and distance (remember 23:8–9).

As elsewhere, Job's integrity is apparent in a number of ways in this final speech. For instance, in remembering his past, Job speaks first about his lost friendship with God (29:1–6), as if that loss hurt him most. This is echoed in 31:6, where we are reminded that, however harshly or lopsidedly he might state it, Job's constant desire is to enjoy relational rightness with God again. It is also significant that Job never once asks for his blessed life back; his losses are enlisted as evidence only of his innocence, not some secret desire to wrangle a comfortable life from God.[84] Furthermore, a significant part of his lament is Job's lost opportunity to do justice to others (29:11–17). So far from producing any selfishness in Job, God's blessing on his life meant Job could be generous to the widow and orphan in a way he cannot be now.

'The words of Job are ended' (31:40). Job's desire to be cleared of all false charges and to have his integrity with God publicly demonstrated is entirely justifiable. Nevertheless, the way Job has framed things may make us a little uncomfortable: the only two possible responses to chapter 31 seem to be the Almighty's producing evidence of some sin of which

---

[83] See further Dick 1992: 321–334 for more on this and for some Mesopotamian parallels.
[84] Murphy 1996: 40.

Job was unaware, which would explain Job's suffering, or apologizing to Job for treating Job like a wicked sinner when he is not one. It is thus perhaps somewhat fortunate that before God appears, a young man rises to speak.

Elihu (chs. 32–37)

The Elihu chapters have traditionally been interpreted in two mutually exclusive ways. On the one hand, some commentators view Elihu positively, as someone speaking hard truths to Job in order to prepare him for the encounter with God in chapters 38–41.[85] Interpretations of this type tend to argue that Elihu's rebuke of Job's sins differs from that of the friends in that Elihu claims Job has sinned not before chapter 1, in such a way that would explain the suffering there, but after chapters 1–2 in the course of the debate; as a result, Elihu confronts Job's pride in criticizing God and prepares him for the profundities of the theophany.[86] On the other hand, some read Elihu negatively by understanding him to promise a new angle on the debate (32:14) and then to repeat the doctrines of the friends; Elihu promises Job a new answer, but cannot avoid condemning Job in the same way the friends did. According to this reading, chapters 32–37 are intended to prompt the reader to conclude that there is no possible human answer to Job's predicament, because Elihu, for all his bombastic insistence to the contrary, has done no better than the friends.[87] As a result, Elihu's speeches are meant to make us ever more anxious for God to speak, for only God can resolve the questions that flummox Job and his friends. Since no explicit evaluation is made about Elihu when God vindicates Job and demotes the friends (42:7–9), the reader is thrown back on Elihu's words as the only basis on which to decide whether he is a wise friend to Job or not.

I find myself unconvinced by the positive interpretation of Elihu because I cannot find the new insight into Job's problem Elihu promises in 32:14. It is especially glaring on this score to read Elihu's statement of the retribution principle in 34:10–12, which seems identical to the

---

85 See e.g. Seow 2011 and Andersen 2015.
86 Ash 2014: 329 lays great stress on this point.
87 Representatives of this view are Waltke (2007: 936–939) and Habel (1985: 442, 502). Waltke provides a convenient summary of the structure of Elihu's four speeches in 2007: 938.

definition of this principle given by Job's friends.[88] Other suspicions accumulate when one surveys the broader trajectory of Elihu's argument. For instance, Elihu's answer to Job's complaint about God's silence (33:13) is to point to dreams that expose hidden pride and sin (vv. 15–18) or sickness that brings sinners to their senses (vv. 19–22). True as this may be in a general sense, one wonders how this is supposed to help Job or prepare him for his encounter with God when it was no sin of Job's that brought the suffering of chapters 1–2. Furthermore, how different is this explanation from that of the friends? Both make sin central in the explanation of pain. Some commentators detect a difference in that Elihu thinks of pain as preventing future sin instead of standing as punishment for past misdeeds.[89] But even if this is the case, it is hard to see how telling Job that God allowed the deaths of all of his children in order to prevent future pride in him is any less cruel than telling him that God is punishing him for something he has already done. Besides, Job's dreams and physical pain do not reveal any sin, only terror (7:4–6, 14). Even if God can communicate this way, he has not chosen to do so with Job.[90]

Elihu never seems to be able to transcend the suffering-as-punishment framework the friends have already insisted on at such tiresome length. For example, in 35:9–13, divine silence is explained because people either ignore God (vv. 9–11) or ask with wrong motives (vv. 12–13); either way, humans are at fault. In chapter 36, God exalts the righteous (v. 7); but if they lose their privileges (v. 8), God reveals the sin that caused their downfall (v. 9) and calls them to repent (v. 10). If they listen, they are restored (v. 11), but if not, they die in their sin (vv. 12–14). Even the final

---

[88] As a supporter of Elihu, Ash tries to distinguish Elihu's claim in this passage from the similar-sounding claim of Bildad in 8:3 by writing that while Bildad focuses narrowly on the judgment of the wicked, Elihu asserts more broadly God's 'good and fair government of the world in every respect' (2014: 347). But both aspects of God's governance of the world – punishing sin and restoring the penitent – are emphasized by Bildad in 8:2–6, as well as by Eliphaz (5:8–27) and Zophar (11:10–20). I cannot see any difference between these earlier passages and Elihu's statement of retribution in 34:10–12.

[89] Walton 2008: 339, 342.

[90] Some positive readings of Elihu make much of his description of the heavenly intermediary, who has a ransom for sinners in 33:23–24, connecting this figure with Job's witness in 16:18–22 and the redeemer of 19:25–27. A Christological connection may be valid here. It is significant, however, that the role Elihu attributes to this figure does not comport with Job's hope in chs. 16, 19. Job's redeemer works as a witness on his behalf without condemning him; Elihu's intermediary, on the other hand, shows the sinner what is upright (v. 23) so that the sinner can repent and avoid the wages of sin in death (vv. 27–28). Elihu is still assuming some sin on Job's part and thus failing to distinguish himself from the friends, as he claimed he would (32:14).

poem about the storm (36:22 – 37:24) uses the common Semitic theme of the deity's power in thunder and lightning to speak again about God's inviolable justice and judgment (36:31; 37:13, 23). The rhetorical questions Elihu puts to Job as part of this speech (36:22–23; 37:15–20) are intended to make Elihu's overall conclusion about Job unavoidable: Job is under God's judgment (34:7–8, 17; 35:16; 36:17).

Rhetorical questions are, of course, prominent in God's speech in chapters 38–39 as well. This prompts some to see a positive connection between Elihu's last speech and God's first, such that Elihu's questions help to prepare Job for the questions God puts to him. A different intention informs God's rhetorical questions, however. As will be seen, God's purpose in asking Job questions is not to win a confession of sin from him; although he does confront the false claims Job has made, he is far gentler with Job than are any of the friends, including Elihu. Furthermore, the intention of the divine speeches is not to insist on Job's ignorance about divine matters, or at least not in the same way, for while Elihu imagines that human beings will simply have nothing to say to God (37:19–20), all the questions God asks Job turn out to be very easy to answer: Who made the earth? Who feeds lions? Who orders the world? Even if the subject of God's question is beyond Job's knowledge, the question God asks about it is not.[91] This suggests that Job does not need any preparation before the encounter with God and removes one important argument in favour of reading Elihu's speeches positively.

Suspicions also accumulate around Elihu when we compare his introduction to his speeches with those of the other participants in the debate. Whereas Job and his friends typically take three to four verses to call on the others to listen, Elihu speaks for almost thirty verses before making his first point (32:7 – 33:7). Not only that, but his self-introduction shows Elihu's referring to himself four times in a single verse, literally saying, 'I, I myself, will answer you, I will impart knowledge, I myself' (32:17, my tr.). Norman Habel also points out that his self-description in 36:4 as one 'perfect in knowledge' is the same phrase he uses to describe God's knowledge in 37:16.[92] It is difficult to avoid the sense that Elihu thinks too highly of himself. His self-importance does not generate much confidence in his theology.

---

[91] Fox 2013: 3.
[92] Habel 1985: 502.

In the light of these considerations, the relationship between the speeches of Elihu and God is best described as one of ironic contrast. Their main purpose is to demonstrate that the human participants in the debate are absolutely unable to resolve Job's problem: none of the human participants in the debate understands God's ways in the world in such a way that explains why a godly man like Job would (apparently) be punished so terribly without insisting on claims that turn out to be completely false (either Job is wicked or God is). Additionally, the Elihu chapters prevent any impression that God allowed himself to be summoned or arraigned by Job's self-imprecation in chapter 31 by giving some space between Job's final speech and YHWH's reply. God does respond to Job's self-imprecation, but not because Job subpoenaed him.

The above interpretation of the relationship between chapters 32–37 and 38–41 is not meant to imply that Job has escaped all sin in the course of the debate. Doubtless many of his harsh criticisms of God, however understandable they might have been, were simply sinful to utter. How can it be anything but morally blameworthy to claim that God laughs when innocent lives are ruined (9:22–24)? The only point here to emphasize is the difference between how Elihu and YHWH interrogate Job and to what different purposes they use rhetorical questions. For all the questions God asks, there is never a hint that Job deserved what he got.

Evaluating the debate between Job and his friends

At this point in the book of Job, the discussion at the human level has exhausted itself. If God stays silent, no resolution is possible.[93] Michael Fox rightly says that

> [i]t is as if everyone believes that the terrible problems of existence can be wrestled to the ground by talk, lots of it. But they only talk their way into a blind alley. They accuse each other of being deaf, blind, and stubborn – and they are.[94]

---

[93] Fox 2005: 358.
[94] Ibid. 355.

The narrator has used both Job and the friends to test different theological stances, but all of them are found wanting.[95] It is deeply and tragically ironic that Job sees suffering as unjust punishment when it is exactly his integrity that has caused it, and that he thinks of himself as so small when he rates very highly with God. But this irony should prompt self-reflection on the reader's part, for 'Job's limited and distorted vision exemplifies the human predicament. The target of these ironies is not God but humanity, in particular its *interpretive* ability.'[96] The friends, of course, are no better. In Derek Kidner's words, the friends 'overestimate their grasp of truth, misapply the truth they know, and close their minds to any facts that contradict what they assume'.[97] The book of Job thus persistently raises the issue of how much of what we see we ignore or distort because of hidden assumptions and 'how unwise it is to extrapolate from our elementary grasp of truth'.[98]

It is time for YHWH to speak.

---

[95] Ibid. 359. Fox rightly points out that Job is not a mouthpiece for the author any more than the friends are; in fact, if readers identify too closely with Job's protests, they will be humbled along with Job in 42:1–6.

[96] Ibid. 358; italics original.

[97] Kidner 1985: 61.

[98] Ibid.

3
Yнwн's first speech and his rule over creation (Job 38:1 – 40:5)

The reader of the book of Job probably reaches yнwн's first speech in chapter 38 with a mixture of frustration and relief – frustration at the exhausting lengths at which the friends have attacked Job and Job has attacked God, all without producing any helpful answers, and relief at the prospect of God's setting things straight. As we will soon see, however, the way in which yнwн engages with the debate completely contradicts what both Job and his friends expect, and perhaps what the reader expects as well. But the surprising way in which God addresses Job in no way means that he fails to give a satisfying response. Attention to God's speech in chapters 38–39 reveals that it directly answers key aspects of Job's complaint, as well as implicitly destroying the theology of the friends. Although this is not God's final answer to Job, God's first response is crucial for understanding the way in which he governs creation this side of the eschaton and how we respond to suffering. Since the first three sections of this speech in 38:4–7, 8–11, and 12–15 are especially significant, more attention will be given to them before moving more quickly through the rest of chapters 38–39.

'Then the Lord answered . . . and said' (38:1): yнwн's introduction

A single verse is given to yнwн's appearance at the beginning of chapter 38. He enters the scene without much anticipation or fanfare, and his speech begins in the same way as the human participants in the debate ('Then ───── answered and said'). This is very hopeful for Job, of course, and not only for the obvious reason that it breaks the silence and distance Job earlier lamented (23:3, 8–9). The exact phrasing of

YHWH's introduction also echoes the verb by which Job cried out for an answer towards the end of his self-imprecation in 31:35 (*'ānah*, 'let him answer me!').[1] As a result, when YHWH 'answers' Job in 38:1 we are to understand him responding directly to Job's assertion of innocence and unjust punishment. Furthermore, as God recognizes the validity of Job's oath by answering but inflicts none of the punishments Job called down on his own head in chapter 31, Job is being vindicated: God's speech validates that Job has committed none of the sins listed in chapter 31. Whatever the reasons might have been for his suffering, Job should not interpret his ordeal as punishment from God.[2]

The way in which God receives a similar introduction to Job and the friends is hopeful in another way: it implies that God is condescending to enter the debate entirely on its own terms, in a way understandable to Job, speaking like one of the sages and offering a disputation of his own. This implication is borne out by the use of frequent wisdom terms[3] and techniques[4] by YHWH in his speeches. Job will not be burdened by any incomprehensible mystery in these chapters: everything God says to him will be perfectly understandable.

The one difference between YHWH's introduction and those of Job and the friends is that YHWH speaks 'from the storm' (*sĕʿārâ*; ESV has 'whirlwind'). While this word sometimes refers to purely natural storms (Pss 107:25, 29; 148:8), it more frequently refers to a storm within which God appears theophanically to battle against chaos and evil (Isa. 29:6; Jer. 23:19; Nah. 1:3; Zech. 9:14; cf. Ezek. 1:4). With these other uses of the word in mind, the way YHWH finishes his second speech from this storm to Job by describing the chaos monster Leviathan takes on new significance. It looks as if the ancient Old Testament pattern of theophanic storm warfare is being activated. Elsewhere in the Old Testament, YHWH's appearance in the storm, with thunder and lightning, is a way of presenting God's victorious warfare against supernatural chaos and evil and the salvation of those who trust him (see Job 26:11–14; Pss 18; 29; 74; 89; Isa. 27:1;

---

[1] Ham 2013: 529.

[2] Keel 1978a: 28.

[3] Just in regard to vv. 2–4, the repeated use of the *ydʿ* root (as a noun in v. 2 and a hiphil verb in v. 4) as well as the reference to *ʿēṣâ* (counsel) and *bînâ* (insight) are very familiar from books such as Proverbs.

[4] Such as rhetorical questions, imperatives and recourse to nature to substantiate theological claims; see further Newsom 1996: 596; Timmer 2009b: 292.

51:9–11; Joel 3:15–18; Hab. 3:3–15).[5] This connection between God's appearance in the storm and his warfare on behalf of his people is easy for modern readers to miss, for the symbolic resonances of the storm in Old Testament poetry are very foreign to our context. It is probably easy for us to assume that ʏʜᴡʜ's thunder and lightning in these texts are a way of describing divine power in a general sense, yet fail to appreciate the full implications of God's action in the storm. In the symbolic world of Old Testament poetry, however, the thunder and lightning of God's storm have a dual function: they both repel the raging sea and the monsters in it and renew creation with rain after the battle. In other words, ʏʜᴡʜ's manifestation in the storm occurs not just as a display of divine power but specifically for the purposes of driving back darkness and chaos and restoring order, fertility and fullness of life. The same thunder and lightning that drive back the raging waters also bless and nourish creation. As modern readers, we must constantly remember that in this cultural and religious context, thunder and lightning are not just fireworks but divine weapons by which God saves and renews his people and all creation.[6]

The exact manner of God's appearance would have been very significant to Job as an ancient Semite. Even if the pattern of divine warfare from the storm does not take exactly the same form at the end of the book of Job as it does elsewhere in the Old Testament, it is no accident that after ʏʜᴡʜ describes Leviathan and promises his defeat (41:1–11), Job is restored to fullness of life before God (42:7–17). Even if there is no battle in Job 38 – 41, there are indications that God's appearance in the storm in 38:1 should be read in line with other texts describing divine warfare – a very hopeful sign for someone who has repeatedly mourned how close he is to death, how dominated he is by darkness (e.g. 30:26).

---

[5] Helpful secondary literature on storm theophanies and divine warfare includes Anderson 1994; Ollenberger 1987; Niehaus 1995: 81–141; Keel 1978b: 49–55.

[6] Some modern commentators understand the storm to be significant only in that it hides God's transcendent otherness (Wilson 2007: 424) or in that it 'enhance[s]' his 'majesty and grandeur' as he speaks with Job (Belcher 2017: 284). Neither of these explanations is entirely wrong, but neither does full justice to the common motif in the OT of ʏʜᴡʜ's appearing in the storm in order to do battle on behalf of those who trust him. Others understand ʏʜᴡʜ's appearance in the storm to reflect Job's subjective experience in suffering; e.g. the storm is a symbol for Job's inner anguish, and God appears in this way to show Job that he is present with him in suffering and understands it (Ash 2014: 375 and, with a slightly different nuance, Luc 2000: 111). But nowhere else in the OT (so far as I am aware) is the appearance of the deity in the storm intended as a reflection of an individual's subjective experience. It is normally a vehicle for describing how God triumphs over his enemies and restores order in creation.

All this is to say that God's introduction in 38:1, unassuming as it may appear at first glance, gives Job the best of both worlds: his long-lost divine friend speaks in a way perfectly intelligible to him, but God speaks (as it were) dressed in full battle armour, ready to defeat enemies no human can. Entirely contrary to Job's complaint in 9:17 that God is crushing him in the storm,[7] YHWH's appearance in the storm here (so it is implied) shows he is ready to go to battle on Job's behalf as his saviour.

YHWH's opening challenge to Job (38:2–3)

Despite YHWH's comforting introduction in verse 1, his first words are ones of challenge: Job is one who 'darkens counsel by words without knowledge' (v. 2). 'Counsel' ('ēṣâ) means either advice or guidance (e.g. Prov. 1:25) or a decision or strategy (e.g. Ps. 33:10–11; Isa. 14:26), especially that recommended to or enacted by the king (e.g. 2 Sam. 15:31; 16:20; 1 Kgs 1:12; 2 Chr. 10:13). Since God proceeds to speak about different parts of creation and the animals that live there, the 'counsel' Job has been obscuring is probably God's policy decisions for governing creation, the way in which he rules over all things. We should not miss how this directly addresses Job's criticism of God as administering creation in an unjust, amoral way (9:22–24; 12:13–25).[8]

God says that Job has darkened God's counsel 'by words without knowledge' (v. 2). Two significant implications are made in the wording of this verse. First, it is impossible to miss a note of gentleness here. After all, YHWH could have finished verse 2 by saying that Job had obscured the way God runs the world 'with arrogant speech' or 'foolishly' or the like. Despite Job's integrity in refusing to curse God, I do not think such characterizations of parts of Job's speeches would be inaccurate (e.g. remember the incredible violence with which Job imagines God to have attacked him in 16:12–14). In sharp contrast to this, however, God begins essentially by saying, 'Job, when you impugned my goodness and claimed I care nothing for justice, did you really know what you were talking about?' This is an extraordinarily mild way to respond to the man who

---

[7] Fox 2005: 352 makes this connection.

[8] That Job specifically *darkens* counsel (hiphil of *ḥāšak*) may also recall the cosmic darkness Job called down on creation in ch. 3 (Good 1990: 342).

has portrayed God 'as a merciless hunter, an insidious spy, a capricious destroyer, and a sinister ruler'![9]

Second, there is an implication in the phrase 'words without knowledge' that Job should have known better than to accuse God in this way. Yhwh is not going to reveal some ineffable mystery in these two speeches, for, if he were, Job could not be faulted for obscuring it.[10] Rather, it is implied that the essential orderliness and goodness of God's manner of ruling over creation are evident and available for anyone to see – Job included.[11]

The gentle tone of God's initial challenge may also be implied by the use of the question 'Who is this?' (*mî zeh*). There may even be a hint of pride here. This is the case because the use of this phrase elsewhere in the Old Testament seeks information only rarely (the sole instance of the question being used this way is 1 Sam. 17:55–56, but even here an awed tone may be present as Saul asks about the impressive young warrior who has just saved Israel). More often it expresses awe at someone or something that is already known (e.g. Egypt in Jer. 46:7). Often God is asked about this way (Ps. 24:8; Isa. 63:1; Jer. 49:19; 50:44). It is also used to single out someone from a group (Ps. 25:12; Lam. 3:37). Detecting tone in a written text is tricky; but is there a note of pride as God confronts his servant Job, who, among many foolish claims, has persevered in his desire to meet with God and not cut off his relationship with him? Is there an echo of the pride of 1:8 in this question?

If I have emphasized the gracious way in which God delivers his initial challenge to Job, verse 3 helpfully balances this by making it clear that a challenge is being given. To 'dress for action' (literally, 'gird up your loins') means to tuck one's shirt into one's belt so one can work unhindered. Job must get ready to engage with yhwh. Although angry accusations from God are conspicuous by their absence, God is directly confronting the foolish and false claims Job has made about how God rules the world. Furthermore, yhwh, not Job, will be the one asking the questions (v. 3b). God will not be submitting to any cross-examination, as Job imagined as a hypothetical possibility (13:22). The sternness of the challenge implies no hostility or severity on God's part, however: to 'brace yourself' or 'dress

---

[9] Habel 1985: 536.
[10] Fox 2013: 3.
[11] Ibid.

for action' like a man is not condescending, but meant to engage with Job as a worthy participant.[12]

There is a further reason why the challenge of verse 3 is good news for Job, for if the Almighty had structured the encounter such that he gave Job a chance to ask questions first, thereby submitting to interrogation by a mortal, he would have lessened himself in doing so.[13] As John Walton writes, Job's protest against God has involved 'pursuing options that will mean that God loses'.[14] On the one hand, if God explains himself or apologizes to a mortal, God denigrates himself as sovereign Lord over all things. Even worse, if God is unable to give an explanation to Job's questions, then Job has created a situation in which the Almighty faces embarrassment before a creature. Either way, God becomes less worthy of worship.[15] When God tells Job to gird up his loins and that he will be the one asking the questions, he avoids both of these unfortunate possibilities. This is a point to which we will return.

It is important to emphasize that the word 'challenge' fits verses 2–3 better than 'rebuke'. While a confrontation is unmistakable, the exposure of Job's 'words without knowledge' and his preparation for a series of questions in no way implies sin on Job's part that would explain the suffering of chapters 1–2. This is very different from what Job's friends expected! God is dealing with his servant in grace here, not counting Job's sins against him even as he challenges Job's unworthy theology. Perhaps part of the reason for God's kindness is Job's persistent desire in chapters 3–31 to meet with God, regardless of some of the foolish things Job has said. Furthermore, without excusing some of the accusations Job has levelled against God, the question animating those speeches is not inherently proud or sinful. Job wants to know why he met with such terrible punishment when he had done nothing deserving of it: why (so to speak) did $2 + 2 = 5$ in his case? Even if he expresses this question in ways of which he later repents (42:1–6), the question itself is not wrong to ask.[16] And God, in his faithfulness, answers.

---

[12] Andersen 1976: 270.

[13] Kidner 1985: 72.

[14] Walton 2008: 341.

[15] Ibid.

[16] *Pace* McKenna (1992: 386–388), who understands Job's questions to be an overreaching attempt to penetrate the mind of God founded on the presumption that God owes him an explanation: 'By demanding that God explain his suffering, Job assumes that he can be as wise as God' (1992: 388). But the question driving Job's complaints is really very simple (did he

Who was it that founded the earth? (38:4–7)

Having appeared in the storm (v. 1), appropriately framing the problem that will be addressed (Job's darkening of God's counsel, v. 2) and the way in which it will be addressed (God will interrogate Job, v. 3), God first asks Job about the founding of the earth (vv. 4–7). Each question in these verses has a clear and obvious answer: Job was not present at the founding of the earth, but God was (v. 4); Job did not and cannot measure its dimensions (v. 5), but God can and did; Job does not know what deeper foundation secures created reality (v. 6), but God does. Creation is being presented in these verses within an architectural metaphor, such that the solid earth is the first storey of a building (cf. 1 Kgs 6:37), measured perfectly according to its blueprints (v. 5), with pedestals and a cornerstone to keep it stable (v. 6b). It is not uncommon to describe creation in this way elsewhere in the Old Testament (e.g. Ps. 104:1–5; Isa. 51:13). Whenever the stability of creation is in focus in the Old Testament, the consistent goal is to highlight God's goodness and care for everything he has made; this 'building' shows not just divine power, but God's attentive goodness to his world.[17]

The implication of creation's stability in God's initial question to Job is twofold. First, Job knows so little about the construction and dimensions of creation that he is not in a position to draw the sweeping generalizations about it and the way God governs it that he has drawn. In fact, the reference to the founding of the earth ('ereṣ) in verse 4 may be meant specifically to contradict claims Job has made about the same place; for example, that God is the one who destroys the earth (9:6) and puts the earth under the control of the wicked (9:24). Since Job does not have God's all-encompassing grasp of creation, he is not in a position to make those claims.

But second and more importantly, the earth is not the sinister, chaotic mess Job has portrayed, where innocent lives are trampled and God does nothing (9:22–24; 24:1–17). When God put creation together, beings higher than Job could not restrain themselves, but burst out singing in joy

---

deserve what looked like the punishment of chs. 1–2 or not?) and desiring an answer does not involve grasping after a wisdom equal to God's.

[17] Of course, modern readers know what the circumference of the earth is (just over 24,855 mi [40,000 km]). But it is very easy to think of comparable questions that put a modern reader in the same humbled position as Job: Who is the one person who completely understands the paradoxes of quantum entanglement? Or unified field theory? But God is addressing an ancient Semite, and so invokes a framework and imagery common to that culture.

over what God made (v. 7). God redirects Job's vision away from Job's wish that the twilight stars will go dark (3:9) or his claim that God snuffs the stars out (9:7) to reveal the whole host of heaven hymning the Creator as he put together the place Job earlier cursed into darkness in chapter 3. The imagery of dawning light at the beginning of creation in verse 7 is especially significant because it speaks directly to the cosmic darkness Job evoked in his first speech.[18] The difference between God's joyful view of creation in these verses and Job's curse on it in chapter 3 could hardly be starker or more striking. Surely Job has been 'darkening' God's counsel! And surely God's all-encompassing perspective on the place he founded at the beginning of time means his happier view of creation has more validity than Job's. Whereas Job sees only a tiny part, God sees the whole – and it is a much more joyful whole than Job ever suspected.

Rhetorical questions and the issue of tone

At this point, further attention should be given to the fact that God engages Job not with direct statements but rhetorical questions, both in this passage and throughout his speeches. Such attention is necessary because our understanding of these questions has a significant impact on our view of God in the book of Job. Some read these questions quite negatively as expressions of sarcasm and contempt from God. David Wolfers, for instance, writes of God's 'sarcasm and abuse' and the 'brutality' with which God humbles (one might say humiliates) Job. According to Wolfers, Job has been trying to take God's place, presuming that Job knows better how to run the universe, and must be squashed.[19] Edward Greenstein goes even further, claiming that the God of chapters 38–41 is 'not significantly' different from how Job has described God in the debate with his friends; God 'demeans' Job and 'mocks his ignorance and incompetence' in this speech, confirming Job's earlier fears about how an encounter with God would proceed (e.g. 9:3). According to Greenstein, this is the same 'sadistic and self-centred deity of the prologue' who allows

---

[18] This verse's equation of the stars with the angels or sons of God would have been much less strange to Job than to modern readers; stars were regarded as divine in the ANE, and while the OT insists they are not to be worshipped (Deut. 4:19), it occasionally makes a poetic equation between stars and divine servants (e.g. Isa. 14:13) or the resurrected dead (Dan. 12:3).

[19] Wolfers 1995: 209, 212.

the death of Job's children over a bet. Greenstein thinks that protest against God provokes only the worst in the Almighty.[20]

If this is true, of course, the book of Job is significantly less comforting than many readers would hope: when God allows terrible suffering, even honest questions provoke only defensiveness and accusation on his part! And it is admittedly possible to read the phrases 'tell me, if you have understanding' in verse 4 and 'surely you know!' in verse 5 and hear a sarcastic tone. Michael Fox has, however, presented persuasive reasons against hearing a wounded, snarky tone from the Almighty here, and even understands God to be affirming Job though these questions. Two considerations Fox puts forward are especially helpful.

First, Fox points out that if straightforward indicatives were given instead of questions in verses 4–7 – 'You were not there when I founded the earth' – the tone would be more obviously harsh. As questions, however, the tone becomes gentler, 'drawing Job in' so that he can 'participate in the knowledge' the questions are meant to provoke. Straightforward indicatives would more easily run the risk of 'merely rubbing Job's face in his own feebleness'.[21] Rhetorical questions, on the other hand, have the effect of drawing Job back to what he should have known about God but has forgotten. Related to this is the consistent use of rhetorical questions, one aspect of instruction in wisdom, as elsewhere in Old Testament wisdom literature. In a wisdom text, whenever the father asks the son rhetorical questions about things the son may not fully understand, the intent is not to humiliate but to help the student grow so that he can receive the blessings of wisdom.[22] God is, in other words, passing wisdom on to Job through these questions as teacher to student, not demeaning or embarrassing him. As a result, the questions in Job 38 – 39 and 41:1–7 need not be read as condescending or humiliating any more than those found in, for example, Proverbs 5:16, 6:27–28 or Isaiah 40:12–28[23] (significantly, this last passage is addressed to a similarly wounded audience).

Second, Fox points out that although many of the questions God asks in chapter 38 have to do with things Job does not understand, they are always phrased in such a way that points to the one Creator who enjoys

[20] Greenstein 2009: 353.
[21] Fox 1981: 59.
[22] Timmer 2009a: 10.
[23] Fox 2013: 14.

effortless mastery of what is beyond Job.[24] In other words, if God were to phrase verse 5 as, 'What are the dimensions of the earth?', it would be easier for Job to feel humiliated: What ancient Semite would know that? But this is not the question. Job is asked only who the one person is who does know the earth's dimensions, because he has personally measured them. The answer is obvious. In fact, we will quickly see that this very obvious answer is the same to all the questions of chapters 38–41: only God understands and can control whatever aspect of creation is under review. In the light of this, it becomes clear that his intention with Job is not to win an argument or score points against him by demonstrating Job's ignorance, but to refocus Job on God himself, giving him a different vision of creation and the deity ruling it.[25] As a result, although it is possible to hear sarcasm when God says to Job, 'surely you know', the obviousness of the answer makes it more likely God is speaking as an encouraging teacher, reminding a student of something he or she knows very well:[26] 'I know you know this, Job!' In Fox's words, God speaks in chapter 38 'with compassion and gentleness, albeit a stern gentleness'.[27] The question of 38:5 is meant to evoke 'awe, not information'.[28]

> [I]f God had merely tried to shut Job up by demonstrating Job's ignorance, he would be saying that there was no possible way for Job to see God's equity and orderly rule and thus would in effect be excusing him for speaking of God as arbitrary and immoral. Rather, God is saying to Job, You know very well that I and I alone created order and maintain it in the world, and I know that you know, and you know that I know that you know.[29]

In fact, far from sarcastically humiliating Job or bullying him into submission, God's questions in these chapters can be said to draw Job even closer to God. This is the case because, as Fox writes, rhetorical questions create a 'special intimacy of communication' between God and his scarred servant as Job is made aware 'of a body of knowledge he shares' with God. God's questions 'thus bind speaker and auditor closer together while

---

[24] Ibid. 3.
[25] Ibid.
[26] Fox 1981: 58.
[27] Ibid. 59.
[28] Fox 2005: 354.
[29] Fox 1981: 59–60.

making the auditor accept the speaker's claims out of his own conscious-ness rather than having the information imposed on him from the outside'.[30] In engaging with Job this way, God avoids 'bully[ing] Job into submission' (as Job feared would happen in 9:20) and 'invites him into his counsel, making him an intimate'.[31]

The 'swaddling' of the raging sea (38:8–11)

To return to our survey of YHWH's first speech, it is important to remember when reading of the sea in verses 8–11 that the ocean is a recurring symbol for cosmic chaos in the ANE, the Old Testament and the book of Job specifically (see 7:12; 26:12). Modern Western cultures do not tend to make this connection, but it is not hard to imagine why ancient Semites would have found the ocean a suitable symbol for that relentless, unorganizable force that would swallow and drown the fertile order of creation if not contained by the Creator. After all, the watery depths cannot be mapped or divided or tilled, as the earth can; no human can impose any boundary on them. Consider as well how ancient Semites would have known only as much about the sea as they could have learned from swimming in it. To them, it would have felt bottomless, murky, the opposite of fruitful and ordered creation. As a result, when the ocean bursts forth in our passage (v. 8) and God sets a limit to it (v. 11), we should understand this as God's action that prevents chaos from destroying his world; exactly the same image is used in Jeremiah 5:22 with the same meaning. God's self-portrayal is obviously very different from the cosmic destroyer Job imagined (9:5–10) and thus directly answers a central aspect of Job's complaint: God is the Creator who constrains and limits chaos, not the one who sets it free. But two other less obvious aspects of verses 8–11 show how comforting God's challenge to Job in these verses would have been.

The first is the maternal imagery used. When the sea bursts from the womb (v. 8), God uses clouds as a swaddling band for it (v. 9). Familiarity with other passages describing what action God takes against the raging waters reveals how unusual verses 8–9 are. Elsewhere, YHWH thunders

---

[30] Ibid. 58. Fox perceptively adds that, like Job, readers answer these rhetorical questions internally as they move through the passage; as a result, a new vision of creation opens up for us as we read.

[31] Fox 2005: 352.

against the waters (Pss 18:13–15; 29:3), or cleaves them in two (Ps. 74:13), or rebukes and makes them dry (Isa. 51:10; Nah. 1:4), or tramples them (Hab. 3:14). Twice he is said more generally to rule over the waters (Pss 89:9; 93:3–4); Psalm 65:7 uniquely shows YHWH soothing them. In Job 38:9, however, when this baby is 'born' – a metaphor for the creation of the waters – God puts a swaddling cloth on the sea! Not unfairly, Norman Habel calls the image 'deliberately absurd'.[32] Are we to imagine the Almighty cooing and singing to this newborn as he cradles it in his arms? Even if this goes too far, the gentleness of the image against the background of the normal biblical portrayal of YHWH's thunderous defeat of the waters is very striking, and speaks strongly to the gentleness of the God whom Job has maligned as amoral and violent. If God is this gentle with the raging waters, surely he is a much kinder person than Job has imagined?[33]

A second surprising dimension of this passage is the implication that God's care for the sea endures even as the sea continues to resist him. That the sea resists God in this passage is not universally agreed upon; in the light of the unexpected maternal imagery used for God's care of the sea in this passage, some conclude that the ocean does not here take on the full significance of a great chaotic power over which God triumphs in battle, as it does elsewhere in the Old Testament.[34] But we should probably understand the sea to play the same hostile role described elsewhere in the Old Testament, and only God's action to be portrayed differently. This is the case because of the limit God places upon the sea: Why else would bars and doors be needed, except that the waters are trying to overwhelm creation? The reference to the 'proud waves' ending verse 11 substantiates this. The word suitably translated 'proud' (gā'ôn) literally means 'exaltation', in either a positive or negative sense, either describing God's exaltation (Exod. 15:7; Job 37:4; Isa. 2:10; cf. Mic. 5:3) or negatively for human pride (Lev. 26:12; Job 35:12; Ps. 59:13; Prov. 8:13). A different noun

---

[32] Habel 1985: 538.

[33] Robert Alter (2011: 123) sees here another allusion to ch. 3 in a reversal of Job's wish that he had never been born: whereas Job was sorry the doors to his mother's womb had not been shut (3:10), here God hedges in the sea with doors when it bursts from the womb (38:8). If this is correct, the implication is that God guides a birth where Job wishes one never happened. Perhaps more obviously, that God 'hedges' (sûk) the sea also contrasts with Job's complaint that God hedges him in (3:23).

[34] E.g. Fox allows that the sea in this passage is 'unruly' but thinks it is 'not an antagonist' (2018: 13).

from the same root describes the raging, rebellious sea in Psalm 89:9 (*gēʾût* instead of *gāʾôn*), and even though the word is not repeated, the same image is used in Psalm 93:3. This implies that the ocean continues (but unsuccessfully!) to defy God proudly even after being 'swaddled'. This 'absurd' image demonstrates God's goodness like no other: if God nurtures even the chaos and evil present in his creation, and if he does so even as it (unsuccessfully) strikes out against him, then his goodness truly knows no bounds.[35] This is God's *ʿēṣâ*, his plan or counsel or strategy, for how he administers his realm, a plan Job has obscured.

In the light of the criticisms Job has levelled against God and the way Job thinks God runs the world, these short verses would have been significant in multiple ways for him. First, Job is not God's cosmic enemy, as Job wondered in 7:12. Second, Yнwн reveals that there is chaos which he allows to remain in creation. The world is not some kind of perfect paradise where nothing is ever allowed to go wrong; one aspect of the order God imposes on his world is to allow for some contained disorder.[36] But this in no way means that God's world is the violent inner-city ghetto Job has decried, or that the one ruling over it is at best indifferent to injustice and wrongdoing. God both keeps this chaos within strict limits and is far kinder with it than Job has imagined – even to the point of caring for and nurturing it. In fact, since darkness is another image for chaos and death in the Old Testament, the fact that 'thick darkness' is used by God for the ocean's swaddling clothes may imply that God even puts aspects of chaos to use in limiting the power and influence of chaos.[37] As it turns out, God has a much happier purpose for darkness than the one Job called for in chapter 3.

The moral significance of the sunrise (38:12–15)

Comforting as the imagery of verses 8–11 is, one might wonder whether it means that God takes no further action against the forces that resist his

---

[35] If the *wayāsek* beginning v. 8 intentionally echoes the 'hedge of protection' of which Satan complains in 1:10, the note of the goodness of God's treatment of his opponent is strengthened: so far from oppressing Job like an enemy, God treats even his enemies well. Making this connection requires understanding three different Hebrew verbs to be by-forms of one another: *skk*, *śûk* and *śkk*, each of which means something like 'to shut off' or 'hedge in' (*HALOT* 754, 1312, 1328).

[36] Ash 2014: 381.

[37] Fyall 2002: 94.

rule in creation and oppress others. Are the only limits he gives to chaos those imposed at the beginning of time? The next section prevents any such misunderstanding by poetically showing the moral implications of the sunrise (vv. 12–15). This passage is strange to modern readers, because even if we can appreciate the beautiful image of each sunrise giving definition to the topography of the earth like clay rising under a seal or a rumpled garment (v. 14), we do not think of the sunrise as having any moral implications at all, much less of breaking the arm of the wicked (v. 15) or shaking them out of the earth like someone shaking ants out of a picnic blanket (v. 13). For ancient Semites, however, natural and moral order paralleled and reflected each other, such that an ordered and stable creation reflected and supported the moral order of the world. Contrariwise, disorder or disaster in the natural realm implied some moral problem (recall how idolatry leads to famine, drought and disease in Deut. 28). David Clines captures the thought nicely by writing that in the Old Testament, 'the principles on which the world was created' mirror 'the principles according to which it is governed'.[38] In fact, while all aspects of nature reflect moral reality in this way of thinking, there are multiple examples from both ancient Mesopotamia and Egypt showing that the rising sun was singled out in an especially significant way as reordering the world morally after night-time.[39] As a result, God's choice of the sun would probably have been particularly significant to Job and the book's first readers.

In the light of this, we see in verses 12–15 that there is something about the regular order of creation that continually frustrates the plans of the wicked (v. 15; 'arm' stands for strength). It also keeps them from getting an established place from which to work (v. 13). Strikingly, even when the sun rises the humans who oppose God enjoy no light (v. 15a). Even if it is not meant literally, God's description of the sunrise speaks clearly to a central aspect of Job's protest: far from an amoral dictatorship in which the earth is under the power of the wicked (9:24), God's strategy for creation structures the natural order in such a way that it works against human evil, shaking the wicked out of the earth (v. 13). Job cannot command the sunrise or teach the dawn its place – but God can, and does,

---

[38] Clines 1989: xlvi.

[39] Cornelius 1990: 25–43. Cornelius points out that the presence of winged sun-disc scarabs in Palestine implies that the kind of significance granted to the sun in Egypt would have been known in the north of that country.

to blessed effect. Taken together with verses 8–11, we see God's nurturing gentleness with and containment of his enemies (whether human or supernatural) nuanced by his defeat of them. In sharp contrast to Job's criticisms, justice matters to God, and the orderliness of his creation enacts it.[40]

God's tour through different parts of the cosmos (38:16–38) and the animals inhabiting it (38:39 – 39:30)

In my opinion, although all of chapters 38–39 are important, the most crucial aspects of YHWH's first response to Job are found in 38:4–15. As a result, we will proceed more quickly through the rest of YHWH's first speech before drawing some conclusions about it and engaging with other interpretations of it.

After the sunrise, God turns to the outer boundaries of creation: the depths of the sea, the underworld and the vast expanse of the earth (vv. 16–18). Job has never traversed these depths or comprehended their expanse; as a result, his claim that the 'order' of creation teaches God's unjust rule (e.g. 12:5–9) is disqualified. There may also be a hint that even if 'the gates of death' (v. 17) are the 'deepest, the darkest, and the worst extremity in creation', the darkness of this place 'is no threat to the goodness of his creation or the ultimate triumph' of God's purposes.[41] Nor does Job understand where light and darkness dwell (vv. 19–21, 24). This does not mean that ancient Semites would literally have imagined light to have a home; Job is only being reminded of the one person who perfectly understands the nature and working of both light and darkness. Contrary to 12:22, in which Job claims that God sends forth the shadow of death as light (thus confusing the most fundamental categories of creation), God gives a place to both, imposing order by separating them.[42] Furthermore,

---

[40] Edward Greenstein complains about these verses that the role given to the sunrise means that 'God has given . . . night for the thriving of the bad', who, regardless of what the sunrise accomplishes, return each sunset to pursue their immoral ends (2009: 351). But this is sophistical: God is not claiming that he stops all evildoing everywhere quickly and permanently, but that he allows it some limited agency – and that this decision does not mean he is an unjust tyrant or cares nothing for fair play.

[41] Ash 2014: 384.

[42] Habel 1992: 35.

Job has never been to the storehouses of snow and hail (vv. 22–23). Since these are stored for the day of battle, when a nation is in trouble and needs to defend itself, and since God sometimes fights on behalf of his people with hail (Josh. 10:11; Isa. 30:30),[43] the implication in these two verses both emphasizes Job's ignorance and reaffirms God's goodness in intervening on behalf of the helpless.

Nor can Job control the storm – if it were up to Job, the world might soon turn into a desert; but under God's care, even those places far from human habitation are renewed (vv. 25–27). While Job claims that God's control of rain is the worst of both worlds in that the only relief to a drought is an overwhelming flood (12:15), God shows how he renews life in places far beyond Job's ken. Furthermore, Job cannot generate the rain, cold or frost (vv. 28–30); nor can he guide the stars (vv. 31–33).[44] He does not even know the 'ordinances' of the heavens, the laws by which they function (v. 33). God made the heavenly lights to rule (Gen. 1), but if it were up to Job, this part of creation would fall apart. Nor can Job control or even fully understand the lightning (vv. 34–38).

The second half of God's speech transitions from different parts of his creation to the animals living in it. God's care for lions and ravens is presented first (38:39–41), the point being much the same as above: Job cannot provide or care for these animals, but God both can and does. Divine sovereignty is clearly emphasized in this short passage. But more importantly, the goodness of God's sovereignty over everything he has created is in view. The same creation both Job and Job's friends pointed to in order to substantiate their theological claims (e.g. 4:10–11) takes on a happier meaning when interpreted by its creator.

It should be noted that the lion and the raven were almost certainly not chosen as random examples of God's sovereign goodness. These two animals would have had a particular significance in an ancient Semitic context that would have deepened YHWH's message to Job. The point is worth some attention.

To begin with, although both lions and ravens take on different symbolic charges in the Old Testament, both are sometimes portrayed in

---

[43] Habel 1985: 542.

[44] The chains and cords in v. 31 'refer to these heavenly bodies being under constraint as they do metaphorical duty governing events on earth' (Ash 2014: 387). Robert Alter here sees another response to Job's cry for cosmic darkness to cover him in ch. 3, as if God is asking Job 'whether he has any notion of what it means in amplitude and moral power to be able to muster the dawn (verse 12) and set the constellations in their regular motion' (2011: 122).

a strongly negative way as 'chaotic' animals. For example, with regard to ravens, we read on the one hand of Noah's raven (Gen. 8:7), the raven-black hair of the young girl's husband (Song of Songs 5:11), and the ravens that feed Elijah (1 Kgs 17:4, 6) – all positive examples. On the other hand, ravens are scavengers and thus unclean (Lev. 11:15; Deut. 14:14). They are also one of the animals inhabiting Edom after the final judgment of God (Isa. 34:11); that unclean animals live where Edomites used to is a way of saying that the land will be irredeemably given over to uncleanness and death under God's judgment. The portrayal of the lion is similarly multifaceted. On the one hand, we read of the messianic 'lion of Judah' (Gen. 49:9; Rev. 5:5), as well as the leonine prowess of the blessed tribes Gad and Dan (Deut. 33:20, 22). Furthermore, God himself is compared to a lion both in judgment (e.g. Jer. 2:30; 49:19) and restoration (Hos. 11:10). But there are negative portrayals of the lion in the Old Testament as well. Although they are not listed as such in Leviticus 11 or Deuteronomy 14, their role as predators would have made them unclean. They are also a common metaphor for the wicked enemies of the godly (Job 4:10–11; Pss 7:3; 10:9; 22:14; 91:13).

What symbolic value do the lion and the raven have in God's first speech in Job? Are these animals inspiring examples of the beauty of creation? Or are they, like the ocean of verses 8–11, examples of those more threatening aspects of creation God keeps within boundaries even as he cares for them? A number of factors suggest the latter. For instance, Othmar Keel points out that the rationale behind the choice not only of the lion and raven, but all the animals in Job 38:39 – 39:30, cannot be their impressiveness (although some are doubtless impressive), because other animals enlisted as impressive species elsewhere in the Old Testament are missing here, such as the falcon in Jeremiah 8:7 or the ant in Proverbs 6:6–8.[45] Additionally, the ostrich is hardly presented in an impressive way in this passage! Nor can it be that all these animals are dangerous, for neither the raven nor the ostrich qualifies in that regard. The only characteristic shared among all these creatures, and the only clue to the rationale for including some animals in this list and excluding others, is their status as chaotic animals – 'chaotic' being defined here as that which stands opposite to and finds no place within orderly human society and culture. Thus, the wild donkey (39:5–8), which cannot integrate in human

---

[45] Keel 1978a: 71–86. I am indebted to Keel for my understanding of this passage.

society, is repeatedly a symbol for hostility and unruly isolation (Gen. 16:12; Job 24:5; Isa. 32:14; Jer. 14:6; Hos. 8:9; Israel's unfaithfulness to YHWH is compared in Jer. 2:24 to a wild donkey sniffing the desert air for a mate).[46] The ox (39:9–12) is often, like the lion, portrayed positively (Num. 23:22; 24:8;[47] Deut. 33:17; Ps. 92:11) – but together with the mouth of the lion David begs in Psalm 22:22 to be delivered from the horns of the wild ox (the oxen slaughtered in Edom's destruction in Isa. 34:7 may also be significant in this regard). The ostrich is not mentioned elsewhere in the Old Testament, but if 'chaotic' is defined as something like 'that which stands opposite and hostile to the fruitful orderliness of God's creation and human society', the portrayal of the ostrich's bizarre treatment of her young in 39:13–18 unambiguously puts this creature in the 'chaotic' category.[48] The hawk (39:26–30) is mentioned elsewhere in the Old Testament only as an unclean predator (Lev. 11:16; Deut. 14:15).

The only possible exceptions are the mountain goat or ibex (39:1–4) and the warhorse (39:19–25). The former is mentioned elsewhere only in Psalm 104:18, as one of the creatures satisfied by the Creator's goodness (see vv. 16–18), as well as in Proverbs 5:19, in a metaphor for the loveliness of the wife of a man's youth. Despite the fact that mountain goats are not as threatening as lions, however, the emphasis in the description in Job 39:1–4 is their complete independence – they flourish independent of human oversight, and even independently from one another (v. 4).[49] Mountain goats are not a part of livestock that help grow crops or can be offered in sacrifice; they thus fall within the 'chaotic' category, even if they are not necessarily threatening or sinister to human life. The warhorse, on the other hand, does serve human interests – but, as will be discussed further below, the description of this frightening animal deliberately echoes other descriptions of chaos in ways easier to see in Hebrew than in translation. The horse's neck is literally clothed with 'thunder' (ra'māh), and the word translated 'leap' in verse 20a is literally 'shake' (rā'aš), sometimes denoting the shaking of the heavens and earth in a theophanic appearance (Judg. 5:4; Pss 18:7; 69:8; Joel 3:16). This verb is repeated in verse 24a to describe

[46] The references to the donkey in Job 6:5 and 11:12 seem more neutral.
[47] Ash understands the reference to the ox in these two verses to underscore the terror the creature would have had for ancient Israelites (2014: 396).
[48] Using a different word, Lam. 4:3 also refers to the cruelty of the ostrich to its young, outdoing even the jackal.
[49] Habel 1985: 545.

the way the horse charges towards battle, along with *rōgez*, suitably translated as 'rage' by the ᴇsv, but also sometimes showing the shaking that happens after a theophany (Job 37:2; Ps. 18:7; Joel 2:1, 10; Hab. 3:2, 7, 16). In other words, even if the warhorse can be integrated into human society, the way it is described in Job 39 makes it an instantiation of chaos.[50]

It is also significant that each of these eight animals was portrayed as chaotic in the ANE. Othmar Keel has surveyed in detail the 'Lord of the Animals' motif from Assyrian and Babylonian reliefs, a theme in Mesopotamian art stretching for over a millennium, in which each of the eight animals from Job 38:39 – 39:30 can be found depicted as an agent of chaos, either hunted by the king as part of his role of protecting his realm, or fed by him.[51] Examples of the former include Ashurbanipal (668–627 BC), who wrote about a hunt of lions preying on his people in order to highlight his role as a just king.[52] The palace reliefs of Sargon II (722–705 BC) also portray hunting and warfare as activities of similar significance in that both protected the country from violence and predation.[53] Similarly, John Hartley reports that the Egyptian pharaoh Thutmose III (1479–1425 BC) commissioned a scarab in which he boasts he killed seventy-five wild oxen on a hunt.[54] The significance of the 'Lord of the Animals' feeding these creatures will be considered below, but for now we should consider how modern readers used to seeing animals in zoos will have to use their imagination to appreciate the terror lions would have inspired for ancient peoples, and how impressive their rulers would have appeared in their mastery over them.[55]

In the light of the larger significance these animals had in the Old Testament and Job's cultural context, the description of how God provides food for both lion and raven was probably intended not only to confront Job again with his limited perspective and ability (thus casting doubt on the conclusions he has drawn about God and his world), but also to

---

[50] Keel points out how the horse as a symbol for military power is not infrequently presented negatively in the OT (e.g. as a synecdoche for oppressive foreign powers in Josh. 11:6; 2 Kgs 18:23; Ezek. 23:6); see Keel 1978a: 70.

[51] Ibid. 71–81, 86.

[52] Luckenbill 1968: 2.363.

[53] Keel 1978a: 78.

[54] Hartley 1988: 508.

[55] Keel compares the level of terror a lion would have inspired for an ancient Semite to that of a deadly car accident for a modern person (1978a: 82).

highlight God's perfect goodness in providing for these creatures (similarly to 38:8–11).[56] In other words, the world is not a chaotic mess God does nothing to address. God's goodness is rather so broad that he provides even for the helpless young of the raven. The same is true for the other animals described: although Job is completely unaware of the schedule by which mountain goats propagate (39:1–4), God both knows and cares for this species so that it does not die out. Similarly, even if the wild donkey lives completely independently of human society, it does so because God sends it to live in the most inhospitable regions (v. 6) and provides for it exactly in that place (v. 6). Another animal existing completely outside human society is the wild ox (vv. 9–12), which will not serve Job (v. 9) and does not depend on him to flourish (v. 11) – but, it is implied, the ox does trust God, who does care for this creature (cf. the same idea in Ps. 104:21). God's care and goodness are not limited to those creatures most familiar to human life and concerns; they encompass every creature, even those totally outside ordered human existence.

In 39:13, we move from the sinister to the strange: the flamboyant ostrich (vv. 13–18) flaps its wings proudly (v. 13) and laughs at the horse ridden by a human (v. 18), but she also foolishly leaves her eggs on the ground, where they may be crushed (vv. 14–15). Since this creature's behaviour does not fit into the patterns wisdom analyses, it seems to be presented as an exception, a kind of deliberate non sequitur – a bird that cannot fly, and one that forsakes her young (vv. 14–15), but is too quick for any predator (v. 18).[57] But God has deliberately made it this way (v. 17), and somehow the species survives. God's goodness and care are not mentioned, but surely they are part of the implication of this passage. In other words, God's sovereign care extends both to animals dangerous to Job (38:39–40) and incomprehensible to him (39:17).

There is nothing strange, however, about the indomitable warhorse (vv. 19–25). The 'chaotic' hints in this animal's description were listed

---

[56] Keel argues further that since many of these animals appear in depictions of royal hunts from Ugarit, Mesopotamia and Egypt, and since these hunts were one means by which the king did justice to his subjects by protecting them, the same nuances inform YHWH's descriptions of these animals (Keel 1978a: 71–81, 86, 125). In other words, according to Keel, just as a royal hunt shows the king's sovereignty over and protection of his realm, so God's realm is not the unpredictable chaos Job has portrayed. God is a good king who protects his subjects and maintains order in his realm. This connection to ANE thought may be present, but if it is it seems to be muted by the lack of any reference in 38:39 – 39:30 to hunting: it is said only that God understands, guides and cares for these animals, not that he kills them.

[57] Clines 2011: 1124.

above; we can now see that the significance of these hints is to move the warhorse beyond the expected role of a powerful weapon in the ancient world to that of 'a quasi-divine, supernatural, eerie, terrifying creature', whose sole business is killing.[58] Furthermore, part of God's administration of creation involves the choice to create and strengthen animals like this; within the orderly patterns of creation, God maintains animals that stand outside these patterns.

The last animal described for Job is the hawk. It is not from Job's wisdom that the hawk lives where few creatures can and employs skills as a predator few can match (vv. 26–30). Strikingly, verses 26–27 imply that it is by God's command that hawks live as predators, killing other animals.[59]

God closes with a final question about whether Job will continue to find fault with God's plan for creation (40:2) – all without making explicit what conclusions he wants Job to draw.[60] The tour has now finished, and God's first speech is over. What was Job supposed to think? What was he supposed to conclude from God's description of the world and its animals?

Human limits, divine goodness and the continuing presence of evil: the significance of YHWH's first speech to Job

In reflecting on the meaning of YHWH's first speech to Job, it is crucial to remember as we proceed that God has allowed Job to fall into a position where Job wrongly but understandably views God as someone who cares nothing for personal integrity and faithfulness – as a cruel dictator uninterested in treating people fairly or proportionately. By the end of YHWH's second speech, however, Job is entirely reconciled both to God and his manner of running the world, even though it sometimes allows unimaginable pain, as Job knows all too well. Whatever God says moves Job from resisting this rule as a matter of principle to celebrating it.

Three main implications are unstated but evident in chapters 38–39 that help Job make this transition, each of which has been broached above

---

[58] Ash 2014: 399.
[59] Ibid. 401.
[60] Good 1990: 365.

and can be summarized here. The first is that God's world is much vaster, more complex and more mysterious than Job has recognized. There is much he does not know. It is important for Job to hear this because he has continually extrapolated outwards from his own tragedy to make sweeping generalizations about God's mismanagement of creation, imagining that God lets evil run free. Yhwh's questions repeatedly and emphatically show Job that he is not in a position to make such an extrapolation – he simply does not know enough (this is especially apparent in 38:2, 4, 16–24; 39:1–4, 13–18).

> Because humans lack the understanding to account for the mysterious happenings and processes in the various parts of the creation, it is impossible for them to have the perspective by which to accurately prove that God is guilty of mismanaging the created order.[61]

By analogy, if a man sailing in a rowing boat in the Pacific Ocean were to run into rough weather, it would be an unwarranted inference to conclude that the entire Pacific Ocean were nothing but a raging storm. In other words, when Job insists on his innocence, he speaks in knowledge, but when he says God is hostile, he speaks in ignorance.[62] Strikingly, Yhwh's first speech becomes a sermon about the *limits* of human knowledge.

Second, Job is meant to conclude from chapters 38–39 that there is a great deal of order and goodness in God's world and how it is administered. The world God created in Genesis 1 is not a sinister, dark place, as Job has insisted. In the Old Testament, the goodness of creation is closely bound up with its orderliness and organization as a secure and fertile environment for life; thus, in Genesis 1, God pronounces creation 'very good' after and because it has been fully ordered as a perfect environment for life to flourish. This is an important emphasis in Job 38 – 39 as well. God is not the cosmic destroyer (9:5–10), but the great Sustainer and Provider, caring even for creatures totally outside human control and understanding. Part of the reason for the choice of creatures in chapter 39 – the raven and ostrich and hawk, which live outside the spheres of

---

[61] Hartley 1997: 793.
[62] Fox 2005: 355.

human control and interest – is to imply how God's goodness overflows normal human standards and expectations. God protects and provides for creatures humans may find ridiculous, dangerous or even unimportant. Indeed, in contrast to some of the ANE presentations of the same animals of 38:39 – 39:30, nothing is said about hunting or killing them; the emphasis falls only on providing for them and their defenceless young (see esp. 38:39, 41; 39:4, 14–16, 30).[63] Although Job has invoked the animal kingdom as evidence of God's mismanagement of creation (12:7–9),[64] no cosmic tyrant would rule God's realm in the way described in chapters 38–39. This is especially noteworthy in 38:12–15, where God insists on his concern for justice by showing that he has put creation together in such a way that it resists and counteracts human evil.

A third implication from God's first speech is that his plan for creation does allow some evil and chaos within certain limits – but that this allowance does not mean God is an amoral, uncaring tyrant. The decision God has made about how his world will be governed is to allow pockets of disorder to exist within a much larger order, without immediately annihilating every threatening or violent aspect of creation. These two chapters 'do not reveal a utopian theocracy in which evil is summarily expunged as soon as it appears'.[65] 'God has arranged for the care of all creatures but not the elimination of pain, dangers, and death.'[66] Furthermore, God's decision to allow these chaotic elements to continue to exist is not a mismanagement of creation and does not show an indifference to justice. To claim it does show this would be to darken yhwh's counsel, to obscure his good purpose in the massive order and the good he has sown in creation, despite its occasionally sinister elements.

It should be emphasized that this is not the same as claiming that death and predation are somehow good in themselves or good within some larger harmonious whole. Alexander Pope expresses this idea quite strikingly when he writes in his 'Essay on Man':

All nature is but art unknown to thee,
All chance direction that thou canst not see,
All discord harmony, not understood,

---

[63] Ash 2014: 393.
[64] Perdue 1991: 215.
[65] Baldwin 2018: 374.
[66] Fox 2013: 7.

All partial evil, universal good,
And spite of pride, in erring reason's spite,
One truth is clear, whatever is is right.

The expression is lovely, but the idea finds no purchase in YHWH's speeches. Lions are for ever dangerous to humans, and no appeal is made to some larger order that justifies their presence in God's world. The only claim here is that God's decision about how he rules over both orderly and chaotic elements in creation, both domestic and dangerous animals, is unworthy of the charges Job has brought against it.[67] His decision to feed lions and other predators does not imply predation is somehow good from a larger perspective, but only that God is not the corrupt authority Job has railed against. Quite the contrary: even if we remain a little in awe of some of the terrifying creatures God has made (39:19–25), his kindness far outstrips anything Job has imagined in the debate with his friends.

Perdue also helpfully points out how this aspect of YHWH's first speech is as much a challenge to the theology of the friends as it is to Job's protests. Whereas Eliphaz imagined the wild animals that symbolize the wicked to be quickly punished within God's retributive justice (4:10–11), God redescribes his relationship with dangerous predators in a way that implies a far deeper kindness on his part to these creatures than Eliphaz ever imagined.[68] God's world is a very good one, but not one in which all evil is punished neatly and immediately.

We can thus summarize YHWH's first challenge to Job's protest in the following way: Job's accusation against God's unjust administration of creation is invalid because it has been made without sufficient warrant (there is too much Job does not understand), in the face of the massive goodness of creation and God's care for everything he has made, and in contradiction of the way God both contains and cares for the pockets of chaos and violence he does allow to continue to exist. God's first speech directly answers Job's protest about his supposed indifference to right and wrong by showing how he rules his realm as a good and caring king. The world is a far more joyful place than Job has imagined (38:7), and justice a far deeper concern to God than Job has claimed (38:12–15). God is also far kinder to those elements of chaos he allows to continue.

---

[67] Kidner 1985: 84.
[68] Perdue 1991: 215.

It should be emphasized that the interpretation of chapters 38–39 offered here differs from one frequently found in literature on the book of Job, especially among evangelical publications. One not uncommonly reads that Yhwh's description of the different parts of creation and the animals living in it demonstrates and vindicates his limitless power and wisdom in a way that comforts Job.[69] According to this reading, divine power and wisdom are the focus of chapters 38–39 and the emphasis on these divine attributes satisfies Job and answers his complaint against God. This interpretation is not totally wrong: after all, as stated above, for all the varied questions Yhwh asks, the answer is consistently the same: 'Only you, Lord – only you understand this and exercise sovereignty over this, not me.' But it cannot be divine wisdom and power in a merely general sense and those divine attributes alone that produce so great a change in Job, for several reasons. The first is that Job credits them to God in 9:4 and 12:13. As a result, if all God is trying to convince Job of in chapters 38–39 is his strength and wisdom, God is trying to convince Job of something Job already believes, and so it becomes impossible to explain why Job stops arguing. Furthermore, God's power and wisdom are not in themselves a comfort to Job, so an emphasis on these divine attributes alone will not lead Job to worship, but only to a deeper terror of God. We saw earlier how it was exactly God's power to destroy and skill in running the world (as Job thought he experienced in chs. 1–2) that make God so frightening to Job (see e.g. 9:4 in the context of vv. 4–19).[70] Finally, the friends have already insisted at length on God's omniscience and omnipotence (11:6–9; 15:8; 25:2). As a result, if God speaks only of the same, it is difficult to see how his speech differs from that of the friends. For these reasons, recourse to omniscience and omnipotence alone is insufficient to explain why Job retracts his argument against God in 40:3–5.

---

[69] E.g. Tremper Longman writes that God's questions point to Job's lack of power and wisdom (2016: 426; similarly Kidner 1985: 71; Alden 1993: 369; Estes 2005: 114; Wilson 2007: 426, 30, 35, 50).

[70] Of course, this statement needs to be qualified somewhat, because wisdom in the OT has moral and spiritual connotations (e.g. Prov. 1:1–7) that Job definitely denied to God during the debate. But even if OT wisdom literature frequently insists that one cannot be truly wise without also being morally upright, one does find passages where 'wisdom' denotes a kind of know-how or skill in some area of life that does not take on explicit moral qualities. One such passage is Eccl. 2, where the wisdom that remains with the Preacher as a successful ruler (v. 9) is distinguished from that spiritual 'light' denied to fools (v. 13). When Job ascribes wisdom to God in his protest, he is thinking of wisdom in this sense; i.e. the divine tyrant is very skilful in ruining innocent lives.

If God's speech is more complex than only a justification of his power and wisdom, it is also striking to note that it differs from the kind of answers most Christians typically give to the problem of evil, each of which is biblical and valid in its own way. God does not say that all things, even evil, work out for good (Rom. 8:28), or that the sufferings of this present age will be outbalanced and resolved in the eschaton (Rom. 8:18; 2 Cor. 4:17). Nor is Job given some mystical or ineffable experience that resolves his trauma. Job has been criticizing God's plan for creation (38:2), and God demonstrates that his care for his world is very different from Job's portrayal of it – and that is all.

Maintaining the fullness of God's first speech to Job

One final aspect of the present interpretation of YHWH's first speech that should be remembered is that each of the three dimensions discussed above – Job's epistemological limits, God's goodness and the continued but limited existence of evil – must be kept in play and given equal attention. If only one (or two) is invoked to interpret YHWH's first speech at the expense of the others, the speech collapses and it becomes difficult to understand why Job retracts his protest (40:3–5). For example, if one emphasizes only the limits to Job's knowledge in chapters 38–39, it is difficult not to read these chapters as if God were saying to Job, 'I know a lot more than you, so stop questioning me – there are mysteries too deep for you to grasp, so just take my word for it that you're wrong.' David Clines seems to reflect this unbalanced emphasis on Job's ignorance in chapters 38–39 when he concludes that the first speech is meant to teach Job that 'Job has no right to an explanation for his suffering, any more than he has a right to have the purpose of crocodiles explained to him'.[71] In fact, according to Clines, Job is not even 'entitled' to be told if he is innocent – God is under no obligation to explain anything, in the natural order or the moral order of his world.[72] H. H. Rowley agrees, arguing that chapters 38–39 show Job he understands so little that he should just bow before God.[73] David Wolfers writes in the same vein that the implication of chapters 38–39 is the 'incommensurability' between Job and God, and the

---

[71] Clines 1998: xlvi.
[72] Ibid.
[73] Rowley 1983: 241. David McKenna offers the same interpretation (1992: 389).

higher, unknowable, inscrutable wisdom of God; as a result, Job should not criticize how God runs the universe because Job is only human and not God.[74] According to Wolfers, the putatively anthropocentric orientation of wisdom is being challenged; Job should accept his smallness and 'rejoice in the complexity of the universe' he can never fully understand.[75] If this is the case, of course, it is difficult to see why Job withdraws his charge against the Almighty of unjust dealings with humans on the basis of his tragedy in chapters 1–2, for there may well be many things beyond Job's comprehension, and God may still be doing things that are unjust. God's counsel or plan for creation (38:2) may still be dark and sinister, and Job be ignorant of many things, at the same time. A different view of God's world in no way follows from merely emphasizing Job's limits. Wolfers admits this when he writes that the first speech is 'no more nor less than the timeless parental evasion'; God is only 'pulling rank' with Job and telling him to shut up.[76] If this is true, it is very difficult to see what comfort the book of Job has for suffering Christians; but God's first speech is, thankfully, more complex than these commentators allow.

Moreover, the purposes for which God points to Job's epistemological limits are not always well understood by the commentators quoted above. Othmar Keel points out that if God gives absolutely no explanation to Job and only plays up Job's ignorance, God is not really different from the friends, for Zophar argued in much the same way in 11:2–6.[77] But, as discussed above, this is not exactly what God says to Job. While it is true that the answers to almost all of the questions in chapters 38–39 are, 'I don't know, Lord – only you do,' Yнwн does not merely assert Job's ignorance, but leverages Job's limited perspective so that he can draw new inferences about God and his world from 'public and verifiable evidence' about it.[78] God thus 'implies that the *'ēṣâ*, his plan for the world, is essentially manifest and known, and that Job is to be blamed for obscuring it, for obscuring a truth that he is really aware of'.[79] As a result, the emphasis

---

[74] Wolfers 1995: 215, 222.

[75] Ibid.

[76] Ibid. Wolfers goes on to claim that ch. 39 teaches that 'the universe is fundamentally cruel, and randomly so', portraying the relationship between God and humanity in a way different from the rest of the OT (ibid.). If Wolfers' interpretation is correct, this conclusion follows; but his reading of the first divine speech is narrow and unconvincing.

[77] Keel 1978a: 46.

[78] Fox 1981: 60.

[79] Ibid.

in chapters 38–39 is not on Job's limited horizon in a simple or reductive way, as if God were only asserting the privilege of his office or avoiding the question. God is simultaneously pointing to what Job can and should know in order to push him to new and happy conclusions about God and his rule.[80]

In distinction from those commentators who focus only on Job's ignorance, it is possible to emphasize the goodness of God's creation in chapters 38–39 to the exclusion of Job's ignorance and the continued presence of evil in such a way that results in a similar anticlimax. Robert Gordis takes this misstep when he writes:

> When man steeps himself in the beauty of the world, his troubles grow petty, not because they are unreal, but because they dissolve within the larger plan, like the tiny dabs of oil in a masterpiece of painting. The beauty of the world becomes an anodyne to man's suffering.[81]

But it is ridiculous to imagine Job's contenting himself with beautiful sunrises and impressive animals as an anodyne or substitute for dead children. Indeed, it may be argued that beauty in the world that continues heedless of suffering can increase individual pain instead of resolving it.[82] Furthermore, to emphasize only divine goodness in chapters 38–39 is to reduce their message in such a way that God says only, 'Things go well most of the time.' But if all God can muster in response to a charge of unfair dealing with his creation is to point to its beautiful aspects, there is no reason for Job to retract his charge, for terrible injustices in which saints are treated like sinners may still occur and thus implicate the entire order of creation, beautiful as this order often is.

Finally, if the interpreter of chapters 38–39 focuses only on the violent or sinister aspects of creation described there, such that God speaks only

---

[80] Together with ch. 28, this has implications for our articulation of natural theology. While the book of Job does clearly teach that the natural order witnesses to God's character and action, none of the human participants in the debate seem to know how to interpret the data correctly, because they come to opposite conclusions about the God ruling over the world and are all found wanting in the end. Even though yhwh is pointing to evidence potentially available to any human being in the natural world in chs. 38–39, it appears that we need a revelation from on high in order to interpret it correctly.

[81] Gordis 1965: 133–134.

[82] Tsevat 1980: 25.

to his care for the chaotic elements in his world, without any corresponding emphasis on the light and joy and orderliness of his world, then God appears suspiciously similar to how Job (wrongly) portrayed him during the debate. As a result, it again becomes difficult to understand why Job retracts his accusation against God in response. Not surprisingly, no-one has interpreted these chapters in this way.[83] But there is an influential reading of Job 38 – 39 that, although not identical to this hypothetical one, is nevertheless close.

A significant rival interpretation of yнwн's first speech

One interpretation of yнwн's first speech that has received some sophisticated articulations in recent years and that differs significantly from the one offered here is to understand chapters 38–39 as intentionally denying any justice in the world. According to this reading, Job 38 – 39 teaches that God does not care about human definitions of justice, and so Job's complaint is not so much given a positive answer as simply dismissed. God is, as it were, excused on a technicality; the argument of chapters 38–39 does not vindicate God's justice in his providential ordering of all things (even suffering) but reveals that there is no justice in how God governs creation. As a result, because God does not care about justice, Job has been asking the wrong question. This is not identical to the third possibility listed immediately above, but it ends up giving a similarly sinister presentation of God's character. It recurs frequently enough in recent scholarship on Job – Fox calls the position a 'near consensus' on yнwн's speeches[84] – that it is worth considering in detail.

Matitiahu Tsevat first made this proposal in his essay 'The Meaning of the Book of Job'.[85] He writes that the first divine speech implies that Job's standards simply do not apply to the world God describes in chapters 38–39. God denies any validity to the doctrine of retribution, 'demoralizing' the world, and so takes away any basis Job has for complaint at his treatment.[86] In support of this reading, Tsevat interprets the rising sun that (symbolically) breaks the arm of the wicked in 38:12–15 to mean that

---

[83] Although Brenner 1981 comes close; see further discussion below.
[84] Fox 2013: 1.
[85] Tsevat 1980: 1–39.
[86] Ibid. 19, 28, 33.

each dawn provides an opportunity to punish the wicked, but this punishment never comes.[87] What opportunities God does have to exercise justice, he deliberately forgoes; according to Tsevat, the sun shines on just and unjust alike. Similarly, when 38:25–27 describes the rain that falls on the uninhabited desert, the fact that this rain benefits no-one and thus (in a sense) goes to waste suggests to Tsevat that human ideas of proportion and merit are being denied.[88] This means that retribution and fair dealing with God's faithful saints are not written into God's blueprint for creation.[89] As a result, Job's complaint about the lack of justice finds no traction.[90] There is nothing about which to complain.[91]

As we will soon see, Tsevat has been joined by some other significant voices in this reading of Job 38 – 39. But before moving on to consider these other developments of his argument, it can briefly be pointed out that Tsevat has arguably misinterpreted the rising sun in 38:12–15 and the desert rain of 38:25–27. The former describes the breaking of the arm of the wicked (v. 15), implying their powerlessness, and portrays how the rising sun (symbolically) shakes the wicked out of the earth (v. 13). As argued above, this shows that justice matters to God and that he has put creation together in such a way that it frustrates the designs of the wicked. Further, the rain that falls on land where no-one lives can just as easily be a sign of God's goodness and generosity as a sign of his indifference to justice and fairness. Fox justly points out that the rain which does not fall where humans tend flocks nevertheless makes the wilderness sprout grass (v. 27), thus rendering it habitable. This is in no way a sign of God's indifference to humanity, but shows exactly his spreading goodness as he makes

---

[87] Ibid. 30.

[88] Ibid. 30–31.

[89] Ibid. 31.

[90] Ibid. 28.

[91] David Clines agrees when he writes that the divine speeches 'refuse the categories of the dialogues' (2011: 1203). Similarly, William Dumbrell appears to align himself with this view from a slightly different perspective when he writes that the divine speeches make 'no allusion' to suffering and so should not be understood as an answer to Job, only a correction to the overly rigid theology of the friends (2000: 91–92). In Dumbrell's words, 'God's speech avoids the problem of innocent suffering in general and Job's case in particular' in such a way that 'the world is not answerable to Job' and 'the divine plan cannot be interpreted solely in human terms' (2000: 93). All that Job can do is 'view his case in light of the total cosmic design of his Creator' in which no simple or direct response to the problem of innocent suffering is available (ibid.). For reasons stated above and developed further below, however, this is arguably an underdeveloped reading of the ending of the book of Job that cannot explain Job's worship at the end.

the desert blossom.[92] On a slightly different note, it is also helpful to remember that (in Fox's words) 'it hardly demonstrates an absence of justice in the world that God cares for creatures that Job cannot even approach'.[93] His providential care 'for wild animals does not show indifference to human needs'.[94] We will return to these considerations further below.

Carol Newsom has given a sophisticated restatement of Tsevat's argument in which she explores some of its theological implications in a way Tsevat did not.[95] Newsom begins by writing that '[a]lmost every commentator notes that the divine speeches refuse to engage Job's arguments on his terms'.[96] Newsom agrees with this trend by pointing to what she perceives as a crucial difference between Job's speech in chapters 29–31 and God's in chapters 38–39: whereas Job takes divine and human definitions of justice to be commensurate (e.g. 31:2–4), God's questions 'eliminate' Job 'from presence, participation, or knowledge ... of the cosmos even as they address him'.[97] In other words, while Job imagines '[d]ivine and human beings [to] occupy the same familiar territory', God presents the cosmos in his speeches in ways totally other than how Job and other ancient Israelites would think of it.[98] According to Newsom, the different portrayal of animals in both speeches supports this. Instead of farm animals integrated into the covenant community (such as when livestock participate in the Sabbath [Exod. 20:10]),[99] God turns to those that cannot thus be categorized because they will not serve human interests (39:5–12).[100] She also notes how the two divine speeches begin with the stable founding of the earth (38:4–7) and end with the chaos monster Leviathan in the sea. Newsom concludes from this sequence that a literary 'uncreation' has been enacted in which Job is led 'progressively closer to a sustained and intimate encounter with the primary symbols of the chaotic'.[101] According to Newsom, a similar effect is achieved by the

---

[92] Fox 2013: 5, 7; 2018: 13.
[93] Fox 2013: 7.
[94] Ibid.
[95] Newsom 2003: 234–258.
[96] Ibid. 239.
[97] Ibid. 239–240.
[98] Ibid. 240.
[99] Newsom admits that Job does not speak of domesticated animals in chs. 29–31, but justly writes that 'one would have no difficulty in inserting them' into the way he portrays life in these chapters (ibid. 241).
[100] Ibid.
[101] Ibid. 243.

contrast between the ordered and happy metaphorical shape of Job's world, with the children gathered around their father (29:5) and the elder held in honour at the city gate (29:7–8), and the way space is represented in God's speeches, which persistently push 'to the remotest parts of the cosmos'.[102] As a result, the 'confident moral realism that Job takes for granted finds little anchorage in the divine speeches'.[103] But what is offered instead?

Newsom answers by pursuing the question of what relationship obtains between the symbols of chaos in chapters 38–41 and God himself. According to Newsom, this is 'the key interpretative question' for under-standing these chapters.[104] The animals of chapter 39 are especially significant on her reading, because the lion (38:39–41), the wild donkey (39:5–8) and the hawk (39:26–30) all 'destabilize . . . the customary binary oppositions of order and the chaotic, culture and nature, blessed and godforsaken' in such a way that their creator is associated 'in positive fashion with these creatures in the fearful beyond'.[105] Similarly, God's care for the donkey (39:5–8) is understood to count as 'an inversion of the values of human culture', especially its moral values, because the wild donkey is more than once enlisted as a symbol for rebellion against God (Gen. 16:12; Job 11:12; Jer. 2:24; Hos. 8:9).[106] For Newsom, God's 'celebration' of these creatures seems 'unnervingly to place him in con-siderable sympathy with the emblems of the chaotic'.[107]

Somewhat in anticipation of the next chapter, we can note here how Newsom's argument is taken even further in relation to Leviathan. Newsom is especially struck by 'a curious level of identification between God and Leviathan' in 41:10–11, and points to how parts of Leviathan's description echo God's theophanic appearance (e.g. Leviathan breathes fire in Job 41:19–20, just as YHWH does in Ps. 18:8, 12).[108]

For Newsom, all this contributes to focus on 'the nonmoral and non-rational aspects' of God: with Leviathan in view, Job and the reader learn 'something of the monstrous' that inheres in the 'numinous, wholly other-ness of God'.[109] Simultaneously, Job receives 'a devastating undermining

---

[102] Ibid. 240.
[103] Ibid. 241.
[104] Ibid. 243.
[105] Ibid. 245.
[106] Ibid. 246.
[107] Ibid. 247.
[108] Ibid. 251.
[109] Ibid. 252.

of his understanding of the unproblematic moral continuity between himself, the world, and God'.[110] Human ideas of justice do not apply, either to God or to the world he governs.

Newsom states the theological implications of her interpretation in somewhat subtle and academic language. Others are blunter. James Crenshaw, for example, agrees that the divine speeches show that God's universe is amoral, such that Job should not expect any answer about his supposedly undeserved punishment in chapters 1–2.[111] But, according to Crenshaw, chapters 38–39 show more than that God is indifferent to human ideas of justice. They show he is positively hostile to them. Crenshaw claims that God's references to predators in chapter 39 demonstrate that the strong prey on the weak under God's rule and with God's approval.[112] This is God's sinister *'ēṣâ* (plan) for creation. Furthermore, Crenshaw asserts that God is both malevolent in and absent from the book of Job and that when he does speak, he ignores Job's questions and mocks Job's smallness.[113] As a result, yнwн's two speeches are 'completely irrelevant' to the book because they contain no answer about undeserved suffering and punishment from on high.[114] All Job can acknowledge in them is divine power, but this is hardly satisfying, both because the subject of God's power is never in question, and because divine power divorced from divine goodness makes God a monster.[115] According to Crenshaw, Job is right when he characterizes God as an uncaring bully (9:22–24).

Edward Greenstein agrees. Like Newsom and Crenshaw, his starting point for reading chapters 38–41 is the majority consensus among scholars

---

[110] Ibid. 255. Newsom's earlier commentary on Job pursues much the same line about the divine speeches: while Job's categories for understanding God 'had been derived from the social and moral assumptions that structured community life and social roles in his own experience', God's speeches reject these categories as anthropocentric (1996: 336). It is significant to Newsom that human beings are never directly mentioned in chs. 38–41 (ibid.); God is, according to Newsom, not addressing human concerns. Job's legal language of right and wrong, just and unjust, does not apply to God's cosmos in the way Job thinks it does (ibid. 337). As a result, any desire for a reply to Job's argument about justice is frustrated: God talks about Job's limits and does not address the issue of justice at all (ibid. 595, 601).

[111] Crenshaw 1998: 109.

[112] Crenshaw 1995: 456.

[113] Ibid. 67, 459. Crenshaw does not explicitly say this, but the flow of his discussion suggests that he primarily has the way God allows the death of Job's children in mind when he speaks of God's malevolence. Crenshaw understands 2:3 to be an admission that the Accuser provoked God to act against his better judgment; he elsewhere speaks of God's permission to the Accuser to cause the death of Job's children as 'murder' (1993: 12).

[114] Crenshaw 1998: 99.

[115] Ibid.

that God does not directly engage with Job's protest about his unjust treatment.[116] But, as above, this does not mean the speeches have no semantic content; the sinister creatures in God's world and God's care for them are taken as a reflection of God's character in a negative way, such that, if God cares for predators, then there is something predatory about him as well.[117] This is very bad news for Job, for God 'makes a mockery of the principle of just retribution', listening to the cry of the raven (38:41) but ignoring Job's (19:7), setting the wild donkey free (39:5) but keeping Job imprisoned under the taskmaster (3:18–19).[118] This means that YHWH's speeches to Job at the end of the book do nothing more than confirm Job's worst fears from the debate with the friends: God is as uncaring towards Job as he is towards one of his creatures.[119] Greenstein goes so far as to name God 'an abusive victimizer',[120] who 'demeans' and 'mocks [Job's] ignorance and incompetence' at the end of the book while saying nothing about justice. According to Greenstein, this proves that God is 'sadistic' and 'self-centred'.[121]

In response to Newsom, Crenshaw and Greenstein, it should be admitted that God's relationship to the raging sea in 38:8–11 and other predators in chapter 39 is very unexpected. Furthermore, after hearing YHWH's extended description of Leviathan in chapter 41, Job does not respond with a shocked admission that he sees Leviathan more clearly, but that he sees God (42:5). This might superficially be taken to support an identification of God and Leviathan, such that God takes on chaotic aspects.

---

[116] Greenstein 1999: 301.

[117] Greenstein 2009: 354–355.

[118] Ibid. 356. Greenstein is drawing connections between specific words used in God's speech that echo the same words used earlier by Job: Job uses the root *šwʿ* to express his anguish over God's silence in 19:7, and God repeats it to ask who listens to the raven's cry in 38:41. It does not seem to feature in Greenstein's discussion that Job laments in the same verse that God does not 'answer' him (*ʿnh*), the same verb used for YHWH's answering Job from the storm wind in 38:1. In the light of this, one might just as easily conclude from God's care for the raven that he is especially attentive to Job's cry, since Job is worth more than many ravens. It is also worth pointing out that Greenstein's connection between the wild donkey, which is 'free' from human civilization, and Job's dismal portrayal of the soul in Sheol in 3:18–19 does not work, for Job says the unfortunate dweller in Sheol *is* free from his former master. Furthermore, Job leaves the despair of ch. 3 behind as the dialogue proceeds (17:15–16), but Greenstein does not appear to take this into account. It looks as if evidence is selectively assembled to argue for a sinister conclusion about God.

[119] Ibid. 357. The same sort of argument is made in Good 1990: 369; Habel 1992: 26; Wolfers 1995: 222–223; Clines 1998: 257; 2004: 235–236, 241, 250.

[120] Greenstein 2009: 342.

[121] Ibid. 353. Elsewhere Greenstein insists that God treats Job no better than the dungheap Job is sitting on (1999: 304).

Even granting this, however, three considerations make this sceptical reading untenable. (A fuller discussion of the relationship between God and Leviathan will be saved for the next chapter.) First, as argued above, it is impossible to read 38:4–15 and conclude from it that God is indifferent to the demands of justice or other human concerns. Why else would God put creation together in such a way that it works to counteract the plans of the wicked (vv. 12–15), unless it matters to God that the faithful and godly be protected and cared for? Why else would God contain the sea so that it does not overwhelm everything (v. 10; cf. Jer. 5:22) unless the flourishing of his creation and the people living there mattered to him? Are the angels wrong to break out in joyful song at this world's construction (v. 7)? Reading Tsevat and those who follow him, it is hard to see how anyone could rejoice in a world ruled by a God who does not care about fair treatment. But beings higher than us, granted a perspective on the world no human can ever gain (vv. 4–6), cannot help but sing.

Second, it is untrue to conclude from God's care for the dangerous or wild animals of chapter 39, which live outside civilized humanity and human concerns and activities, that his character must resemble these animals as uncaring towards human ideas of justice. Othmar Keel's very thorough study of the significance of the animals described in 38:39 – 39:30 in the ANE, already mentioned above, is again relevant here. Newsom is well aware of Keel's work and cites it approvingly.[122] But the evidence Keel assembles does not support Newsom's blurring of the distinction between instantiations of chaos and the deity who supports and provides for them. The 'Lord of the Animals' theme was introduced into the discussion above,[123] as was the fact that the animals in these glyphs are almost always the same as in Yнwн's first speech to Job.[124] Although sometimes the king is portrayed as hunting and killing these animals, he is just as often shown feeding and providing for them.[125] In other words, it is the task of the 'Lord of the Animals' to care for every creature under his rule, even those unable to be tamed by humans. Lions

---

[122] Newsom 2003: 245. Neither Crenshaw nor Greenstein interacts with Keel in the pieces cited above.
[123] Keel 1978a: 86–125.
[124] Ibid. 87.
[125] Ibid. 82. There are, however, examples of the hero taking a weapon to the animal (ibid. 7, 103), which does not occur in Job 39.

or wild birds do not serve in the ordered sphere of human existence, but their Lord is still sovereign over them, and is the one who keeps them laughing and free.[126] But never is the lordship of the king or god portrayed in Mesopotamian art in such a way as to blur the character of the sovereign with the subject in the way Newsom and others suggest. Mesopotamian deities are never thought of in 'chaotic' ways because they care for 'chaotic' animals. It is rather the uncontested rule and care of the deity that is on full display – the emphasis falls exactly on the god's status as an agent of order, ruling over these chaotic creatures. He is never portrayed in such a way that implies he takes on chaotic characteristics. Since the 'Lord of the Animals' theme was present in Mesopotamian culture for over a millennium,[127] this consistency is significant. In fact, one Neo-Babylonian example of the 'Lord of the Animals' theme with an ibex contains a short prayer: 'Marduk, great Lord, is the one who gives life. Let your radiant light shine on me!'[128] Light, not darkness; life, not death – although Marduk is hailed as lord of the animals, he is not an agent of chaos.

These considerations do not necessarily mean, of course, that a blurring between God and chaotic animals has not occurred in Job 38 – 39, for this could be one place where the Old Testament is breaking with its cultural context in a surprising way. But it does imply that ancient Semites were used to thinking of their gods and kings as ruling over and caring for animals that stand outside ordered human existence without drawing the conclusion Newsom does. One suspects Newsom's reading of chapters 38–39 owes more to her postmodern 'polyvalent' approach to the book of Job than the text itself as an ancient Semitic document.[129] Postmodern

---

[126] Ibid. 82–83.

[127] Ibid. 86.

[128] Ibid. 90.

[129] Newsom describes her approach as 'polyvalent' in the sense that the different parts of the book of Job and the different perspectives they represent (the prose prologue and ending, the debate between Job and the friends, the Elihu speeches and the divine speeches) are set in play in such a way that none is given a primacy that might provide closure to the whole text (2003: 29–30, 236). According to Newsom, each part of the book can be related in multiple ways to others, with multiple interpretations arising from these relations; but Newsom is disinclined to 'privilege' any one perspective in the text as the hermeneutical key to establish 'the' meaning of the book (ibid. 234). In other words, reading Job amounts to 'a series of different but juxtaposed ways of exploring the potentialities of the Job tradition' (ibid. 238). Instead of a text with a single message, it is as if the reader is caught in an unresolved and ongoing quarrel between the different parts of the book (ibid. 23). But Newsom does not always succeed in arguing for so fraught and indeterminate a text. She points out, for instance, that Job's restoration matches nicely the friends' description of Job's bright future if he will only admit his sin (ibid. 30, 235) and interprets this irony as destabilizing any sense of closure Job's restoration

approaches tend to blur distinctions and dismantle hierarchies; but significant evidence exists that ancient Semites would not have done so when presented with a picture of a deity caring for a dangerous or 'chaotic' animal.

This point requires nuance because there are examples of identification between the deity or king and a wild animal from ancient Mesopotamia. The most prominent of these comes from the lion hunt from Assyria, in which the king is symbolically identified with the victim and thus, in the words of Michael Dick, 'becomes the lion'.[130] However, this does not, as one might think, support any characterization of the king as an agent of chaos. Dick writes that this identification between king and lion is leveraged in such a way as to present the king as the powerful warrior, 'extending his rule beyond the city' to the chaotic wilderness and spreading civilization.[131] 'The king as identified with the lion (or with the wild bull) is then a "creature of nature" who rules over his (domesticated people), as a shepherd.'[132] The identification of king with lion, in other words, is in no way thought to give the king chaotic or predatory characteristics, but just the opposite. Indeed, Dick writes that ancient Assyrian lion hunts amounted to a cultic act by which chaos is defeated and the boundary between order and chaos reinforced. Strange as this identification may be

---

may provide for the reader. According to Newsom, Job rails against the friends in his speeches and God says they speak wrongly, but apparently they are right after all. That God describes Job's speech about himself as right (42:7) after Job has criticized God so fiercely is taken in a similar way: '[t]hus, what is seemingly settled by the intervention of God is disclosed as still subject to question, comment, and contestation, even if obliquely' (ibid. 235). But neither of these interpretations is convincing. The first fails to take into account that Job's restoration happens for the opposite reason the friends predict: instead of confessing some secret sin that could explain chs. 1–2, Job continues to cling to God, even while criticizing him. Similarly, it is surely significant that God's approval of Job's speech in 42:7 comes only after Job has repented in dust and ashes for speaking what he did not know against God (42:1–6). In other words, Newsom does not seem to take into account all the exegetical considerations one could and should take into account, thus weakening her claim that the book is 'polyvalent'. Furthermore, in a more general way, it is difficult to sustain the claim that every perspective in the text should be kept equal: while the friends' advice sounds very sane if taken out of context, surely we remain suspicious of it in the light of what we learn about Job and the divine throne room in chs. 1–2? And surely Job's criticisms of God are similarly impossible to read in a straightforward way, since we know God is not Job's antagonist. It looks as if the narrator/ poet means to privilege some perspectives in the book over others (see further Dempster 2005: 350). But the main point for the present discussion is that Newsom's way of handling the book is very widely different from how ancient Semitic poets and audiences would have written and received texts. This weakens her interpretation.

[130] Dick 2006: 244.
[131] Ibid.
[132] Ibid.

to modern readers, the boundary between the distinct characteristics of ruling king and defeated predator is never blurred, even when the king is presented as a lion.[133]

If God's goodness and concern for justice are established (38:4-15), and if his care of animals considered to be 'chaotic' in the Old Testament does not necessarily lessen or confuse his goodness, we are in a better position to read the rest of chapters 38-39 in such a way that explains why Job retracts his accusation of divine injustice instead of claiming he was right all along to protest (40:4-5). This is the third factor mitigating against the more sinister reading offered by Tsevat and others: if it is true that God is indifferent or hostile to human ideas of justice, this is hardly different from Job's protest in the debate with the friends, and so it is difficult to explain why he puts his hand over his mouth (40:4-5).[134] But if God's care for wild or dangerous animals does not imply his lack of care for humans, but suggests the wideness and generosity of his care for all creatures, a much happier vision of the world is opened up that explains Job's retraction. In fact, consideration of the weaknesses of the proposal by Tsevat and others can put us in a position to appreciate how profoundly Job's world of pain and chaos is being redescribed by the person who created it. All those aspects of the world that were most sinister to Job have become signs of God's goodness and care, but not because they have been sanitized or defanged. Lions do not stop being dangerous predators just because God cares for them! Job's prior perception of dangerous animals as creatures that could easily kill him are now seen in the light of God's limitless and providential care. The chaotic nature of lions, ravens and hawks is not changed by the first divine speech, but their significance is. They become

---

[133] Fox insightfully points out that if God's pleasure in dangerous creatures implies an identification with them, then one may claim the same for the creation of the sea monsters in Gen. 1:21; but no-one reads the verse that way (2013: 10).

[134] Fox makes this observation (2005: 352, n. 3). Crenshaw even admits that on his own reading Job's response is puzzling (1998: 99). Greenstein, by contrast, understands Job's response to confirm his interpretation: on his reading, Job is 'defiant to the end'. Because God only intimidates people who challenge him and bullies them, Job simply has nothing to say; his non-response is tantamount to a vindication that Job's criticisms of God have been confirmed (2009: 357). But as will be shown below, the normal meaning of placing a hand over one's mouth in the OT and the ANE is to express deference and submission to a superior, not some tacit claim to victory in an argument. Another way of attempting to claim that Job continues to criticize God in his response is by translating the first verb Job uses in v. 4 (*qll*) as 'I am held in contempt by God', as if Job, instead of withdrawing his protest, is still smarting under God's sarcastic and contemptuous response to him (see Perdue 1991: 216-217; Dumbrell 2000: 94). But this fits better with the piel or hiphil use of *qll*; the qal stem, which Job uses, means 'to be insignificant' (*HALOT* 1103-1105).

signs of divine goodness, without ceasing to be chaotic. If God cares even for lions, ravens and hawks, then his goodness is truly without limit. The dark and sinister world Job thought he was seeing for the first time after his tragedy is profoundly different from God's vision of creation. And surely if God cares for lions, his care for Job is no less profound.[135]

But this implication of the first speech is not stated: God speaks only of his goodness towards all his creation, not his goodness towards Job. In fact, none of the implications traced above about human limitations and divine goodness even for predators are explicit. A moment's reflection will, however, reveal why this is so. If God were explicitly to speak of his care for Job, it would be difficult for God to avoid sounding like a father trying to pacify a child throwing a tantrum: 'Look at all the nice things I do for you, Job! Don't criticize me!'[136] In a similar way, God cannot respond to Job's criticisms by pointing to God's reward of faithful saints, for to do so will put God's speech uncomfortably close to the speeches of the friends. Furthermore, the entire point of the book is that this reward is not always quick or uninterrupted.[137] This is why God speaks only indirectly and by implication.

It is, of course, possible to respond at this juncture that God should not allow any predation at all – the sea should be annihilated and all wild animals be killed, and God is wrong to run creation in any other way. But to insist on this is to put ourselves in such a position that the full weight of YHWH's full speech bears down on us: we do not know enough to conclude from the fact that dangerous elements in creation persist that God is unjust; massive evidence exists entirely to the contrary, pointing to God's limitless goodness; and even those sinister and frightening parts of life reflect that goodness.

Job's response (40:1–5): Is he satisfied? Is the reader?

God concludes his first speech by asking if Job will continue to argue with him or presume to instruct him in the governance of the cosmos (40:2). The question is not rhetorical: God is giving Job a genuine opportunity to

---

[135] Fox 2013: 7–8.
[136] Ibid. 15.
[137] Ibid. 17.

continue to insist on the moral wrongness of God's strategy for ruling all things, which does allow some limited agency to chaos and danger. Surely if anyone would have good reason to do so, it is Job, who has experienced this chaos and danger with such terrible intimacy.

However, Job does not do so. In verses 3–5, although he does not retract his claim to innocence, Job does legally withdraw his protest, setting aside 'his demand for formal vindication as the injured party'.[138] Earlier Job worried that, even though he was right, he would be so overwhelmed that he would not be able to argue his case. Ironically, when God does speak, Job finds himself overwhelmed, but for the opposite reason: God has reasoned with him and redescribed the cosmos in such a way that silences Job's protests. Everything in these two short lines expresses Job's submission before God's happier vision of creation and his abandoning of his claim against God: Job spoke once, but will not speak again (v. 4). That Job places his hand over his mouth also shows his reversal from criticism to silence before God (v. 3). This gesture has rich symbolic connotations in the (relatively few) other places it is found in the Old Testament. For instance, the 600 Danite thugs insist that Micah stop arguing and submit to them by telling him to put his hand over his mouth (Judg. 18:19). Job earlier used the same phrase to express the astonishment his friends should have felt as they saw the extent of his suffering (Job 21:5; the same connotation is found in Mic. 7:16). Proverbs 30:32 even ties this gesture to stopping proud or evil speech. It is also worth mentioning a relief of a courtier bowing before King Darius and covering his mouth with his hand.[139] One can see all of these connotations coming into play here: Job is submitting before God, ceasing his inappropriate criticisms of him and expressing astonishment at what he has just heard.[140]

So far, so good: God's speech has addressed Job's criticisms of the way God governs creation. We have seen how God allowed Job to fall into a position in which Job understandably but mistakenly thought God was punishing him as a rebel and sinner without any sufficient cause. As a result, Job extrapolated outwards from what he thought of as wrongly applied punishment to draw sweeping and terrifying conclusions about the world under the rule of this putatively arbitrary deity. God responds

---

138 Dumbrell 2000: 96; cf. Fox 2005: 354.
139 See *ANEP* 463 on p. 159, cited in Newell 1984: 311.
140 See further Glazov 2002: 30–41.

by sternly but gently challenging Job's description of his rule, emphasizing Job's epistemological limits, the massive goodness of the world Job has ignored, and the way God contains the chaos and violence he allows to continue in creation and is much kinder to it than Job has imagined. No charge is brought against Job of any sin that may explain his suffering; and in this silence, Job can infer that God is not angry with him, and not all suffering is punishment.[141] Job responds in turn by submitting and refusing to argue further. As mentioned above, Job 38 – 39 is not a timeless or general defence of God's policies, but one specifically geared towards the criticisms Job has levelled against them. This is an appropriate answer that gives some closure to the debate of the book and remains relevant to anyone tempted to draw dark conclusions about God's character and reign when he allows suffering.

At the same time, it is impossible to avoid the sense that it is not a complete answer. After all, this is a man whose children are dead – who furthermore knows (even if he cannot perceive everything happening in the divine realm) that supernatural agency was involved in their death (1:16). To speak only of how the sea is contained (38:8–11) or how creation does have some mechanism for blocking the designs of the wicked (vv. 12–15), however appropriate it may be in response to some of the false claims Job has made, appears underwhelming and anticlimactic if it is the only response given to Job.

This lack of closure – without denying the direct relevance of the claims God makes in chapters 38–39 to Job's speeches – is also seen when one compares Job's first response (40:3–5) with his second (42:1–6).[142] This latter response fairly jumps off the page as Job goes far beyond placing his hand over his mouth to repenting in dust and ashes – far beyond refusing to criticize again, all the way to admitting he had no idea what he was saying at all (42:3). In the light of this contrast, one might wonder if Job is being a little cold here, a little formal. His first response is good: he accepts that his criticisms of God's rule were wrong. But will Job admit only that he has nothing to say in response (40:4) when angels existing on a higher order than Job sang for joy when the cosmos was created (38:7)? Does the new vision of creation that has been revealed to Job give him no

---

[141] Fox 2005: 354.

[142] In the following comments, I am assuming the interpretation of 42:1–6 that will be argued for in chapter 5: that Job despises himself and repents. These verses are, however, strongly contested by some commentators, whose arguments are discussed further below.

joy at all? Similarly, Job's admission that he is insignificant (qal of *qll*) is psychologically realistic after his guided tour of the farthest reaches of creation and the strange animals inhabiting it. Job's smallness and insignificance were, however, never in doubt in the debate (e.g. 9:3, 19). As a result, this admission does not have as much force as his self-abasement in 42:1–6.

All this is to say that, without in any way detracting from the relevance of YHWH's first speech to the main issues of the debate in chapters 3–37, it is good that the book does not end here. God has more to say to Job, and Job has a more profound breakthrough awaiting him in new knowledge of God (42:5).

4

YHWH's second speech and the defeat of Leviathan (Job 40:6 – 41:34)

The last chapter closed by noting that Job's response to God's first speech, while appropriate, may be guarded in a way which suggests that Job needs a further breakthrough: however good it is for Job to withdraw his protest, doing so does not in itself imply a healing of the distance between God and Job and a complete resolution of Job's trauma. This helps to explain why God continues to address Job in 40:7, repeating the challenge of 38:3 but linking this challenge not to his plan for creation (38:2) but more specifically to his justice (40:8).[1] This verse defines the subject and trajectory of YHWH's second speech in an important way. Although the subject of God's justice was certainly not absent from chapters 38–39, God will address more directly Job's accusation in his second speech that God is unjust both in his character and in how he administers his kingdom. After this introduction (40:6–8), the speech unfolds in three parts: the preparation of the divine warrior (vv. 9–14), followed by the description of Behemoth (vv. 15–24) and Leviathan (41:1–34). (Job's response to the second speech in 42:1–6 is enough a part of his restoration that it is saved for the discussion of chapter 5 below.)

'Will you break my justice?'[2] (40:6–8)

The issue of the moral rightness of God's administration of his world is, as mentioned above, very important in his first speech. As a result, the

---

[1] ESV's 'put me in the wrong' glosses what could be rendered more literally as 'break my justice'. The verb 'break' (*prr*) means to 'frustrate', 'deny' or 'invalidate' something (Job 5:12; 15:4; Ps. 89:34).

[2] This is my translation.

opening question signals to the reader that God's second speech will not move in a completely different direction from the first. But neither does the second merely repeat: while God's first speech investigated his plan for the natural order, his second quickly moves to the supernatural as we read of the preparation of the divine warrior (40:9–14) and his warfare against the two monsters Behemoth (40:15–24) and Leviathan (41:1–34; I use the word 'warfare' because of the sword of 40:19 and the spear, harpoons and battle of 41:7–8). God's second speech also advances upon the first in that it will concern Job more personally. Job is not mentioned in 38:1 – 39:30, for the first speech focuses on the natural order external to Job. Now the supernatural evil that has so terribly interrupted Job's life will be brought to the foreground. Like two parallel clauses in a Hebrew poetic line, the second speech both overlaps with the first and advances upon it, simultaneously opening a transcendent horizon for YHWH's scarred servant and speaking to him more intimately than before.

These comments are, however, based on the assumption that 'justice' in 40:8 (*mišpāṭ*) is meant in the legal sense of a fair moral standard – that God is insisting his way of administering creation is right, the very point Job has repeatedly denied. The Hebrew word sustains a wide semantic range, however, and some would understand the word differently here. Just within the book of Job, in addition to 'justice' as moral uprightness in an abstract sense (see 8:3; 9:19; 32:9; 34:4), *mišpāṭ* can shade into one's legal right, or the justice or recompense to which one is entitled (19:7; 27:2; 31:13); upright behaviour enacted by humans (29:14); the case or legal argument of someone in court (13:18; 23:4; 31:13); the verdict of the court about a case (9:19, 32); or, more specifically, the judgment of the court, which inflicts punishment (36:17).[3] One might imagine an argument for one or more of these shades of meaning being present in YHWH's reference to his *mišpāṭ* in 40:8, but doing so would not greatly change the present argument.

Sylvia Scholnick goes further, however, by arguing that God's question about justice in 40:8 should not be taken in a legal sense at all. She distinguishes two senses of justice in the book of Job: the juridical and the executive.[4] According to Scholnick, while the friends think in terms

---

[3] See further Timmer 2009b: 294–295, for a good reading of the fine nuances with which Job uses the word. The use of *mišpāṭ* elsewhere in the OT conforms with its use in Job.

[4] Scholnick 1982: 521–529. Newsom expresses agreement with Scholnick on this verse (1996: 596), as does Good (1990: 353–354). Clines takes a somewhat different line, understanding

of legal justice, God in chapters 40–41 talks of sovereign right and prerogative as ruler – the ruler's 'executive authority' – that transcends any human legal system.[5] According to this sense of 'justice', God 'may treat his people and their property according to his own interests without their prior consent' as an all-powerful ruler, not a just judge.[6] She would thus translate the question in verse 8 as, 'Will you impugn my sovereignty?'[7] In support of this, while recognizing that the majority of the uses of the word in the Old Testament fall within the sphere of legal justice, Scholnick points to how 1 Samuel 8:9 uses this word to describe the way a king disposes of the materials of his kingdom purely as he sees fit.[8] As a result, '[t]he author of the book is trying to expand the understanding of the nature of God to include a realization that He is King of the universe'.[9] God's decisions about allowing Job's suffering 'reflect His use of sovereign authority' such that 'God is acting as Ruler to test his subject, not as Judge to punish him for wrongdoing'.[10] Job thus responds by bowing before divine power and retracting his lawsuit.[11]

If this is correct, it would remove any question of whether God is right to allow some evil in his creation: God is asserting his sovereign prerogative as king to do whatever he wants, and no-one is allowed to question him. Two weaknesses hinder Scholnick's interpretation, however, and suggest that God in his second speech is in fact defending the moral rightness of his manner of ruling creation. The first is that the supposed closure Scholnick's interpretation grants to the book – a realization on Job's behalf that God is King – would create a massive anticlimax, since Job has never disputed God's role as king of the universe and his undisputed sovereignty (see e.g. 9:12). Indeed, as we have seen, it is just these qualities (divorced from any sense of goodness) that make God so terrifying to Job. Since divine sovereignty was never at issue for Job, it would

---

God's *mišpāṭ* as 'my cause' in the sense of the legal case in which Job has involved God (2011: 1147). But it was argued above that God does not submit to a cross-examination by Job; while directly answering him, he resists entanglement in the hypothetical lawsuit Job earlier imagined (9:2–24; 13:13–25; 23:2–7).

[5] Scholnick 1982: 522.
[6] Ibid. 527.
[7] Ibid.
[8] Ibid. 522.
[9] Ibid. 523.
[10] Ibid.
[11] Ibid. 521.

be strange for God to ask Job why he has impugned it, and a reaffirmation of divine sovereignty alone would not prompt Job to withdraw his case against God and reconcile in worship. Second, although the distinction Scholnick draws between types of justice in the Old Testament is valid, she arguably pushes it too far. This is the case because those few instances in which *mišpāṭ* is best translated as 'sovereign right' always have some reference nearby to the moral rightness (or lack thereof) of the king's royal prerogative; even if the legal or moral aspect does not strictly fall within the use of this word, it is never absent either. This is the case in 1 Samuel 8, for the whole point of the passage is that the king will use his executive privilege wrongly, to oppress the people (vv. 11–18). Other possible examples of 'executive' (as opposed to legal) justice in the Old Testament are the same. For example, Psalm 89:15 speaks of *mišpāṭ* being the foundation of YHWH's throne in a way that could possibly be translated as 'sovereign right' – but the verse pairs it with 'righteousness' (cf. also Isa. 40:14 in the context of vv. 12–31). The distinction between legal and 'executive' justice in the Old Testament is valid but cannot be pushed in such a way that divorces the moral rightness of the king's rule from his right as sovereign. And this is, after all, clearly seen in Job 40:8, where God asks Job whether Job will continue to condemn him (hiphil of *ršʿ*, 'to be wicked') so that Job can be right (*ṣdq*). The moral quality of God's rule seems to be clearly in view in this question.

And it is not unfair for God to put this question to Job. In his desire to understand the tragedy of chapters 1–2, Job has been putting God in the wrong. From Job's perspective, only he and God were involved – and since there is nothing Job can think of to explain God's warfare against him, Job is forced to the conclusion that God was wrong to allow chapters 1–2, and to draw some troubling conclusions about God's character as a result. Job has some distant notion of a cosmic struggle (26:11–14), but does not know how to connect this to his own suffering. As a result, Job has understandably but wrongly cast God in the role of his enemy (9:24). Job has already learned that his characterization of God's world was wrong (chs. 38–39), but God will press more deeply into Job's protest in this speech by unmasking the real enemy[12] and expanding his vision so that Job can be innocent while he suffers, and God still be sovereign over evil

---

[12] Fyall 2002: 141.

without being unjust.[13] Furthermore, although Job's second speech in 42:1–6 is not easy to interpret, it will be argued that Job does repent and worship – whatever it is that Job discerns in God's speech entirely reconciles him to God's present administration of creation and moves him far beyond his first guarded admission that he was wrong to criticize. So how is it that God defends the justice Job denied so thoroughly?

The preparation of the divine warrior (40:9–14)

The central point in the first part of God's second speech is that the references to his arm, voice and radiant majesty are an Old Testament way of describing his preparation for battle (vv. 9–10) against his enemies (vv. 11–13). The same combination of theophanic glory with God's thunderous voice and upraised arm, all for the purpose of defeating those who resist his rule, is found repeatedly in the Psalms: in Psalm 18:12–13, it is from the brightness before yнwн that coals of fire come as he thunders in the heavens against David's enemies; in Psalm 89:11–16, the upraised arm that scatters God's enemies is hymned by the people walking about in the light of his presence; in Psalm 93, God is clothed with majesty, reigning high above the storming waters; in Psalm 96, splendour and majesty are before him (v. 6) as he comes to judge the earth (v. 13; this is the same 'glory and splendour' [hôd wehādār] in Job 40:10b). Isaiah 30:30 is also relevant as it describes God's making the splendour (hôd, 'glory', as in Job 40:10) of his voice to be heard and the descent of his arm to be seen as he defeats Assyria and saves Judah. Divine theophanic warfare in the Old Testament is a major way God beats back the powers of darkness and executes his blessed rule on the earth, and it is just this theme being activated in this passage.

It can be easy for modern readers, unfamiliar with this idea, to revert to abstractions in explaining yнwн's radiant theophany from the storm in these texts and assume it is only a poetic way of emphasizing divine power. While God's power is on display in these passages, we must not miss how the theophanic display of his arm and voice shows not just

---

[13] J. C. L. Gibson astutely points out that while the friends condemned Job to exonerate God and Job condemned God to exonerate himself, God is asking Job if he can be just and Job innocent at the same time (1988: 401). Perdue aptly phrases the same insight by writing that the second speech 'denies that the innocence of Job depends upon the guilt of God' (1991: 219).

divine power in a general sense but his action both to save those who trust him and to judge those who rebel. This is true in Job 40:9–14 as well, for the reason why God is adorned with splendour and majesty, raises his arm and thunders with his voice (vv. 9–10) is to humble and judge the wicked (vv. 11–13).[14] This is the salvation God's right arm wins (v. 14; cf. Job 26:2; Isa. 51:9–11). In other words, verses 9–14 show Job how God executes justice in the earth (40:8) – the very thing Job complained that God fails to do (10:3; 21:7). Nor is this judgment restricted to the here and now, for it ends with these wicked being 'hidden' in the 'dust' (v. 13).[15] The 'grave' connotations of dust in the book of Job were already argued for in relation to its use in 19:25, and I think they should be understood here as well. The verb 'to hide' can also evoke death and the underworld (in 3:16, Job expresses his wish that he were stillborn in Sheol as being 'hidden' there). This means that when God describes his judgment of the wicked as 'hiding them in the dust', it means that his judgment of the wicked is not partial in the ways that frustrated the Preacher (Eccl. 8:11–14). It is rather a judgment of death – as total and final as could be imagined. What complaint about a supposed lack of concern for justice can be brought against a God who acts in this way?

The question that closes this section in verse 14 is not intended as a sarcastic put-down.[16] As with the rhetorical questions of chapters 38–39, it pertains to an activity no human would feel ashamed of for being unable to accomplish. The point to the question is not to mock Job for being unable to perform a judgment of human sin so total it extends into the

---

[14] The rĕšāʿîm, 'wicked', mentioned in v. 12, always elsewhere refers to human evildoers (e.g. Job 3:17; 8:22; 11:20; 38:13; Ps. 1:1; Eccl. 8:10; Isa. 13:11; etc.). The parallel word in the first clause of the verse, gēʾeh, 'the proud', can also be used for human evildoers elsewhere (Pss 94:2; 140:6).

[15] In addition to being hidden in the dust, v. 13 also makes reference to 'binding the face' (ḥbš with pāneh); but since this phrase is found nowhere else in the OT, it is more difficult to say what it means. One common interpretation is that it refers to the wicked being imprisoned in the underworld (Habel 1985: 553). Or perhaps it speaks of an unending shame and disgrace (cf. 2 Sam. 15:30; Esth. 6:12; Jer. 14:3–4). In comparison with the peaceful and noble burials spoken of elsewhere in the book of Job (such as 3:14–15; 21:32–33), Hartley wonders if this phrase implies these wicked will not get the burial for which they hoped (1988: 521).

[16] As with the rhetorical questions in chs. 38–39, some discern an insult in the question of 40:14. Clines reads the challenge to Job to do something he clearly cannot as unambiguously sarcastic (2011: 1178). Good similarly understands God to be setting Job an impossible task in ironic fashion and wonders if YHWH will gloat when Job inevitably fails (1990: 357). Crenshaw seems to go farther on this point when he writes that the question of 40:14 betrays a divine defensiveness about God's own failure to do justice, such that God is essentially saying, 'Well, you can't do any better!' (1998: 112). Enough has been said above, however, to show that this interpretation is in no way necessary, and does not fit with the portrayal of God elsewhere in the book of Job and the rest of the OT.

afterlife, but, as in chapters 38–39, to show that God does in fact accomplish the judgment described in verses 9–13 no human being can accomplish.[17] God is refocusing Job's attention on himself and the justice he works out, giving Job insight into the radiant divine energy God devotes to executing justice in this life and after it. Humiliation is not the desired response, but awe and trust in an active and just God is desired. However, if Job wants to insist he has a better idea than the Almighty of what justice looks like, God clearly shows him what is needed to confront human sin fully – a radiant power Job clearly does not possess. Job stands with the rest of humanity in needing a Saviour on high to act on his behalf (v. 14). In other words, the question of verse 14 is sincere: God is not merely 'pulling rank', but describing what the execution of justice in the world really entails. If there is an irony in this verse, it is one meant in Job's favour, for Job really does have a Saviour who will thunder in the heavens on his behalf. This is God's justice, which Job has been denying (v. 8). Will Job continue to argue, or will he repent?

Significant as this passage is for Job, there is a great deal more ʏʜᴡʜ has to say to him in ʏʜᴡʜ's second speech. The just judgment of human wickedness is only the beginning of God's work as he confronts the evil loose in his creation on a much larger scale. But to see how this is so is to enter one of the most contested areas of the book of Job, and one of the most difficult to interpret.

Behemoth: the 'Superbeast' (40:15–24)

It was mentioned above, in relation to chapters 38–39, that the divine poetry uttered to Job and recorded for us does not state what conclusions Job and the reader are meant to draw from it. The same is true in the description of Behemoth and Leviathan: 'Nothing is stated, yet much is evoked.'[18] All ʏʜᴡʜ gives Job is an extended description of the physical characteristics and prowess of these creatures – and something about these verses prompts Job to break into worship. What it is that provokes such a strong reaction in Job is, of course, not immediately clear. Even though I have already indicated in a general way what argument will be

---

[17] Fox 2013: 16.
[18] Newsom 2003: 247.

made about the significance of these two creatures, I would like to follow the lead of the text by attending as much as possible to the details of these descriptions on their own before turning to possible interpretations. I want to put ourselves as much as possible in the position of hearing or reading them for the first time, and being forced to puzzle out what YHWH may be saying to suffering saints through them. Doing so seems to be the best way of following the lead of the text itself.

It is important to remember at this juncture that outside Job 40 – 41 physical descriptions in the Old Testament tend towards extreme brevity. For example, Rachel is 'beautiful in form and appearance', but Leah's eyes are 'weak' (Gen. 29:17) – that is all we are told. David, on the other hand, is entitled to three whole phrases: 'ruddy', 'handsome', with 'beautiful eyes' (1 Sam. 16:12). The exception that proves this rule is found in Goliath, who is given four whole verses to impress upon the reader how, from a human point of view, Israel's opponent is unbeatable (1 Sam. 17:4–7). From this perspective, the nine verses devoted to Behemoth and the thirty-four given to Leviathan are very striking! They are surely the longest physical description of any creature in the entire Bible. It appears there is no way to reach Job's ecstatic worship except by considering these creatures in the same detail the text uses. Even if nothing is explicitly stated, much is evoked.

Behemoth's hulking strength and deep vitality are portrayed for us first (vv. 16–19). Even if he eats like an ox (v. 15), his impenetrable muscle distinguishes him: his bones are bars of iron (v. 18) and the sinewy muscles of his thighs intertwine (v. 17).[19] We pull back to see the creature's habitat in verses 20–24, with Behemoth dwelling beneath the lotus in deep shadow (vv. 21–22), unperturbed and unmoving before disturbances that set other animals to flight (v. 23). The creature is intimidated by no-one

---

[19] The clause about Behemoth's tail in 17a is difficult to make sense of for two reasons. First, on the supposition that Behemoth is a hippopotamus, it is hard to understand how Behemoth can have a tail 'like a cedar' when a hippo's tail is short and thin. Second, the verb *ḥpṣ* everywhere else in the OT means 'to delight', but it is difficult to understand how Behemoth could delight in his tail 'as a cedar'. Commentators go different ways, none entirely convincing; perhaps an otherwise unattested homonym of the verb is being used here, such that the tail 'hangs down' or 'is stiff' like a cedar, or perhaps a euphemistic reference to the creature's sexual potency is being made. As he always does, Clines gives an exhaustive discussion of different options (2011: 1150–1151) and translates as 'it stiffens its tail like a cedar'. The overall impression of strength in vv. 16–18 is not affected much regardless of how one takes the line. It should be noted, however, that this is the one point of the description that does not easily square with the picture of a hippopotamus.

and totally untamable (v. 24).[20] Williams evocatively refers to Behemoth as 'that savage, massive *thereness*'.[21] The total effect is one of solid brawn, lurking, lurking, deep in shadow, sliding silently through the water, an effect deepened by the repeating sibilants in verses 21–22:

Under lotus he lies, in the secret	*taḥat ṣe'ĕlîm yiškāb bĕsēter*
place of reed and swamp;	*qāneh ubiṣāh*
the lotus shades him with its shadow,	*yĕsukuhu ṣe'ĕlîm ṣilălô*
ringed by willow trees of the river.	*yĕsubuhu 'arbe nāḥal*
(My tr.)	

No other animal dares compete with Behemoth: poetically, all the beasts of the field bring him tribute and sport before him (*śḥq*, v. 20). This is their recognition of Behemoth as king; the same verb in 2 Samuel 2:14 describes a military contest that takes place as part of David's being crowned over all Israel. Realism is sacrificed for impressionistic vividness as all the other animals (as it were) hold court before their ruler.

Thus we see Behemoth. What is Job supposed to think after having this creature's power and watery dwelling place narrated? Four clues in verses 15 and 19 will be introduced into the discussion here and explored further below. The first is the name 'Behemoth' itself. This is not the name of any species, but rather the Anglicization of the feminine plural of the Hebrew word *bĕhēmâ*, which refers either to animals in general or livestock in particular (*HALOT* 112). Hebrew avails itself of the plural in situations English does not, sometimes as an honorific, and this is the most common explanation of the form here: not 'an animal', but 'The Beast' or 'Superbeast'.[22] This is significant because, although the description seems

---

[20] V. 24 is not specifically marked as a question, but should be read that way, similar to the rhetorical questions surrounding Leviathan in 41:1–11. GKC 150a gives numerous examples of questions that are unmarked but discernible from context. The image of capturing Behemoth by his eyes is obviously strange, but since the answer to the question is, 'No, of course not,' the image may be deliberately absurd (Clines [2011: 1157] lists other options for emendation). Dhorme quotes Herodotus' report that Egyptians used to capture crocodiles by putting a plaster over their eyes, which may lie in the background here (1984: 625).

[21] Williams 1992: 370; italics original.

[22] This apt designation is Ash's (2014: 410). Pope points out that the singular verbs used with the plural noun Behemoth also suggest the noun is a plural of majesty (1973: 269). It is noteworthy that Leviathan is described with the plural 'sea monsters' (*tannînîm*) in Ps. 74:13 (WOC 7.4.3a).

most closely to resemble a hippo (with the exception of the difficult v. 17), the name does not seem to point to any one species of animal.

Second, Job is told God made Behemoth along with Job (v. 15). It is significant that we are told this first, because everything else in the description sets Behemoth apart as unlike any other animal. The intention of almost every line describing the creature is to distinguish the creature from normal animals. This juxtaposition creates a striking effect: on the one hand, Behemoth is no sooner named than his status as a creature of God along with Job is emphasized (v. 15); but on the other hand, no other animal is treated as a king by the others (v. 20). Is Superbeast being presented as a creature, but more than an ordinary one? If this is on the right track, it suggests a finesse in the presentation of Behemoth that would have been very important in an ancient Semitic context. This is the case because ancient Canaanites, Mesopotamians and Egyptians frequently portrayed their gods in animal form (including, as we will see, the hippopotamus). The implication seems to be that Superbeast is no ordinary animal, but this suggestion is no sooner registered than it is made explicit that Behemoth is as much a part of God's creation as Job is, and is thus no dualistic competitor with the Creator. At the same time, he is unique among his fellows in a way to which no other animal species quite compares (v. 20). What exactly this means will be explored further below – it is enough here to register these clues so they can be enlisted in a later discussion. We can, however, anticipate that later discussion by comparing Behemoth to the serpent in Genesis 3, who is presented in a similar way: on the one hand, it is introduced along with the other creatures of the field created by God (v. 1), but, on the other, the serpent has the ability to talk, and knows things only God does.[23] We will return to the significance of this connection below.

A third clue about Behemoth is found in verse 19, where the creature is called 'the first of the works of God' (v. 19a; esv's 'works' correctly interprets the word 'ways'). The word 'first' can refer either to temporal priority (Gen. 1:1; Mic. 1:13) or the most important part of something (Jer. 49:35; Dan. 11:14; Amos 6:1, 6). Either nuance may be in play here. On the one hand, the reference to Behemoth's creation in verse 15 may

---

[23] This latter characteristic is seen when comparing Gen. 3:6 with v. 22. God warned the man only that he would die if he ate (Gen 2:17), not that he would become like God, knowing good and evil – even though this turned out to be true (v. 22).

point to Behemoth's being the first animal created by God. However, this does not square with either creation account in Genesis 1 or 2, for land animals are not created first in either account; and if Behemoth represents supernatural chaos, no mention is made in Old Testament creation accounts of God's creating chaos. The distance between the reference to Behemoth's creation in verse 15 and verse 19, together with the next verse's portrayal of Behemoth's superiority to every other animal (v. 20), suggests that Behemoth is 'first' in God's ways in terms of importance. This fits more generally with the emphasis in verses 16–24 on the creature's uniqueness. In what way Behemoth carries such a significant place in God's plans is, of course, not at all easy to see and will require further reflection. For now, we can imaginatively continue to put ourselves in Job's position, seeing this massive, muscular creature moving through the water, a creature that has a prime place in God's plans – whatever that exactly means.[24]

Fourth and finally, it is striking that we are no sooner told of Behemoth's prime place before God than that the very God who created the beast is bringing his sword near (v. 19b). Some find the reference to a sword jarring in context and emend the phrase to 'the one made as tyrant among his companions' (the Hebrew of both is very similar).[25] While this would fit well with the general emphasis of the passage, it is not reflected in any of the ancient versions and so remains speculative. Further, coming on the heels of the preparation of the divine warrior in verses 9–14, it is not unusual to have a reference to the weapon of that warrior. Other divine warrior passages refer to the sword God uses in battle (Isa. 27:1; 34:5–6; 66:16). This suggests that the MT is the better reading, and means that immediately after reading of Behemoth's importance, we are told of his slaughter at God's hands. The significance of this sequence will be considered further below.

---

[24] Many commentators point out how the only other thing in the OT granted this honour is Lady Wisdom in Prov. 8:22, called 'the first of God's ways' because she was there before any of God's other work in creation. The particular phrasing of the verse suggests the temporal aspects of 'first' are in play in this verse in Prov. 8 (Fox 2000: 280; Waltke 2005: 408–410). This connection, while striking, does not perhaps help us very much with Job 40:19, for while it is unsurprising that Wisdom would be there at the first and act, as it were, as a kind of blueprint for creation (Prov. 3:22), this does not in itself shed light on how a hippo-like creature could play a similar role.

[25] E.g. Dhorme 1984: 621; Newsom 2003: 250. Where the MT has *hāʿōśō yagēš ḥarbô*, this proposal would emend to *heʿāśû nōgēś ḥăbērāw*; the consonantal text is changed in only one letter (from yod to nun in the verb).

Collectively, these aspects of Behemoth's description suggest a creature of immense strength but entirely under the rule of God; a beast no less a creation than Job, but not fitting into the normal categories the Old Testament uses to describe animals. Behemoth has a rank of first place in God's plans for his world, but God is also going to destroy him. What is Job supposed to think? Before answering, let us attend to the description of Leviathan, which is similarly suggestive without being explicit.

Leviathan: the twisting, fleeing serpent (41:1–34)[26]

The description of Leviathan falls broadly into two parts: a series of rhetorical questions concerning Job's powerlessness before the monster (vv. 1–11) and God's praise of the creature's fearsome attributes and prowess (vv. 12–34). In the first section, the repeated questions each end on the same note of Job's helplessness. Job could not subdue Leviathan by any of the means humans normally use to capture crocodiles or other sea creatures (vv. 1–2).[27] Leviathan certainly would not beg Job for mercy or try to strike a deal with him or submit as a slave (vv. 3–4). It would be ridiculous for Job to think of using this creature for entertainment (v. 5) or economic advantage (v. 6). Spears normally used for fish are useless against Leviathan (v. 7). Merely to touch the creature would be the experience of a lifetime; it would take only one encounter to convince Job that any battle with Leviathan was totally impossible and never to be attempted again (v. 8). Any confidence a hypothetical combatant might have would be destroyed by the mere sight of this creature (v. 9). As with chapters 38–39, these rhetorical questions intend not to humiliate Job but to highlight the active power of God, who both can and does accomplish victories impossible for Job.

The last two verses of this section broaden the perspective of verses 1–9 as YHWH includes himself in the utterly unequal comparison between Leviathan and Job. If Leviathan is so unapproachably and overwhelmingly cruel when aroused, then who, by comparison, could possibly take a stand

---

[26] English Bibles sensibly begin a new chapter when Leviathan is introduced, but the Hebrew continues with 40:25 through to 40:32 (English 41:8) before it begins ch. 41. I use the English numbering here.

[27] See Clines 2011: 1192–1193 for references in ancient literature to fishing techniques similar to the language of this verse.

against God (v. 10)?[28] Even more, who could confront God so that God would have to repay or make restitution to that person (v. 11)?[29] It is striking that just as YHWH singles out Behemoth and Leviathan as unique, exemplary and unapproachable in relation to other creatures, YHWH also presents himself as unique and incomparable in contrast with these monsters.[30] If there is no way Job or any other human could oppose Leviathan, there is absolutely no way they could oppose the God who easily masters that beast. In fact, God applies his transcendent uniqueness directly to Job by making another echo to Job's first speech in verse 10, repeating the verb 'arouse' (*'ûr*), which Job used in 3:8 as he spurred on those mysterious priestly figures ready to rouse Leviathan and destroy creation.[31] God implies to Job that Job did not know what he was asking for when he called for the chaos monster to be stirred up, but God makes this claim in relation to himself, not Leviathan alone. This surely must have been a sobering reproof to Job the arguer from chapters 3–31 – but it was probably very hopeful as well, for reasons to be seen below.

God also seems to find a kind of unique joy in his opponent: 'Under all the heavens, he is mine!' (v. 11).[32] One of the ways in which God leverages

---

[28] Hithpael *yṣb* with the preposition *lipnêy* normally implies a hostile confrontation (see Exod. 8:16; 9:13; Deut. 9:2; Josh. 1:5; Job 33:5; two exceptions occur in Josh. 24:1 and 1 Sam. 10:19, where the phrase means only to assemble before God). The first clause of v. 10 is usually translated to the effect that no-one could be so fierce as to arouse Leviathan (ESV, NIV); however, Gibson (1992: 105) points out that if the verse were pointing to a hypothetical human combatant with Leviathan, we would expect *'ên*, 'there is not/no one', not *lô*. As it is written, the negative particle rhetorically points to Leviathan's cruelty, not to that of his hypothetical opponent: 'Is he not cruel when he is aroused?'

[29] Some prefer to emend the pronouns in vv. 2b–3a so that they are all third-person masculine singular, such that the attention on Leviathan alone continues: 'Who is so cruel as to rouse him? Who would take his stand before him? Who would confront him and come out safe? Under all the heavens, not one!' However, the MT represents a more difficult reading and the textual evidence for this alternative reading is spotty. Although BHS n. 2b shows that many other Hebrew manuscripts show a third-person masculine singular pronoun in the second clause of v. 2, the LXX, Syriac and Vulgate all reflect the first-person pronouns of the MT in both verses. See further Naselli 2012: 93–94 for a good argument for retaining the MT in these verses on textual and contextual grounds.

[30] I am indebted to Henry Rowold on these verses (1986: 104–109), although he reads v. 2b a little differently from the interpretation given here, taking it to mean Leviathan may be fierce when aroused, but when he stands before God, who is he? Nobody (ibid. 106).

[31] Fyall 2002: 161.

[32] The phrase is normally translated, 'Whatever is under the whole heaven is mine' (e.g. NIV, ESV), which makes sense coming right after v. 11a. However, when the exact phrase *taḥat kôl-haššāmayim* occurs elsewhere in the OT it is usually (rightly) translated 'under all the heavens' or 'under the whole heaven' or the like (Gen. 7:19; Deut. 2:25; 4:19; Job 28:24; 37:3; Dan. 9:12), suggesting the translation given above. The more common translation given in the NIV and ESV for this verse would fit better if *kôl* came before *taḥat*.

his unique power and sovereignty in relation to Leviathan is to refuse to give the job of defeating Leviathan to anyone else. Not only is God the only one who can draw out Leviathan with a hook (v. 1), fill his side with spears (v. 7), lay his hand on him in battle (v. 8) – God absolutely will not delegate this task to anyone else. Just let someone try to stop him!

So far, what YHWH has said to Job in verses 1–11 would have been deeply meaningful to God's mistrustful and argumentative but still faithful servant. But perhaps surprisingly, YHWH continues his speech in verses 12–34 by praising his opponent's physical prowess.[33] The use of 'graceful' (NIV) or 'goodly' (ESV) to describe the creature's physical arrangement in verse 12 is especially surprising, since the Hebrew word[34] is commonly used elsewhere to describe 'favor . . . in the sight of God and man' (Prov. 3:4) or God's grace (Ps. 84:12; Zech. 12:10); it also can refer to graciousness or some pleasing attribute in more general ways (Prov. 5:19; Eccl. 10:12). There is certainly no danger of damning one's opponent with faint praise in this verse! Why would God describe Leviathan in so positive a way?

This question takes on greater urgency as we realize that every attribute for which YHWH praises Leviathan is dangerous and frightening to human beings. The creature's impenetrability comes first (vv. 13–17), starting from the outer edges of the monster (v. 13), moving to the teeth as the 'doors' of his mouth (v. 14) and then to the armour of his back, the scales like shields joined so closely not even air can escape (vv. 15–17). No-one can even get close, much less penetrate or strip away Leviathan's armour.

The numinous, fiery attack of the creature is described next (vv. 18–21): fiery sparks and lightning flash forth from his mouth, all beneath his mysterious, glowing eyes.[35] This is more than an exaggerated way of

---

[33] Fyall sees 41:8–11 as the climactic midpoint of the entire poem, providing a framework for everything that follows in ch. 41 (2002: 160).

[34] Strictly speaking, the word in v. 4 is spelled differently from its use everywhere else; but they seem to be two forms of the same word (BDB 336).

[35] That this creature has eyes 'like the eyelids of the dawn' exactly recalls Job's use of the phrase in 3:9, where, just after calling for Leviathan to be roused (v. 8), Job called for the dawn of the night in which he was conceived to be dark, never seeing 'the eyelids of the dawn'. The phrase occurs nowhere else in the OT and there are enough other allusions in YHWH's speeches to Job's first speech that one suspects this echo is not accidental. The implication of this echo is, however, unclear to me. Is God saying that if Job's curse had been successful, the darkness he had hoped for would have been replaced with a more sinister light – the light coming from Leviathan's eyes? That Job's curse on creation and summoning of Leviathan is extremely ill-advised? It is difficult to be sure.

emphasizing Leviathan's power: within the Old Testament motif of theophanic combat, these images describe the warfare of the combatants (the closest comparable text is YHWH's theophanic warfare against David's opponents in Ps. 18:7–15; see esp. v. 8). The only difference is that in Job 41, it is Leviathan who does these things, not God. But that is not surprising, for in other texts of this kind the chaos God defeats mimics the kind of attack he makes on it (e.g. in Ps. 46:3, 6, both YHWH and the raging waters roar).[36] No instability in God's supreme reign over all things is implied in this similarity; only the magnitude and drama of the conflict. The point to Leviathan's mimicry of divine warfare in Job 41:18–21 is to make inescapably clear that Job cannot even approach a monster with such an arsenal at its disposal, much less oppose it; but doing so is an easy matter for God.

YHWH next describes for Job the creature's unbending neck, its impenetrable hide, its immovable strength (vv. 22–24). Terror dances before it (v. 22)! Even the gods[37] are overwhelmed, flummoxed, beside themselves when Leviathan rouses himself (v. 25), and with good reason: weapons are useless against the monster (v. 26) and Leviathan would not even flinch before them (vv. 27–29). Leviathan's description then moves towards a conclusion with the scaly, sharp underside of the beast (v. 30), which makes the deep boil like a pot and the water turn white as the creature swims away (vv. 32–33).

A pattern develops in the second half of chapter 41 in which YHWH alternates between Leviathan's impenetrability and his invincibility in any attack:

A Physical impenetrability (vv. 13–17)
   B Unstoppable attack (vv. 18–21)
A Physical impenetrability (vv. 22–24)
   B Invincible before any attack (vv. 25–29)
A Physical impenetrability (vv. 30–32)

---

[36] The same is true in descriptions of divine conflict in the ANE; see Habel 1985: 572 for examples from *Enuma Elish* and the Baal Epic of hero and monster attacking each other in identical ways.

[37] Hebrew *'ēlîm* in this verse is usually translated as 'mighty' (NIV, ESV), which is appropriate in relation to Ezek. 31:11, where it refers to the mightiest among the nations. But it also refers to subordinate divine beings in Pss 29:1 and 89:7, making 'gods' or 'divine beings' an acceptable translation here. Although the point will be developed below, it is worth mentioning that in the *Enuma Elish* the gods cower before the chaos monster Tiamat before Marduk comes to rescue them (see Pope 1973: 286 for discussion and other references).

Two concluding verses are given in evaluation of Leviathan that repeatedly emphasize his incomparable supremacy (vv. 33–34). He is a king without equal and without fear. Even when emphasizing Leviathan's uniqueness, however, this concluding evaluation recalls verses 10–11 and the creature's inferiority to God. This is accomplished by describing him as 'a creature without fear' (v. 33). The word translated 'creature' is a qal passive participle: 'a thing created'. Just as Behemoth is a creature along with Job (40:15), this final praise of Leviathan as unequalled and without competitor simultaneously keeps Leviathan firmly to one side of the infinite divide between the transcendent Creator and everything else he has made. Terrible as this creature would be to Job, Leviathan is only a creature along with Job in relation to God.

But not an ordinary creature. Two other hints in these final lines suggest no ordinary animal is being portrayed for Job. The first hint comes when we read that Leviathan is without equal 'on earth' (ESV, NIV). This is an acceptable translation of the Hebrew, but the word used is *'āpār*, 'dust', a word that elsewhere in the book connotes the underworld. If we interpret 'dust' in this way here, then presumably Leviathan's kingship over 'the sons of pride' shows the monster at the head of his infernal retinue. On the other hand, if we retain the translation of 'earth' in verse 33, it would be easy to imagine this creature only as king of the beasts. This latter option is confirmed by the only other use in the Old Testament of the word 'pride' (*šāḥas*) to refer to lions (Job 28:8). But a significant echo in the first half of 41:34 to 40:11–13 suggests that we read 'dust' here in its 'grave' connotations. Both passages repeat the image of 'looking on everyone who is proud' in similar language,[38] and both do so in relation to 'the dust': in 40:11–13, Job is ironically commanded to bind the faces of proud rebels in the dust, while in 41:33–34, Leviathan surveys all the proud as king without equal over the dust. This hints that the spiritual connotations of dust are being activated in 41:33–34, such that Leviathan stands as the grim king over a demonic horde that serves him.

But these are only hints. The consistent note sounded as a whole in 41:12–34 is Leviathan's unique danger and threat, which would overwhelm Job but present no problem for God. The final verses show the creature

---

[38] The verb *r'h* is repeated, while *gē'eh* describes the proud in 40:11–13 and *gābōah* the proud in 41:34. The two adjectives are found together in Isa. 2:11–12 and Jer. 48:29.

swimming away, churning the sea white (v. 32). But as Leviathan fades from view, what have we learned? No conclusion is drawn from the description: God does not push Job towards any conclusion on the basis of what he has just said. What was Job supposed to think?

As we consider some of the widely varying interpretations of YHWH's second speech, we must keep in mind that a successful interpretation must explain two issues in particular. First, it must account for God's opening statement that this speech addresses the justice of his rule over all things (40:8). Whatever we are to conclude from the description of Leviathan, it somehow resolves Job's protest about God's apparently unjust administration of creation, as exemplified in his treatment of Job. Second, a successful interpretation must keep in mind Job's very different response in 42:1–6 in comparison with the first speech. Whatever it is that YHWH communicates to Job in his second speech, it provokes an about-turn in Job from protest to self-effacing worship.

Possible interpretations of Behemoth and Leviathan

Behemoth and Leviathan as a hippopotamus and crocodile

The most common interpretation of Behemoth and Leviathan is that these two creatures are a hippopotamus and crocodile – ordinary animals no different from the other animals surveyed in 38:39 – 39:30. This was first proposed by Bochart in his *Hierozoicon* in 1663 and has mostly dominated interpretation since then.[39] According to this reading, the hippo and crocodile show the power and wisdom of God in creation. If they are impressive, their creator must be even more so; if Job is powerless to understand or control them, God certainly is not. These two animals are thus presented to Job to evoke an awestruck trust in God.[40]

---

[39] Wilson 1975: 1. López (2016: 404–405) summarizes other animals that have been suggested (such as the dolphin), none of which is especially convincing.

[40] For a representative sample of this way of reading YHWH's second speech, see Delitzsch 1949: 687–699; Gordis 1965: 120, 133–134; 1978: 558–566; Andersen 1976: 289–290; Rowley 1983: 255–264; Dhorme 1984: 619; Atkinson 1991: 151; Alden 1993: 400; Wharton 1999: 174–175; Clines 2011: 1185–1186; Fox 2012: 261–267; 2018: 14; Brown 2014: 111–118; Wilson 2015: 452; Longman 2016: 441–445; Belcher 2017: 283, 293, 303. See Day 1985: 65, n. 16, for this interpretation in earlier commentaries (e.g. Budde, Duhm, Driver, etc.).

Arguments for this position vary. The specificity of the physical description seems to be significant for most representatives of this view; with all due allowance for poetic exaggeration, the sinewy muscle and bronze-like bones of Behemoth and his watery habitation, together with the teeth and scales of Leviathan, make an identification with a hippo and crocodile natural for many interpreters.[41] The fact that Behemoth is introduced twice with 'Behold!' (40:15–16), as if Job can see the creature right in front of him, is also taken by some to suggest a purely naturalistic interpretation.[42] One also sometimes reads that nothing is said about any conflict between God and these two creatures; Fox writes that '[a]ll Behemoth does here is stand in the river and graze imperturbably'.[43] Similarly, Clines claims it is 'mere speculation' to find evidence of conflict with the mention of Behemoth's maker's sword (40:19).[44] This way of reading YHWH's second speech also usually involves criticisms of the mythological or supernatural view, pointing to difficulties making an exact identification between Behemoth and different chaos monsters known in ANE myth, more general problems in relating the book of Job to its cultural and religious environment, and so on.

Behemoth and Leviathan as hippo and crocodile is an interpretation with a long pedigree and enjoys the favour of some very wise readers of the book of Job. It is, however, almost certainly wrong, for a variety of reasons. First, it is difficult to understand how a description of a hippo and crocodile pertains to the issue of divine justice – the explicit subject of YHWH's second speech (40:8). God's power and wisdom certainly would be displayed by such genuinely impressive animals, if that is what Behemoth and Leviathan are – but divine justice is being addressed in chapters 40–41, not power and wisdom alone. What does a hippopotamus have to do with whether God is just in how he governs creation, sometimes allowing terrible evil to befall his favourite saints?

This interpretation also cannot explain why Job registers such different reactions to YHWH's first and second speech. Why would the sight of a hippo cause Job to repent in dust and ashes (42:6)? Or to claim a whole new vision of God (v. 5)? Job never stopped believing that God was the

---

[41] See e.g. the summary of arguments given by López (2016: 406), who does not himself hold this view.

[42] E.g. Gammie 1978: 219.

[43] Fox 2012: 262. See also Brown 2014: 116.

[44] Clines 2011: 1188.

Creator (see 10:8), and never denied divine power and wisdom (12:13). The only attribute surrendered by Job in the debate was divine goodness, which rendered this still-sovereign, still-wise God monstrous and terrifying to Job. So what is it that sparks Job's profound reconciliation to God in 42:1–6? A hippo and crocodile cannot explain this.

The naturalistic interpretation attracts other problems. For example, the physical descriptions of Behemoth and Leviathan do not neatly fit with any known animal species. This is admittedly easier to see with regard to Leviathan than Behemoth; the only part of Behemoth's description that does not suggest a hippo is the ambiguous reference to the tail like a cedar in 40:17.[45] But it is more difficult to understand why a crocodile would be described in so exaggerated a way that it is said to breathe fire (41:18–21) and swim in the sea (v. 31). A lion would have been just as dangerous to Job as a crocodile, but the former is not exaggerated (38:39–40). So why is Leviathan exaggerated? Indeed, even using the name Leviathan suggests a more-than-natural monster (Job 3:8); and it will be recalled that Behemoth simply means Beast, apparently not intending to refer to any specific species.

In fact, if we have only two normal animals in view in chapters 40–41, it is difficult to understand why the second speech exists at all. A whole catalogue of animals was already given in chapter 39. What do a hippo and crocodile add? Why give them a separate speech? Rowley, who holds to a naturalistic view of Behemoth and Leviathan, goes so far as to acknowledge that his reading cannot explain the presence of chapters 40–41 or what they have to do with God's justice.[46] It is also difficult to understand why YHWH would need to describe the preparation of the divine warrior in 40:9–14 – elsewhere always a prelude to the defeat of cosmic chaos – before describing the physical attributes and habitats of two ordinary animals. Clines, who likewise holds to the naturalistic interpretation, even denies any connection between the description of Behemoth in 40:15–24 and its introduction in 40:9–14; according to Clines, the two parts of the chapter have nothing to do with each other.[47] To my mind, this denial is a significant weakness in his interpretation.

---

[45] Fox 2012: 262, n. 4, points out that the verse does not say Behemoth's tail is as long as a cedar; only that it does something like a cedar – however we are to understand the unusual use of the verb ḥpṣ (usually 'to delight') here. But whatever we make of it, it does not sound like a hippo.

[46] Rowley 1983: 259.

[47] Clines 2011: 1183.

Related to this is the question of why God speaks of bringing a sword near to Behemoth (40:19) or refers to a battle with Leviathan (41:8). No such warfare is even hinted at with regard to the animals in the first speech. It is also simply untrue to say that no conflict is implied between God and Behemoth and Leviathan. Even if the battle is not as explicitly developed as in other similar texts (for reasons discussed further below), this is exactly the implication of the reference to the sword for Behemoth and the battle with Leviathan. It must also be admitted that the force of the rhetorical questions in the Leviathan speech (41:1–11) collapses if Leviathan is only a crocodile, for although Job probably never engaged in such an activity, crocodiles were hunted and killed in ancient Egypt.[48] All the repeated questions about Leviathan's untamable fierceness become meaningless as soon as one remembers that human beings have been capturing and controlling crocodiles for a long time.

But perhaps the most problematic aspect of this very common interpretation is the sinister implications it has for our understanding of God. It was stated above that the way in which a hippo and crocodile count as a defence of God's justice was not clear. Some proponents of this reading of Behemoth and Leviathan, however, do more than claim an ambiguous connection between these creatures and God's justice, arguing instead that the descriptions of the hippo and crocodile count as a positive denial of divine justice. Clines takes this approach by admitting that, according to his reading, the speech has nothing to say about whether God was just to let Job suffer so terribly; as a result, YHWH 'refuses the categories of the dialogues' and simply dodges Job's questions.[49] Little wonder, then, that Clines sees God in this chapter as 'unlovely and not a little chilling' and 'too interested in crocodiles'.[50] Disturbing as this conclusion is, it is difficult to disagree with if Behemoth and Leviathan are only ordinary animals. Walter Brueggemann similarly writes that, in answering Job, 'Yahweh is lordly, haughty, condescending, dismissive, reprimanding, refusing to entertain Job's profound question' and 'refusing to enter into

---

[48] Pope 1973: 320; Day 1985: 65, 77; Waltke 2007: 943, n. 17. Robert Alter misunderstands this when he writes that 'whether hippopotami could actually be captured is not important, for the poet needs to drive home the point that this awesome beast is both literally and figuratively beyond man's grasp' (2011: 134). It is important, for hippopotami were literally not beyond man's grasp, and so Behemoth must not be a hippopotamus for the claims about the creature's untamable power to be true.

[49] Clines 2011: 1202–1203.

[50] Ibid. 1203.

any discussion about justice'; according to Brueggemann, it is 'evident' that YHWH's speech concerns divine power alone, to the exclusion of divine justice.[51] In other words, God overwhelms Job but does not engage with him; moral considerations simply do not apply to this God.[52] Crenshaw agrees that YHWH's second speech to Job is a bare assertion of power and refuses to address the issue of justice: '[s]o much for dreams about a moral universe. No such place exists.'[53] According to this way of reading the book, far from qualifying as a theodicy, the book of Job is an 'anti-theodicy' in the sense of demonstrating God's injustice. Troubling as such conclusions about God are, however, I do not know how to argue against them if Behemoth and Leviathan are two ordinary animals.

The mere fact that God speaks comforts Job

If there are fatal problems with the view that Behemoth and Leviathan are ordinary animals, some commentators do not even go so far as to identify these creatures. The mere fact that God speaks at all is sometimes taken as all the comfort and resolution Job needs, irrespective of the meaning of God's speeches: 'The content of this answer is not important. The only essential thing is that he [God] encountered Job in a theophany and turned towards him as one who also hears the individual person and responds to him.'[54] G. K. Chesterton states the same idea in his own inimitable way when he writes that Job

---

[51] 1997: 390. Brueggemann does not explicitly endorse the naturalistic view, but speaks of the subject of YHWH's speeches as being the 'creative power' of God, which seems to be close.

[52] Ibid. 390–391.

[53] Crenshaw 2011: 153. Crenshaw's agreement with Clines and Brueggemann is, in one sense, unexpected, because he elsewhere argues for a supernatural interpretation of Behemoth and Leviathan, understanding them to be 'mythical creatures' embodying 'evil itself' (2005: 187). For reasons opaque to me, however, Crenshaw nowhere connects these symbols of evil with God's justice (40:8) in their defeat (40:19; 41:8). Other aspects of his interpretation of these chapters are difficult for me to understand. For instance, he somehow reads God's challenge to Job in 40:14 as an admission that the task of subduing the wicked is beyond God's power; according to Crenshaw, this is a defensive put-down on God's part, as if God were saying, 'You couldn't do any better!' because God knows he has failed (2011: 154). Similarly, God's supposed lack of concern for justice in his final speech leads Crenshaw to say that any hope of divine reward is 'a huge lie' in the book, only to admit how strange it is that Job is readmitted to a life of incredible blessing in ch. 42 (2011: 154). It does not seem to occur to Crenshaw that Job's restoration in ch. 42 shows that hope of divine reward is not a lie. Fortunately, there are more consistent and satisfying ways to read the final chapters of the book.

[54] Ruprecht 1971: 231; see also Gowan 1986: 89; Murphy 1996: 44. Polzin takes the same line: 'God's power-play tells Job nothing that he does not already know. It is the impact of his appearance before Job that produces the change rather than anything God says' (1977: 105).

has been told nothing, but he felt the terrible and tingling atmosphere of something which is too good to be told. The refusal of God to explain his design is itself a burning hint of His design. The riddles of God are more satisfying than the solutions of man.[55]

Burrell gives a more philosophically sophisticated account of this way of understanding YHWH's second speech by arguing that the completely unique relation between God and humans, in which the eternally self-existent God extends himself to a created dependent being, is an 'incommensurate good'; as a result, when God activates the relationship by speaking, Job receives this incomparable good, which resolves his suffering.[56] In other words, the comfort that resolves Job's agony is not an explanation of his suffering but being established in a relationship with God when God speaks to him.

In response, it is doubtless true that the mere fact of God's speaking directly to Job was a comfort (Job complains specifically about God's absence and silence in 23:3, 8–9). But this way of reading the ending of Job implies that God could have spoken about absolutely anything and Job would have experienced the same comfort, which is difficult to believe. This interpretation also does not explain God's stated concern for justice in 40:8 or what provokes so great a change in Job after hearing YHWH's second speech – for if the mere fact of divine speech was all that mattered, the first speech would have reconciled Job to God entirely.

Behemoth and Leviathan show that suffering is a mystery

A variation of the interpretation which focuses solely on the fact that God speaks is sometimes offered in which it is allowed that God does communicate something to Job, but it amounts only to the fact that suffering is a mystery that cannot be explained – that is all Job is told. According to this interpretation, Behemoth and Leviathan hint at some greater order in divine providence outside all human understanding, a great mystery

---

[55] Quoted in Glatzner 1969: 234.

[56] Burrell 2008: 108. Burrell even argues that any explanation of suffering in YHWH's speech would disrupt the incommensurate good of Job's relationship with God, because such an explanation would assume that God and Job 'operate . . . on the same level' and would thus damage God's transcendence, in effect destroying the incommensurate good of a relation with a transcendent deity (ibid. 120; see also 109, 118). However, this underestimates how God can speak to Job in an intelligible way without reducing himself or endangering his transcendence.

faith accepts but cannot comprehend. Good writes in this vein that, after reading about Behemoth and Leviathan, we should conclude that '[w]hat from our perspective looks stupendously ugly and evil has a more fundamental beauty from the spacious standpoint of the divine'.[57] Frederick Buechner expresses the same very beautifully when he writes:

> He [Job] had seen the great glory so shot through with sheer, fierce light and gladness, had heard the great voice raised in song so full of terror and wildness and beauty, that from that moment on, nothing else mattered. All possible questions melted like mist, and all possible explanations withered like grass, and all the bad times of his life together with all the good times were so caught up into the fathomless life of this God, who had bent down to speak with him though by comparison he was no more than a fleck of dust on the head of a pin in the lapel of a dancing flea, that all he could say was, 'I had heard of thee by the hearing, but now my eyes see thee: therefore I despise myself and repent in dust and ashes.'[58]

It should be admitted that this interpretation may possibly explain Job's different reactions to yʜwʜ's first and second speech, and may account for what new insight Job gains into God's being and character. It may also account for yʜwʜ's stated concern for justice (40:8) – the point being in this case that divine justice transcends human ideas in such a way that it cannot be explained to Job. Upon further reflection, however, this is unconvincing for several reasons. First, nowhere in the book of Job is it stated or implied that two standards of justice exist, one human and one divine, the latter being incommensurate with the former in a way that is inarticulable or unutterable. On the contrary, justice is always spoken about as if it is basically an open and comprehensible matter and agreed upon by all parties, divine and human; the only problem is the execution of justice, not its definition (see e.g. Job 8:3; 19:7; 23:4; 27:2; 29:14; 31:13). This is borne out in the rest of the Old Testament as well, and perhaps nowhere more clearly than in Psalms 111 – 112. When read back to back, it becomes inescapably clear that human righteousness directly mirrors

---

[57] Good 1990: 365; see the same in Delitzsch 1949: 380; Dhorme 1984: 645–646; Rowley 1983: 325–326; Balentine 2006: 669.
[58] Quoted in Bartholomew 2014: 46.

and mimics divine righteousness (e.g. both God and the pious Israelite are gracious and compassionate [Pss 111:4; 112:4]). This is not to deny God has transcendent and mysterious purposes in how creation is governed, and especially in his sovereign control over evil and suffering. It is only to argue that there is no evidence in the Old Testament for two different standards of justice (one wholly mysterious), as if what is unfair or wrong from the perspective of a human framework is right and just from a transcendent perspective. This makes it more difficult to believe that, from within an Old Testament framework, Behemoth and Leviathan represent some mysterious higher perspective of which Job receives a hint but which he cannot fully see. In slightly different terms, one wonders if an appeal to a transcendent and mysterious standard of divine justice would have comforted Job very much. The problem (from Job's perspective) is very simple: he had done nothing to deserve the judgment due an unrepentant, rebellious sinner, but still suffered judgment. What possible higher perspective would make such a basic category mistake right and just? It is almost like claiming that, from some transcendent perspective, 2 + 2 may equal 5. How is that a meaningful or comforting thing to say? Furthermore, the preparation of the divine warrior in Job 40:9–14 does not suggest that God's justice is beyond human comprehension, but rather that God is about the business of executing his justice in the human realm.

A variation of the suffering-as-mystery interpretation (sometimes given in conjunction with one of the other readings discussed here, such as the naturalistic reading of Behemoth and Leviathan as ordinary animals) is that God's second speech deconstructs wisdom's supposed anthropocentric focus. James Crenshaw thus writes that part of what Job is supposed to learn from YHWH's second speech is that Job is not the centre of the universe.[59] Robert Gordis seconds this when he claims that Job must learn that God and his universe 'cannot be judged by man in anthropocentric terms'.[60] According to Andrew Naselli, Job's understanding of God has been 'too soft, too tame, too domesticated'; Job has been putting himself at the centre of things and must have his vision of reality expanded.[61] Similarly, Norman Whybray sees the resolution to Job's problem in the insight that human beings are not central in

59 Crenshaw 1998: 99.
60 Gordis 1978: 558.
61 Naselli 2012: 84.

God's design and that human 'obsession' with 'rights' is not important to God.[62]

It is not difficult to find claims about Old Testament wisdom's anthropocentric focus in secondary literature on Job.[63] What is difficult, however, is to find specific biblical texts cited in these claims that give evidence of this focus. It seems to have become a staple in scholarship on the wisdom genre, such that it no longer needs to be argued for. It is difficult for me, however, to think of any passages from Proverbs, Job or Ecclesiastes that put human beings at the centre of creation in a way that is culpable or needs correction. Nor has Job's protest fallen into this trap. Job wants to know why he has been treated as something he manifestly is not – a hardened rebel – by an omniscient deity (cf. 10:4–7). Whatever needs to be challenged or corrected in Job's speeches, his question does not amount to elevating himself or assuming he is the most important factor in God's world in a way that needs to be humbled or decentred. Furthermore, although this reading may possibly explain the new insight Job gains into God's character that provokes his worship, if any decentring has occurred in yhwh's speeches, surely it was already accomplished in the first speech? It is difficult to explain the existence of the second speech according to this reading.

Behemoth and Leviathan as ciphers for Job

A third way of interpreting yhwh's second speech to Job is to understand Behemoth and Leviathan as figures or ciphers for Job. According to this line of argument, God describes these creatures in order to help Job understand himself and his suffering differently. John Gammie has given an influential statement of this interpretation.[64] His argument begins by rightly pointing to other animals in the book that are presented for

---

[62] Whybray 1998: 170.

[63] See Naselli 2012: 84, nn. 63–65, for more references.

[64] Gammie 1978: 217–231. See also the same argument in briefer form in Habel 1985: 561; Janzen 1986: 241, 245; McKenna 1992: 399–401; Walton 2012: 408–410 (although Walton distinguishes himself somewhat by arguing that Leviathan stands as a figure for God, a proposal considered further below). David Wolfers gives an allegorical twist to this reading in understanding Behemoth to represent what is beastly in humankind (he compares Job 40:15 with the beasts of burden in Isa. 30:6, implausibly understanding them to stand for the Judeans) and Leviathan to represent Assyria (comparing the hook and bridle in Job 41:1–2 with Isa. 37:29). Job, however, represents the faithful remnant in exile (Wolfers 1990: 474–499; 1995: 166, 179, 190). Wolfers' approach is unconvincing because it involves an overly subtle reading of allusions in OT poetry and because Judah's suffering under the Assyrians is hardly an example of unjust or inexplicable suffering.

didactic purposes (such as the beasts in 12:7), which are always, outside chapters 40–41, ordinary zoological specimens.[65] Behemoth fits into this category because (it is argued) the use of 'behold' indicates he is a creature that can be seen; he is made along with Job (40:15), which Gammie takes to mean the creature is mortal; the creature also eats grass like cattle (v. 15), suggesting to Gammie an ordinary animal.[66]

As a result, Job should see himself as a 'Behemoth' in a variety of ways meant to be consoling. When Behemoth's nose is pierced in 40:24, for instance, since *'āp* can mean 'nose' or 'anger', Job should infer his anger against God needs to be humbled.[67] Similarly, just as Behemoth is calm and trusting when attacked (v. 23), so Job needs to continue to trust even when oppressed; just as Behemoth dwells in dark places (40:21), so Job can take comfort when in spiritual darkness (30:26).[68] Finally, reading a sexual overtone in 40:17, Gammie thinks that Job should infer from Behemoth's sexual prowess that his own life can begin again with another family.[69] With regard to Leviathan, Gammie discerns an implied comparison between Leviathan and Job because both are 'on the dust' (41:33; recall Job's position on the ash heap in 2:8) and both are presented as royal figures (41:34; Job sat 'as a king among his troops' in 29:25). Gammie finds the point of the comparison with Leviathan in the focus on the tongue of Leviathan (41:1–3) and what comes out of the creature's mouth (41:18–21), according to which Leviathan becomes a figure for the protesting Job, and even an affirmation of him. Gammie finds it significant that Leviathan creates light from his mouth (v. 18), taking this to imply that Job brought forth wisdom in the debate with his friends and emerged as a victorious king among them.[70] Gammie concludes by claiming that God approves of Job's protest against his injustice and that God has provided him with defences when under attack from God.[71]

Samuel Balentine makes a similar argument in two essays and his commentary on Job. He finds evidence for a comparison between Job,

---

[65] Gammie 1978: 220.

[66] Although the point will be developed further below, none of these considerations speak decisively against a mythological understanding of Behemoth, for other chaos monsters in ANE texts have specific physical features, can be killed, and sometimes even have specific eating habits.

[67] Ibid. 220.

[68] Ibid. 221–222.

[69] Ibid. 222.

[70] Ibid. 225.

[71] Ibid. 226.

Behemoth and Leviathan in the specific wording of 40:15 ('which I made as I made you') and the royal nature of both Leviathan in Job 41 and humanity elsewhere in the Old Testament, especially Genesis 1 and Psalm 8 (even though the language is not identical, Balentine finds the glory and splendour with which humanity is crowned in Ps. 8:5 similar to the luminous aura with which Leviathan is described in Job 41).[72] Balentine also finds it significant that (in his words) 'Behemoth and Leviathan are figures of strength, pride, and dominion' that are 'celebrated – *not condemned* – as creatures that are the near equals of God'.[73] As a result, the description of Leviathan is a coded way of calling Job to a 'royal responsibility' that is the height of human calling to live out the image of God. In other words, Job should leave behind his protests against divine injustice and get on with living out God's original intentions for humanity for dominion in a sometimes chaotic world.[74] According to Balentine, Job should speak like a god, just as Leviathan does (41:18–21), and be a king over his domain, just like Leviathan (41:34);[75] the message here is that God has 'divinely endowed' Job and humanity in general 'with power and responsibility for their domains'.[76] Specifically with regard to the issue of justice, Balentine thinks that 'Job is to gird up his loins with the strength, pride, and fearless dominion of a Behemoth and Leviathan'[77] and fiercely contend for justice – sometimes even against God when God is unjust.[78] In other words:

> the lesson for Job seems to be that those who dare to stand before their maker with exceptional strength, proud prerogatives, and fierce trust come as near to realizing God's primordial design for life in this world as it is humanly possible to do.[79]

Unfortunately, this interpretation of YHWH's second speech cannot explain why Job reacts so differently in comparison with the first, because

---

[72] Balentine 2006: 84, 682.
[73] Balentine 2002: 509; italics original.
[74] Balentine 1998: 268.
[75] Balentine 2006: 689, 691.
[76] Balentine 2002: 512–513.
[77] Ibid. 509.
[78] Ibid. 513.
[79] Balentine 2006: 686. McCann connects Job 40 – 41 with Gen. 1 in order to make a similar argument (1997: 23–24).

Job claims a deeper knowledge of God on the basis of the second divine speech (42:5), not any new insight into himself. Balentine writes that 'Job's new vision is informed by a new understanding of what it means to be fully and dangerously human', but this is contradicted by the wording of 42:5.[80] There is something Job sees about YHWH on the basis of what YHWH has said about Leviathan. He does not claim new insight into humanity's original creation mandate (or claim that he has been reminded of what he forgot), but claims to understand something new about God beyond what was said in the first speech. This interpretation also cannot explain why God would reprimand Job for discrediting his justice (40:8) when, according to the above argument, God was unjust and Job was right to criticize.

There are other difficulties with reading Behemoth and Leviathan as a cipher for Job. For example, the point to the mixed questions and imperatives in 40:9–14 and 41:1–11 is that Job cannot hope to subdue human wickedness or Leviathan; this makes the comparison between Leviathan's unapproachable fierceness and Job's supposed creational mandate to subdue creation strained. Furthermore, it is surely cruel to say to someone who has suffered in unimaginable ways, who has lost everything and stands at death's door, that he should be fierce and strong and contend for justice. How would this spark awestruck worship on Job's part? The cruelty of saying something like this to Job is sharpened when we remember that Job was already highly sensitive to the demands of justice and right behaviour in all his relationships (ch. 31). Job seems already to have been doing everything he could as God's representative on earth. Can God say nothing more than that Job should do even more? It is also cruel to tell someone who has had to bury his children that (like Behemoth) he can have more. Doing so also completely sidesteps the issue of whether it was just to allow the death of Job's children when they had not sinned in such a way as to deserve it. It will also be argued below that Job withdraws all his former protests against God's supposed injustice in 42:6, which does not sit well with the putative implication that Job should continue to protest against (even divine) injustice.

---

[80] Balentine 2006: 691.

Behemoth and Leviathan as representing the possibility of renewed life for Job

The mention of the possibility of a new family for Job in the third interpretation discussed above leads naturally to that given by J. Gerald Janzen, who understands yнwн's second speech to imply that Job can enjoy renewed life. Citing Elihu's reference to the storm in chapter 37, he interprets the storm within which God speaks as a sign of the possibility of natural renewal, such that all things grow green after so much devastation (citing 37:13).[81] Behemoth and Leviathan, together with the portrayal of the cosmos and its animal inhabitants in chapters 38–39, show a 'vision of creation' so 'awesome' that Job 'is taken out of himself and caught up in wonder of a world teeming, once again, with life', a world 'of powerful, dynamic, teeming vibrancy'. Even if this world is sometimes dangerous, the vision of creation in God's speeches 'bursts human preoccupation with "security first"' and elicits 'an affirmation of life in the face of all its vulnerabilities [which] is the path to true participation in the mystery of existence'.[82] Kathleen O'Connor seconds this by understanding the storm within which yнwн appears to show 'a deity who is wild, beautiful, free, and deeply unsettling'.[83] O'Connor finds no hint of any conflict between God and Behemoth or Leviathan, but only 'pleasure in their beautiful wildness'.[84] As a result, Job is supposed 'to recognize his participation in the beauty and wild freedom of creation and its Creator'.[85] By the same token, modern readers should 'generate harmony and wild freedom in our work and relationships' and work to care for others, as Job did. These chapters 'call us to pulse with life, to be strong, to yell and shout like Job'.[86]

As above, however, this interpretation fails to take account of yнwн's stated concern for his justice (40:8), for if the only point is that Job should re-engage with life, then nothing is said about whether it was right to

---

[81] Janzen 2009: 101.

[82] Ibid. 108–109. It is not clear to me, however, that Job ever was concerned with 'security first'.

[83] O'Connor 2003: 173. O'Connor also agrees with Gammie's interpretation, cited above.

[84] Ibid. 177. O'Connor writes that '[i]f the ancient combat myth ... lurks here, it has been seriously defanged' and that the reference to the sword in 40:19 does not mean God will bring a sword near Behemoth, but only that he can (176).

[85] Ibid. 177.

[86] Ibid. 179.

allow Job to suffer in the first place. It does not explain why Job worships God so deeply after hearing the second speech (42:1–6), or claims new insight into God as a result of it (v. 5).

Behemoth and Leviathan as symbols for God

In a manner similar to the third interpretation explored above, some commentators read Behemoth and Leviathan as ciphers not for Job, but for God; the point of the speech is not to help Job see himself differently, but to gain a deeper insight into his long-lost divine friend. John Walton finds a number of points of contact between Leviathan's untamable fierceness and God's power, laying great emphasis on 41:10, in which God relates his own incorrigible majesty to Leviathan's incomparability.[87] The point of YHWH's second speech, according to Walton, is that because Job cannot 'domesticate' God any more than he could Leviathan, Job should stop protesting against God.[88]

If this is correct, it is the only example in any surviving ancient Semitic text in which the hero/saviour God is compared to those monsters deity usually defeats. This would, in other words, be a surprising comparison. Further, the fact that Leviathan is always elsewhere a chaos monster may also suggest something sinister about God's character. Although Walton does not draw this conclusion, most others who offer this interpretation do so. William Brown, for example, speaks of Behemoth and Leviathan as revealing a 'monstrous' side of God.[89] Carol Newsom lands in the same place,[90] as does James Williams, who interprets God's apparent pride in Behemoth and Leviathan as a sign that they reflect something of the divine nature – God's 'dark, irrational side'.[91] Athalya Brenner attempts to explore some of the metaphysical implications of an identification between Leviathan and God, claiming that such an identification means that God is the ultimate source of both good and evil and is thus both a

---

[87] Walton 2012: 409. Walton refers to v. 10 as an 'outright comparison' between God and Leviathan; but while there is an explicit comparison between the impossibility of standing before Leviathan and the even greater impossibility of opposing God, this need not imply the comprehensive comparison between every aspect of the two that Walton offers.

[88] Ibid. 413; similarly, Lévêque 1994: 217–218. Whether or not Job has been trying (in Walton's words) to 'domesticate' God is questionable; Job's questions about his treatment at God's hands need not necessarily imply any domestication of the Almighty, but only whether the Almighty treats saints and rebels according to just deserts.

[89] Brown 2014: 118.

[90] Newsom 2003: 251.

[91] Williams 1992: 370.

creative and destructive agent (i.e. something close to philosophical dualism).[92] According to Brenner, Job's protest against God in chapter 9 accurately describes who God really is.[93] As a result, human beings must be patient with God, because he has not fully conquered his dark side yet, even though he is aware of the problem.[94] At the same time, Brenner also claims that this God is 'honest, caring, and ethical' and Job can draw near to him in order to be renewed.[95]

More proponents of the view that Leviathan is a reflection of God's dark side could be quoted,[96] but surely readers have already concluded for themselves that this interpretation of the significance of Behemoth and Leviathan completely fails to explain Job's different reaction to YHWH's second speech. Why would a revelation of God's putative chaotic side reduce Job to repentant self-loathing and worship? It also fails to explain how the speeches about Behemoth and Leviathan somehow count as a defence of the divine justice that rules all things but sometimes allows nightmarish pain – a fact that a number of proponents of this view point out,[97] sometimes even claiming that the point of God's second speech is to emphasize to Job divine injustice and the immorality of God's world.[98] This is not a convincing interpretation.

Evidence for Behemoth and Leviathan as symbols of supernatural chaos and evil

These unconvincing attempts to interpret YHWH's second speech do not mean we are stuck with a frustrating anticlimax in the book of Job or a dead-end for YHWH's servant, who trusted him imperfectly but genuinely throughout a horrifying ordeal. A final possible interpretation of Behemoth and Leviathan understands them as symbols for cosmic chaos

---

[92] Brenner 1981: 129–137, esp. 133.

[93] Ibid. 131–132. Brenner makes a number of claims in her article that are difficult for me to understand. The questions of 40:9–14 are somehow taken as an admission of failure on God's part (ibid. 133). She further writes that '[i]f God has conquered them [Behemoth and Leviathan], they have been incorporated in him' (ibid. 133). But surely this inference is unwarranted: How does God's defeat of evil imply it is incorporated into his being?

[94] Ibid. 135.

[95] Ibid. 136.

[96] E.g. Greenstein 1999: 301–312; Patton 2001: 163–165.

[97] Williams says the book's vision of the world 'is practically amoral' (1992: 371); Patton claims the Leviathan speech teaches that chaos 'is a divine attribute, even if it is unjust or illogical' (2001: 165).

[98] Greenstein 1999: 311–312.

and evil.[99] This is an interpretation that is far more exegetically satisfying and better accounts for the resolution of the book of Job. Proponents of this view are in the minority, however, and at a popular level it is not very well known.[100] For these reasons, it will be helpful to survey the evidence for this view and explore its implications for interpreting the book of Job in detail. This will be done in three stages. Evidence of bovine and serpentine chaos monsters in the ANE will be explored first, before moving on to other Old Testament references to Leviathan. It will be argued that, where evidence is available from outside the book of Job (whether from the ANE or other OT books), it consistently supports the conclusion that Behemoth and Leviathan are symbols of supernatural evil. We will then turn to the many exegetical pay-offs a supernatural reading of Behemoth and Leviathan give to an interpretation of the book of Job, in contrast to those interpretations surveyed above. An exploration of what comforts YHWH's second speech would have had for Job will conclude this chapter.

Evidence from the ANE for Behemoth and Leviathan as chaos monsters

One important factor in favour of a supernatural reading of Behemoth and Leviathan is that doing so fits best with other references to creatures of this type from the ANE. An appeal of this kind does not imply that the Old Testament is completely identical to ANE texts, or that the Joban poet is specifically quoting or alluding to or dependent on any of the texts or

---

[99] More specificity is possible within this interpretation; i.e. Behemoth and Leviathan may be taken as purely mythological beings, as real animals representing evil, as figures for Satan, and so on (for more discussion, see López 2016: 401–424). I am not as concerned about this kind of precision with Behemoth and Leviathan, for their descriptions seem intended more to evoke and suggest than classify. At the same time, I do not think Behemoth and Leviathan are real animals that symbolize chaos, because their descriptions do not fit with any known animal species. Real animals can take on symbolic weight in the OT, of course, such as the jackals and ostriches inhabiting the ruins of Edom in Isa. 34:13–14 (symbolizing how this judged nation is given over to uncleanness and death for ever) or the serpent in Gen. 3 (which appears to be a real serpent used as a guise by Satan). However, the way Behemoth and Leviathan are described suggests (to me, at least) that they are not animals one would ever come across, but are purely symbolic of supernatural realities.

[100] It is argued for in Pope 1973: 76–78, 268–270; Keel 1978a: 127–156; Habel 1985: 66; Gibson 1988: 414; Caquot 1992: 69; Carson 1992: 374; Mettinger 1992: 39–49; Fyall 2002: 126–129, 157, 172–174; Sutherland 2004: 91–101; Angel 2014: 71; López 2016: 419–422; Kang 2017: 172–180, 232–234, 237–238; Baldwin 2018: 374. Samuel Terrien takes the same line but draws a different conclusion from the one argued here, emphasizing how these creatures show that evil is mysteriously given some place in God's order without speaking about any conflict with them (2005: 319).

glyphs surveyed here. All that is claimed is that there is significant evidence for supernatural chaos monsters outside the Old Testament that look very much like Behemoth and Leviathan – and, in the case of the latter, even share the same name. This suggests it would have been natural for Job and ancient Israelite readers to draw a similar conclusion about the two creatures described at the end of Job, unless it were signalled clearly otherwise. (As already noted, some think such signals are present in the text; e.g. that there is no conflict or hostility between Yнwн and these creatures, and that they are clearly portrayed as part of creation; objections of this kind will be discussed further below.)

With regard to Behemoth, there are two examples from ancient Semitic culture of a bovine-like monster another god must defeat. In the Epic of Gilgamesh, the titular hero and his friend Enkidu fight the 'Bull of Heaven', sent by Ishtar from her father Anu against Gilgamesh for rejecting her advances. The bull destroys crops and kills people, but Enkidu slays the beast.[101] Even if not identical with the description of Behemoth in Job 40:15-24, it does show that supernatural monsters could take the same general shape as the creature we read about in Job 40.[102] Even more important is Horus' struggle against Set from ancient Egypt, in which the chaotic god Set sometimes took the form of a hippopotamus.[103] This occurs in the text 'The Contending of Horus and Set', which narrates a long struggle between the two deities to see who would rule after Osiris. At one point, Set takes the form of a hippo to sink a boat in which Horus is sailing; at an earlier stage of the story, both take the forms of hippos and fight with each other.[104] The way in which this conflict is both narrated and depicted at the temple of Horus at Edfu is also worth mentioning, because in one panel Set takes the form of a hippo, only to be speared by Horus.[105] At a more general level, Hartley reports that hippo-hunting in

---

[101] See George 1999: 47-54 for a translation.

[102] J. Lévêque, while allowing the mythological status to Behemoth, objects to the comparison with Gilgamesh's Bull of Heaven, because the latter fights with horns, which Behemoth is not said to have (1994: 212). But perfect identity between the two is not being invoked in the present argument, only the presence of generally similar chaos monsters outside the book of Job.

[103] Keel 1978a: 127-131.

[104] See *ANET* 14-17 for a translation.

[105] The conflict between Horus and Set was narrated and drawn on the temple because it was ritually enacted by the priests there (for translation of this liturgy, see Lloyd 2014: 255-289, 308-318). For interested readers, a Google search for 'the temple of Horus at Edfu' will show the picture of Horus spearing Set as a hippo (the faces of these gods were disfigured by later Christians, but the accompanying text still identified which gods are which). The liturgy enacted a complex ritual drama with five acts and lines for various players; Horus and Set as

ancient Egypt was a common royal activity, and a theologically significant one as well, which was thought of as defeating evil and confirming the validity of the pharaoh's reign.[106]

I am not trying to claim too much here. It should be admitted that the evidence for hippo- or bovine-like chaos monsters in the ANE is much sparser than for Leviathan. Further, the hippopotamus as a religious symbol was multivalent in ancient Egypt and sometimes positive (e.g. the fertility goddess Tawaret was sometimes portrayed as a hippo).[107] Similarly, Set was a complex deity who, in some contexts, took on a positive role along with other protector gods.[108] I am also not suggesting any genetic relationship between the portrayal of Set as a hippo and Behemoth in the book of Job, as if the Joban poet were specifically aware of the Egyptian texts cited above and consciously drew on them, or meant to identify Behemoth with Set.[109] Nor is any deep familiarity with the intricacies of Egyptian religion presumed on the part of the Joban poet.[110] All that is claimed is that there is some precedent from the ANE for symbolizing supernatural chaos and evil as an animal that looks similar to the description of Behemoth in Job 40.[111] There are enough other parallels between Old Testament wisdom literature and ancient Egypt for the comparison to be potentially significant as one part of a larger argument.[112]

(note 105 *cont.*) a hippo appear in the fourth act (strikingly, Horus himself later takes the form of a crocodile). In the fifth, Set takes the form of a red donkey when fighting with Horus. For more on this, see Ruprecht 1971: 209–231; Pope 1973: 23, 321; Perdue 1991: 224; Fyall 2002: 131.

[106] Hartley 1988: 524; see also (in much more detail) Ruprecht 1971: 212–217; Kang 2017: 175. Mention may also be made of Atik, the 'divine calf', listed as one of Baal's opponents along with the seven-headed serpent in the Baal Epic (*KTU* 1.3 III 37–41), which is also sometimes enlisted as a comparison with Behemoth (e.g. Day 1985: 80–84). As a calf and hippo are different from each other, this is perhaps not as strong a comparison as the others made above.

[107] Patton 2001: 150–153, quoting Morenz 1992: 106–107, 270–271. Similarly, the Egyptian protector god Sobek was often portrayed as a crocodile (ibid.).

[108] Hart 1988: 194–198.

[109] Although it is unknown when the book of Job was written, the temple of Horus at Edfu was constructed in the Ptolemaic era; certainly after the OT was completed.

[110] This is one reason why Fox, who understands Behemoth to be an ordinary hippo, disagrees with Keel, who takes the supernatural view. Fox quotes Keel as identifying Behemoth with Set and understandably objects against assuming an Israelite poet knew as much as we do now about ancient Egyptian religion, or accepted enough of it to make such an identification (2012: 263). Keel's argument is, however, more modest. He does not claim that Behemoth is the same as Set; only that both stand as a symbol of supernatural evil that humans cannot defeat (1978a: 132). The same argument is made here.

[111] Bernard Batto points out that post-biblical traditions consistently refer to Behemoth and Leviathan as supernatural creatures (1992: 166).

[112] With regard to the book of Proverbs, see the summary of evidence for Egyptian influence on OT wisdom in Waltke 2004: 30–31.

Before moving on to Leviathan, mention should be made of possible echoes Robert Fyall has noted between the description of Behemoth in Job 40 and the language surrounding Baal's opponent Mot, the god of death, in the Canaanite Baal Epic. Although no individual echo between these two figures amounts to as strong a connection as Set's taking the form of a hippo, the echoes do have a cumulative effect that is very suggestive and worth considering. Fyall first points out that when it is said that Behemoth eats grass like an ox (40:15), this is similar to Mot's action of consuming vegetation: under Mot's rule, the vegetation of the earth is scorched as Baal descends into Mot's mouth and throat (*KTU* 1.5 II 2–5).[113] To modern readers, it sounds quite innocuous to read of Behemoth's eating vegetation; but there are enough other echoes between the Baal Epic and the Old Testament to suggest this picture might have conjured more sinister associations for ancient Semites. It is also suggestive that Job 40:16–18 describes Behemoth's strength when Mot is described as strong ('z) and both Baal and Mot gore each other like wild oxen (*KTU* 1.6 VI 17–18).[114] The *bûl* the mountains bring Behemoth in 40:20, translated either as 'produce' or 'tribute' (*HALOT* 115), also echoes the 'tribute' (*ybl*) the chaotic sea god Yam receives (*KTU* 1.2 I 37) and the 'produce' Death scorches (*KTU* 1.5 II 5–6).[115] Furthermore, Behemoth's watery dwelling place (40:21–23) finds a parallel in the watery place where Mot dwells (*KTU* 1.5 VI 5).[116] Fyall concludes by citing a number of Old Testament parallels that complete the 'deathly' connotations of Behemoth's dwelling place: for example, just as Behemoth 'lies' under the lotus (*šākab*, v. 21), so humans often 'lie down' (*šākab*) in death (Job 3:13; 14:12; Isa. 14:8; 43:17; Ezek. 31:18; 32:27–30). Similarly, the 'hidden place of reeds' in verse 21 recalls the 'beast of the reeds' God is called to rebuke in Psalm 68:30.[117]

All of this is to say that what seem to be innocent naturalistic details in the description of Behemoth may have had darker connotations for ancient Israelites. As above, no assumption is made of specific and/or conscious dependence on the part of the Joban poet on the text we now know as the Baal Epic. I am only claiming that there is some compelling

---

[113] Fyall 2002: 133. Fyall also points out how two of Baal's opponents in a fragmentary text are described as *aklm*, 'eaters', the same verb used in Job 40:15 (ibid.; see *KTU* 1.12 I 36).

[114] Fyall 2002: 134.

[115] Ibid. 135.

[116] Ibid. 136.

[117] Ibid. Fyall justifiably concludes from these echoes that the ending of the book of Job presents Death and Hell to the reader (ibid. 137).

evidence from outside the Old Testament to understand Behemoth as a more-than-ordinary creature.

The evidence is much stronger when it comes to Leviathan, since the monster is mentioned (with a different spelling) in the Baal Epic and serpentine sea monsters are common elsewhere in ANE literature. With regard to the Baal Epic, Mot, the god of death, makes reference to a prior victory of Baal over Lotan (claiming it will not help Baal when he fights with Death).[118] Mot describes Lotan, the 'fleeing' and 'twisting' serpent (*brḥ* and *ʿqltn*); the identical description of YHWH's eschatological enemy in Isaiah 27:1 prevents any confusion about the identity of Leviathan in the Old Testament. Further afield, the Mesopotamian gods Ninurta and Tishpak defeat dragons that live in the sea; in the case of Ninurta, his opponent is even said to have seven heads (cf. Ps. 74:14).[119] A seal from Tell Asmar, from the city of Eshnunna, also portrays a deity piercing a seven-headed monster.[120] And of course mention should be made of Marduk's defeat of Tiamat in *Enuma Elish*, the latter sometimes being portrayed as a serpent or dragon.[121]

All of this is to say that there is significant evidence from the ANE that ancient Semites, when hearing about a serpentine, sea-dwelling creature of the name 'Leviathan', would have understood it as a symbol for cosmic chaos. Modern Westerners do not think about evil and chaos this way, of course, but ancient Semites did not turn to abstract or analytical categories when addressing the problem of evil, and YHWH is addressing one such Semite in the book of Job. Although not decisive for how we read the end of the book, ancient Israelites would arguably have understood Behemoth and Leviathan in the same way they are presented elsewhere in the ANE unless it were clearly signalled that these creatures were only ordinary animals.

Biblical evidence for Leviathan as a chaos monster outside the book of Job

It was mentioned above that the extra-biblical evidence for chaos monsters similar to Behemoth is available but sparser than evidence for Leviathan.

---

[118] On the relation of Ugaritic *ltn* and Hebrew *liwyātān*, see Emerton 1982: 327–331.

[119] See further discussion and references in Mabie 2008: 42.

[120] See Keel 1978b: 54, 50–55 for more examples.

[121] See Jacobsen 1968: 104–108 and, more generally (among many possible resources), Keel 1978b: 49–55; Day 1985: 62–86; Uehlinger 1995: 511–515; Mettinger 2005: 92–122.

When we turn to the Bible, something of the same situation obtains in a more extreme form. On the one hand, Behemoth is never mentioned again; the Hebrew word *bĕhēmôt* in the plural always elsewhere refers to ordinary animals (e.g. Job 12:7; Pss 8:8; 50:10; Isa. 30:6; Joel 1:20; 2:22). Moreover, it is difficult to find, in places where the Old Testament describes what supernatural opposition the one trusting in yнwн may face (such as Ps. 91), other creatures that resemble the figure described in Job 40:15–24. The only possible biblical parallel to Behemoth in Job 40 occurs in Psalm 68:30, where God is called on to rebuke the beast of the 'reeds' (*qāneh*, the same word for Behemoth's habitat in Job 40:21). This rebuke recalls the identical action taken by God against the storming waters in Isaiah 17:13 and Nahum 1:4, suggesting a more-than-natural opponent God must repel. At the same time, Psalm 68:30 also makes reference to the peoples who lust after tribute, prompting one to wonder if this beast is a metaphor for Israel's historical enemies. Some commentators think so;[122] others understand a supernatural opponent to be 'embodied in the earthly powers that assert themselves against Israel'.[123] The verse is short enough (and the Hebrew difficult enough) that one cannot be certain. But even if we understand a supernatural opponent to be referenced here, the creature is not described in detail; it is called only a *ḥayyat*, 'living thing' or 'animal'. Its dwelling place is its only connection to Behemoth. As a result, inner-biblical evidence for other supernatural entities similar to Behemoth is very sparse at best.

On the other hand, Leviathan appears by name in several important passages (Job 3:8; Pss 74:14; 104:26; Isa. 27:1). A good case can be made in each passage that Leviathan stands as a symbol for supernatural evil; but, with the exception of Job 3:8, each is disputed, with some commentators interpreting the creature as a symbol for Israel's political enemies or as an ordinary animal. For this reason, it is necessary to consider each passage in order.[124]

Job 3:8 is easily dealt with first. The reader will remember that, as part of his curse on creation, Job referred to those 'ready to rouse up Leviathan' (vv. 8–9). Job must be referring to a supernatural creature here, because rousing an ordinary animal such as a crocodile would not turn the day

---

[122] Hossfeld and Zenger 2005: 167. In Ps. 9:6, God is praised for having rebuked the nations.
[123] Goldingay 2007: 331.
[124] The following argument about Leviathan outside Job 41 is made in more depth in Ortlund 2013: 19–23.

dark, as Job wishes (v. 9); nor am I aware of any commentators who claim otherwise.

The situation is different, however, with regard to Leviathan's presence in Isaiah 27:1. Some venerable commentators on the book of Isaiah take the reference to Leviathan in 27:1 as a coded way of speaking about Israel's historical enemies whom God will one day punish.[125] Certainly, there is enough about the punishment of Assyria and Babylon in the book of Isaiah, and enough emphasis that this judgment is an integral part of Israel's restoration, that this reading is not impossible. Furthermore, the immediately preceding verse speaks of YHWH's coming out of his place to punish the inhabitants of the earth (26:21). In the light of this, one might take 27:1 and 26:21 to describe the same action of judgment against human beings in two different ways.

Despite these considerations, however, the larger shape and momentum of Isaiah 26 – 27 and the role of 27:1 within these chapters speak against interpreting Leviathan in Isaiah 27:1 as a coded way of referring to the nations that had enslaved Israel. Isaiah 27:1 forms the last of three short answers from God to the communal prayer found in 26:7–18, the first two occurring in 26:19 and verse 20. The prayer in 26:7–18 is complex, but it is sufficient for present purposes to note how God has been at work in good ways to restore the effects of past disruptions in covenant life (vv. 13–14). Despite these hopeful signs, however, the prayer ends with the community confessing that they have been unable to bring about salvation on the earth (v. 18). God responds to this prayer first with a promise of the resurrection (26:19) and then with his judgment of the world for its sin (vv. 20–21); the punishment of Leviathan in 27:1 is the final comforting answer for the painful, unfulfilled expectation of the community in chapter 26. The result of God's action in 26:19 – 27:1 is that Israel fills the world with her fruit (27:2–6), reversing the earlier image of God's people as a fruitless vineyard, ripe only for judgment (Isa. 5:1–7).

The location of 27:1 and its contextual significance speaks against interpreting Leviathan as a way of representing Israel's historical enemies. This is the case because Leviathan's punishment answers the community's

---

[125] E.g. Delitzsch 1949: 453; Young 1969: 2.234. The medieval rabbis Kimchi and Ibn Ezra took Leviathan as a symbol for the nations, such as Egypt, Assyria and Rome, that had oppressed Israel (Cohen 1996: 174–176).

inability to bring salvation into being (26:17–18) and makes possible Israel's spiritual fruitfulness on a worldwide scale (27:2–6) – but the destruction of Assyria and Babylon alone would not make such happy results possible. It is more likely that 27:1 describes a greater defeat of a greater enemy in parallel with the defeat of Israel's historical enemies. As a result, 26:21 (punishment of the inhabitants of the earth) and 27:1 (punishment of Leviathan) describe two parallel but unequal acts of judgment: first of earthly, and then of heavenly, powers. Isaiah 24:21 portrays judgment in exactly the same parallel way. As a result, Leviathan in Isaiah 27:1 is best understood as a symbol for supernatural chaos and evil.

A similar sort of question arises in Psalm 74:13–14. This is the case because the reference to yʜwʜ's crushing the heads of Leviathan (v. 14) is preceded by God's dividing the sea in his strength (v. 13), which obviously recalls the exodus. Other aspects of the psalm's language evoke the great victory narrated and hymned in Exodus 14 – 15, such as the references to God's strength (v. 13; cf. Exod. 15:2, 13), yʜwʜ's salvation (v. 12; cf. Exod. 14:13, 30) and the acclamation of yʜwʜ as king (v. 12; cf. Exod. 15:18).[126] Together with Ezekiel 29:3, which compares Pharaoh to a great dragon lying in the Nile, it is possible to argue that Leviathan represents the Egyptians or Pharaoh or both. If the victory God wins against this 'Leviathan' in Psalm 74:12–17 refers exclusively to the exodus, however, it is difficult to understand the references to the creation of the world in verses 16–17.[127] It is better to read the psalmist as simultaneously evoking God's great acts in both creation and the exodus as part of his broader appeal that God renew these victories after the destruction of the temple by the Babylonians (vv. 1–11, 18–23). Modern Western readers would not tend to associate creation and exodus so strongly, but there are a number of other places in the Old Testament where these two divine acts are set parallel with each other while remaining distinct. Bruce Waltke, commenting on the dual motivations for the Sabbath commandment in creation (Exod. 20:8–11) and exodus (Deut. 5:12–15), helpfully clarifies this connection:

---

[126] Goldingay (2007: 431) points out these echoes. Watson (2005: 158, 163–165) argues that all of Ps. 74:12–17 refers to the exodus.

[127] Watson argues that these verses refer not to the primeval act of creation itself, but to divine lordship and the resulting security of the earth in a more general way (2005: 158). This seems unlikely, however, for the verbs used in vv. 16–17 often speak of creation elsewhere (for the hiphil *kûn* in v. 16, see Pss 33:2; 65:10; Prov. 8:27; and for the qal *yāṣar*, see Gen. 2:7, 19; Isa. 43:7; 45:7; etc.).

God's two great works, creation of land out of water . . . and Israel's exodus through the sea . . . are God's two great works of creation and liberation. The Sabbath commemorates both the liberation of the cosmos from lifeless chaos to ordered life and the liberation of Israel from Egyptian bondage to worship *I AM*.[128]

In the light of this, it is difficult to insist that Psalm 74:12–17 speaks only of a defeat of historical Egypt, because this does not fit with the creation language of verses 16–17. On the other hand, a dual reference to both creation and exodus opens up the possibility that a greater-than-historical foe has been defeated in verses 12–15. This also fits better with the rhetorical intention of the psalm than a purely historical interpretation of Leviathan. This is the case because the argument of the poem intends to render as glaringly as possible the incongruity between YHWH's earlier victories in verses 12–17 and his later 'defeat' in the destruction of his temple by the Babylonians in verses 1–11. Invoking enemies of unequal magnitude (the supernatural Leviathan and historical Babylon) suits this purpose better than moving from one national and military opponent (Egypt) to another (Babylon).

The final reference to Leviathan in the Old Testament is found in Psalm 104:26, and this is the one place in the Old Testament where a good case can be made for seeing Leviathan as a completely ordinary animal. The tone and trajectory of Psalm 104 are unmistakably different from the other texts surveyed above, for there is no hint of conflict anywhere in God's world in this psalm until the last verse, which refers only to human wickedness (v. 35). It is striking that when God rebukes the waters to make room for dry land in verses 5–9, the waters do not lift themselves up or roar in response, as in other passages (see Pss 89:10; 93:3; Isa. 17:13). On the contrary, they obey instantly, being completely subservient. Leviathan in Psalm 104 is similar, for we see the creature not breathing fire and churning in the water, as in Job 41, but rather playing![129] This does not sound like the symbol for supernatural evil we have encountered elsewhere in the Old Testament.

---

[128] Waltke 2007: 187. The use of *qnh* in Exod. 15:16, which can mean either 'create' or 'acquire' (in the sense of God's redeeming his people) also speaks to this parallelism.

[129] Or, even more surprisingly, God made Leviathan to play with it; the Hebrew could be taken either way.

The way in which Leviathan is portrayed in Psalm 104:26 is doubtless exceptional. Two considerations suggest, however, that the psalm does not mean to present Leviathan as just one more animal creation, no different from the lions (v. 21) or fish (v. 25) mentioned elsewhere in the poem. First, Leviathan is somewhat set apart from the innumerable other sea creatures in verse 25 by the reference to the ships beginning verse 26 – there is just a bit of syntactical space between them ('living things both small and great. / There go the ships, / and Leviathan, which you formed'). Is this a hint the creature does not quite belong in the same category? Of course, the very next verse speaks of 'all of them' looking to their creator for sustenance (v. 27), which includes both Leviathan in verse 26 and the other sea creatures of verse 25. As a result, not too much can be made of this. At the same time, the text does not quite seem to place Leviathan in the same category as the other sea animals of verse 25.

But, even granting this, it is possible that the poet meant only to present Leviathan as the most impressive example of the animals listed in verse 25, as the very greatest of the creatures 'small and great'. If this were the psalmist's intention, however, this could have been signalled more clearly by writing of the 'great fish' (*dāg gādôl*) that helped Jonah towards his mission field (Jon. 1:17) or even the 'great sea creatures' (*tannînîm*) God makes in Genesis 1:21. The latter would have been especially appropriate to refer to the most impressive example of ordinary animals living in the sea, since the word elsewhere sometimes refers to normal sea creatures (Ps. 148:7), but sometimes to that primeval serpent God himself must defeat (Ps. 74:13; Isa. 27:1; 51:9). Given this range of options, why pick a word that elsewhere refers only to a supernatural creature?[130] The poet's choice of words in this verse perhaps suggests that he understood Leviathan's fearsome reputation and was banking on it as he shows the reader the creature playing in the sea. The point of Psalm 104:26 would thus be to emphasize as strongly as possible the goodness of God's creation: even Leviathan, that writhing monster, to the extent that he is part of God's world, is good. Doubtless it is equally true to say that to the extent this creature rebels against its creator, it is evil and must be defeated – but that is not the point of Psalm 104.

---

[130] Writing with regard to Job 41, Pope states that '[i]f the author . . . wished merely to exercise his poetic abilities on the subject of the power and ferocity of the crocodile, he surpassed his goal at the start with the use of the term Leviathan' (1973: 331). The same is true for Ps. 104:26.

As mentioned above, the portrayal of Leviathan in Psalm 104:26 is exceptional in relation to other references to the monster in the Old Testament. But even here an argument can still be made that Leviathan is not an ordinary animal. If this is correct, then the united witness of the Old Testament outside YHWH's speech in Job 41 presents Leviathan as a creature representing supernatural chaos.

Exegetical benefits of interpreting Behemoth and Leviathan as symbols of chaos

The meaning of Leviathan and Behemoth-like creatures in the ANE and elsewhere in the Old Testament is important for the interpretation of Job 40 – 41, but it is not decisive, for both of these factors are external to the text under consideration. Solely with regard to the book of Job, however, strong reasons suggest that Behemoth and Leviathan should be understood in the same way as in the rest of the Old Testament and the ANE. Most importantly, this interpretation alone can explain the two criteria that other readings cannot: the issue of God's justice (40:8) and Job's differing reactions to the two speeches (40:3–5; 42:1–6). If YHWH moves in his second speech from nature to supernature, this explains why Job responds differently; and if YHWH is understood to speak to Job about a chaos and evil at loose in God's world of which God is aware and which he will one day defeat (40:19; 41:8), this satisfies the stated goal of the speech as a defence of God's justice and explains why Job responds in worship.

This interpretation has other strengths. At a basic level, it explains why the second speech exists at all and how it is different from the first. After all, Job has already retracted his criticism of God's administration of the universe. If God seconds his description of the animals of chapter 39 with two more animals, what else is Job supposed to say? What other response is God hoping for? It also preserves the rhetorical force of the questions and imperatives in 40:9–14 and 41:1–8. Since ancient Egyptians can and did capture and kill hippos and crocodiles, it makes sense for YHWH to ask if Job can pierce Behemoth's nose with a hook (40:24) or draw out Leviathan with a fishhook (41:1) only if Behemoth and Leviathan represent a more-than-natural evil. Finally, this reading explains the preparation of the divine warrior in 40:9–14. Two ordinary animals would not require God to prepare for battle in this way, but the defeat of supernatural evil in his world would.

The hopeful and comforting implications of YHWH's second speech

It was stated above that much is evoked in YHWH's second speech but nothing is explicit. Having considered rival interpretations of the significance of Behemoth and Leviathan and having presented the evidence for understanding them as symbols for supernatural chaos and evil, we can lay out four implications for Job in YHWH's second speech that lead him to the profound worship of 42:1–6.

First, the descriptions of Behemoth and Leviathan reveal to Job a massive, writhing evil at loose in creation – a supernatural force no human can hope to control. As we have seen, Job thought he had experienced the very worst life had to offer, and that his suffering had shown him the truth about God and God's world, which Job's blessed past hid from him. Job was, of course, aware of Leviathan in some distant fashion (3:8; 26:12–13), but misunderstood what relationship this chaos had to his own predicament. Sometimes he urged chaos on to victory (3:8), sometimes he identified himself with the chaotic power (7:12) and sometimes he cast God in that very role (9:5–7).[131] In direct response to this, the long descriptions of Behemoth and Leviathan clarify the real enemy and Job's position in relation to it by giving him a frightening close-up of the monster of which Job is only dimly aware.[132] As the radiant divine warrior speaks line after line to Job about the muscle and strength and fire and scales of these monsters, any suspicion Job might have that God is an agent of chaos is erased, as is any confusion that God is treating Job as if Job were the enemy. Job also loses any desire that Leviathan will finally be set at liberty in the world. It is as if God is saying to Job, 'Job, you think I simply attacked you for no reason – but look with me out at the ocean and you'll see my real opponent, and yours.'

Second, following directly from this, Job would have been able to infer that not all suffering is a direct result of angry punishment from God. Nor is it to be attributed to human sin. Job mistakenly assumed his tragedy was due to direct terrorization from God; the friends, however, were certain it was due to some hidden sin on Job's part. The descriptions of Behemoth and Leviathan helpfully complicate the theology of both,

---

[131] Kang 2017: 232.
[132] Fyall 2002: 163.

implying to Job that suffering can come without God's mysteriously turning into an enemy (13:24), and to the friends that completely innocent people can suffer terribly. Yhwh's second speech thus rebukes the theology of the friends and subtly vindicates Job by severing any necessary link between suffering and sin or suffering and divine anger. When Job earlier asked who else it could be except God who destroyed his life (9:24), his confusion was understandable, but he had completely misread his true situation. Now Job sees that other powers are involved.

Third, yhwh's extended descriptions of the monsters' fearsome and dangerous prowess implies to Job that God understands how greatly Job has suffered. Indeed, to the extent that God is revealing to Job his real enemy, we see that it takes a revelation from God to show the true extent of the evil that God sometimes allows to overtake his saints. This is never stated, however; the comfort of which Job will later speak (42:6) nowhere surfaces in yhwh's speech. But as the descriptions of Behemoth and Leviathan clarify for Job his real enemy, the more fearsome and sinister yhwh makes these creatures appear, and the more God hints to Job that he understands how profoundly Job has suffered under their power. In fact, there is a sense in which only God sees the true dimensions of Job's suffering.

Finally, and most importantly, yhwh promises one day to defeat these evil powers. It was stated above that the obvious answer to the rhetorical questions of chapters 38–39 always points to God only: only he can create, control, guide and provide for the different parts of his world and its creatures. It is important to remember that the point to the rhetorical questions in the first speech is to impress upon Job not merely that God has the potential to do these things, but that God does control, guide and provide, and does so continually. It is equally important to remember that the same intention guides the questions and imperatives of 40:9–14 and 41:1–11 in God's second speech. The point is not just that God could hypothetically adorn himself with radiant majesty (40:10) in order to bring the sword near Behemoth (40:19) and lay hands on Leviathan in battle (41:8), but that he does go to battle against these powers, subduing and defeating monsters Job could not even touch. This is surely what satisfied Job about God's justice (40:8). God's plan for his world is to allow evil – even evil that exists in massive malevolence, which humans can grasp only through symbols. Even as this evil is revealed, however, God assures Job that it is kept within strict boundaries (38:8–11) and he will one day eradicate it (40:19; 41:8), scouring all evil from his creation.

Christopher Ash expresses this superbly:

> Even the mystery of evil is his [God's] mystery. Even Satan, the Leviathan, is God's Satan, God's pet, if we dare to put it like this. This means that as we suffer ... we may with absolute confidence bow down to this sovereign God, knowing that while evil may be terrible, it cannot and will not ever go one tiny fraction beyond the leash on which God has put it. And it will not go on forever.[133]

Some further questions

I hope it is now clear in what ways YHWH's second speech both builds on and far exceeds his first, as well as the ways in which it would have satisfied and comforted Job. But several questions arise naturally from this discussion that must be considered before moving on. First, why does God only imply the monsters' defeat instead of explicitly describing it? Every other text in the Old Testament describing the raging waters or the monsters that live there speaks of the defeat of the enemy and the re-establishment of God's blessed rule over all things. The proportions of Job 40 – 41 contrast sharply with this, containing hints of the battle but focusing instead on the creatures' habitats and prowess. Why is this? Furthermore, why is the Leviathan speech so exceptionally long, especially when descriptions elsewhere in the Old Testament are typically so brief? Finally, since Job already knows about Leviathan (3:8), what is new in YHWH's speech about the creature? What does God say to Job in his second speech that Job does not already know?[134]

---

[133] Ash 2014: 422. In speaking of God's defeat of evil and the comfort this brings to suffering, I am in no way implying that the outcome of the conflict is in any doubt. It may seem strange that this qualification needs to be made, but one sometimes comes across uncertainty on this question (see Brenner [1981: 133] and Crenshaw [2011: 154], who both understand the questions of Job 40:9–14 to be an admission of failure on God's part). Michael Fox comes close to this when he claims God needs help from humans in running the world, calling this belief 'disturbing yet elevating' (2018: 8). Fox does not spell out how it is that God's rule needs humanity except to argue that God allows the test of ch. 1 because he needs honour from human beings (ibid. 18). Fox portrays the God of the book of Job as well-meaning but neither completely sovereign nor omnipotent – but this is contradicted by Job's confession in 42:2–3, where Job worships a God who is unlimited in his power to save.

[134] Although it is somewhat tangential to the book of Job itself, I am also sometimes asked when teaching this part of the book if God's speeches imply that God creates evil. If Behemoth is one of God's creations (40:15) and the creature symbolizes evil, then the question is a natural

With regard to the first question, one should remember that Job has already spoken of the slaying of the twisting serpent in chapter 26, and so merely to repeat this victory at the end of the book would inevitably create an anticlimax. More importantly, however, it is helpful to remember that the restoration soon to meet Job in chapter 42 is still future in chapter 41: as Job listens to YHWH describe Leviathan, he is still on the ash heap, covered in sores, alienated from his wife, still casting sidelong glances at the graves of his children. To speak of Behemoth and Leviathan in a way that breaks with the rest of the Old Testament by highlighting their present (if strictly limited) powers and only hints at their coming defeat is more appropriate to Job's situation. A world in which Leviathan is still at loose is very much the world Job knows.

The focus on the monsters' present powers, with less attention given to their defeat, probably occurs for another reason, one that also helps to explain why the description of the monster is so long (my second question listed above). This has to do with the way in which the Almighty uses the description of Leviathan to imply to Job something about himself (see 41:10–11). The question of tone was raised above in relation to chapter 38, and the same question faces us here, especially when YHWH apparently speaks in praise of his opponent (41:12). Behemoth is praised as well, at least in a sense, for we already read of how that creature is the first of the ways of God (40:19). Whatever this exactly means, the creature ranks very highly with its maker. Detecting tone in YHWH's second speech is as difficult as detecting it in his first, but it seems safe to say that YHWH sounds

---

(note 134 *cont.*) one; but it raises some difficult theological and even philosophical questions about God and evil, a satisfying answer to which would take us far beyond the book of Job. My sense is that evil is not the sort of thing God can create, but only a parasitic twisting and diminishing of what is good; but that is a larger and more difficult question that the book of Job is not intended to answer. Nevertheless, I usually respond to this question in class by emphasizing that the Old Testament teaches that everything God does is utterly morally pure and that his creation was intended to work perfectly without any evil being present in it. The description of Behemoth and Leviathan as created things need not imply that evil comes from God, but clarifies that there is no plurality in the divine nature, no struggle of good gods against evil ones. All evil that exists in God's world is very firmly on one side of the infinite distance between transcendent Creator and his creation. Although elements within God's creation can rebel against him, and although creatures such as Behemoth and Leviathan are appropriate symbols for this evil, they always remain under God's transcendent rule. (In other words, agents can be at work in God's world which are 'supernatural' in relation to human beings, but still very much not on the same level as God.) How it is that these rebellions occur – how it comes about that evil is operative in God's world in the first place – is not explained in the book of Job; the book rather explores what enduring trust in God looks like in the midst of suffering.

anything but morose or worried or defensive when describing Behemoth and Leviathan. Quite the contrary – yhwh's refusal to be silent about Leviathan's 'goodly frame' suggests a happy confidence when surveying the monster in detail with Job. While contempt and insults from one opponent to another might show strength, praise suggests serene confidence. This creates something of an ironic effect, for as the description of Leviathan goes on for so long, and as the creature becomes increasingly terrifying to Job, God stands ever taller in calm mastery of it. The more terrifying Leviathan becomes, the more glorious God is seen to be in his easy mastery of the beast; as Job sees more clearly the scale and fang and fire and claw, the incomparable majesty of God grows all the more irresistible: 'Is Leviathan not fierce when aroused? Who, then, can take his stand against me?' (41:10, my tr.). In other words, the praise of the opponent beginning in verse 12 literarily enacts and activates the contrasting comparison drawn in verses 10–11 between the monster and the God who defeats it. The certainty of God's victory over the powers of chaos is never in doubt in other texts on this theme, of course, and is referenced in the sword of 40:19 and the battle of 41:8. But no other text speaks to yhwh's attitude towards his opponent before that defeat in a way so revealing of God's majestic joy in the battle. It evokes 'the gay, almost mocking courage' with which early Christians were said to have faced martyrdom.[135] This helps to explain both why the defeat of Leviathan is only implied in Job 41 in favour of focusing on the creature's present potency, and why his description continues at such length. The longer the speech continues, the more force the question of 41:10 gains.

God's praise of his opponent does more than just prompt Job to see God differently. God's world would also have looked very different to Job. Yhwh has already spoken of the joy of his creation in his first speech (38:7). As we conclude the second speech, the same effect is produced by God's praise of this terrifying creature. As the Almighty continues at unusual length about the physical characteristics of a creature that could easily kill any human, and does so in an apparently happy and confident way, this produces an indirect comment on the value and beauty of God's world before the redemption of all things, even with supernatural evil at loose in it. God has already spoken of his joy in creation and its animal inhabitants in chapters 38–39. When we listen to God's two speeches as a

---

[135] The phrase is C. S. Lewis's; see Lewis 1972: 206.

whole and take into account his praise of Leviathan together with his joy in his world, surely the world looks different to us as readers? Surely we are prompted to view creation with the same joy God has – a joy not even the chaos monster can diminish? And surely this leads us, without trivializing the suffering that can meet us, any more than God trivializes Leviathan, to engage with life in God's world with a joy and confidence we would never otherwise have – to agree with God's perspective on his world and live as if it were true?

It is important to emphasize that God's praise of Leviathan in no way implies that the evil at loose in his creation is somehow good from a higher perspective. Leviathan is 'nothing but violence and turmoil'[136] and remains utterly terrifying to Job and later readers of the book. When God invites Job to lay his hand on the creature (41:8), both Job and the reader are meant to back away in fear; the very quality of the poetry is meant to convince us of how dangerous and sinister Leviathan is. But it is just exactly the stable meaning of the monster as a monster, when described in a praiseworthy way by its happy creator, that creates the frisson that revisions the world for Job and provokes his about-face.

In fact, it is very striking to survey the consistently joyful tone with which God describes everything in his world in contrast to the human participants in the debate. Job saw the world as one vast inner-city ghetto, filled with the unanswered screams of the innocent (9:22–24; 24:1–17). Eliphaz and his friends describe the world as dirty in God's sight, apparently of value only for providing space for repentance so that the blessings of obedience can be enjoyed (e.g. 15:15–16). For the friends, God's world is like an unpleasant boarding school for rebellious teens; even if one might be thankful for how one grew, one is always glad to graduate. God's perspective on his world is totally different. No other character in the book is so consistently positive about creation, even while being simultaneously utterly realistic about the evil he allows, but only for a time.[137] (This is surely another reason for the unusual length of the descriptions of the monsters: we are being assured that God is entirely familiar with and in

---

136 Clines 2011: 1190.

137 One sees the same in the book's opening chapters, not with regard to God's world, but with regard to Job himself. As already mentioned, God refers to his servant in 1:8 in a way that goes beyond the narrator's already sterling description in 1:1. And even 2:3, difficult as that verse is, can be read as a defence of Job against the Accuser as utterly unworthy of the charges brought against him. God's pleasure and pride in Job in chs. 1–2 are unmistakable and show a consistency to God's character in the book.

control of a massive, supernatural evil of which humans are only distantly aware.[138]) Again, none of this in any way implies that Leviathan is anything but a terrifying monster that must be killed. At the same time, God's joy in his world – even with Leviathan loose! – means that those who trust him can take a similar joy in our sometimes-tragic lives, before the redemption of all things. After all, God's perspective surely trumps all human interpretations of life in the here and now. The one person who most clearly sees everything wrong with his world is the one participant in the debate who describes that world in the happiest terms. God commands the sunrise each day (38:12), knowing and not excusing the horrors humans will visit on one another, or that more sinister evil lurking behind the world's suffering – and he does so joyfully. So we should receive each new sunrise joyfully (cf. 7:3), even when we sense Leviathan is nearby.

This also helps to answer the last question raised above, concerning what is new in God's speech about Leviathan, when Job already knows about the monster (3:8) and its defeat (26:12–13). Perhaps the answer is that Job never imagined the joy with which Yhwh regarded his opponent and God's coming victory. If we might continue to imagine chapter 41 of the book as a conversation between Yhwh and his scarred servant, perhaps we could hear Yhwh saying to Job, who is staring wide-eyed at the huge creature thrashing around in the sea, 'Look at that, Job! Those scales, those huge sharp teeth, the bursting flames from his mouth – what an opponent! I cannot wait for the day when I draw my sword and finally destroy him for ever!' In other words, the question in chapters 40–41 is not only whether Job will trust God's present administration of the cosmos (allowing evil limited but terrible agency), but whether he will also rejoice with God in God's world, before the redemption of all things. This is the new perspective Job receives on the defeat of Leviathan.

This also helps make sense of Behemoth as 'the first of the ways of God' in importance (40:19). If Behemoth ranks first with God, then perhaps God's most important work in all the world is when the Creator brings his sword near the creature to slay it – as implied by the two clauses of verse 19. Far from God being put on the defensive or having to react to some contrary force, Behemoth is the best and most glorious instance of

---

138 Sight in the OT can imply not just perception but comprehension and even mastery (cf. Pss 33:13–15; 92:11; Isa. 18:4–6).

God's ability and joy in defeating evil for those who (like Job) trust him when they suffer. In other words, terrifying evil is 'Exhibit A' for God to show how easily, how joyfully, he defeats everything that opposes him and oppresses his saints.[139]

The limitations of God's second speech to Job

YHWH's second speech and the tone in which he delivers it is gloriously comforting and, at the same time, profoundly changes how we look at a world in which unimaginable evil sometimes occurs. It is important, however, to be clear about what God is not saying in these two chapters. Perhaps most obvious is the difference between God's assurances in Job 40 – 41 and other answers to the problem of evil found elsewhere in Scripture, answers probably more familiar to modern Christians than those found in the book of Job. No assurance is given in Job 40 – 41 that God uses evil to good ends (Gen. 50:20) or that he works all things out for good (Rom. 8:28). Nothing is said about how the joys of the eschaton will completely outweigh and resolve whatever trauma God's saints suffer in the present age (Rom. 8:18; 2 Cor. 4:17–18). No transcendent perspective is invoked that grants resolution to or at least outweighs intractable evil in the here and now. Without in any way denying the beauty and worth of promises of this sort, they form no part of God's speech to his scarred servant here.

Furthermore, God does not unfold his purposes to Job in allowing evil in his world in such a way that Job can verify according to some hypothetical independent standard of judgment that God is right to allow some evil in his present administration of all things and agree with God in that decision. All God does is imply to Job that he is aware of the problem far more deeply than Job is, and will address it one day – that is all. Perhaps in some ways, this is not very much. Certainly, it does not rule out any further protest. After all, Job might have responded to the up-close, guided tour of the monster by saying, 'Worse and worse! Now that I see Leviathan up close, I see that the evil you allow is worse than I ever imagined. How can you tolerate it and still be a good and just ruler?' In

[139] I am thankful to my father, Dr Ray Ortlund, for helping me with this point (private communication, 20 November 2018).

other words, so far from being a complete explanation or defence of God's ways to Job, the vivid description of Leviathan makes it possible for Job (or the reader) to renew and deepen a protest against the God who allows this monster some agency in his world. Were one to do so, of course, one would become vulnerable to all the questions of chapters 38–39; the fact that we were not there when angels sang for joy at the founding of the earth (38:7), that we have no knowledge of the origin of light (38:19), that we cannot create or provide for God's many creatures without giving them what God has already made (38:39 – 39:30), invalidates our sense that we know better than God how his world should be run. If only God can bear the sight of the monster that must be defeated, we can leave the matter to him. But the point here is that God's speech in Job 41 does not fend off all such responses. God does not justify himself to Job by invoking some transcendent perspective or by pointing to some greater good that becomes possible by tolerating Leviathan. God tells Job only that he is aware of the problem far more deeply than any human can be and will fix it one day. Helpful and profound as such an answer is, it does not completely silence any possible objections. This raises the issue of whether (or to what extent) the book of Job is a theodicy in the strict sense of the term. This is a question to which we will return.

The way in which God gives a satisfying answer to Job, but not a complete one, leaves readers at the edge of their seat when finishing Yнwн's second speech. God has answered aspects of Job's complaint, but has certainly not told him everything. Job has just seen a creature far more terrifying than he imagined. How will Job respond?

5

Job's restoration and the question of theodicy (ch. 42)

The final chapter of the book of Job consists of Job's second response to God (vv. 1–6) and his restoration from suffering to blessing (vv. 7–17). It is a short chapter, but contains a number of exegetical problems that have a significant impact on how we read the entire book, as well as the way in which we articulate Job's contribution to theodicy and the problem of evil. In the light of this, we will first work our way through chapter 42 and the questions it raises before turning to focus more broadly on what the book of Job has to say about suffering and evil.

'Now my eye sees you': Job's second response (42:1–6)

Job's final speech falls into two parts, both showing a quotation from God's speeches and Job's response to it (vv. 2–3, 4–6). Against the background of God's happy victory in chapters 40–41, each verse is redolent of a profound joy in God.

Job begins with God's irresistible and incomparable power (v. 2). This is not merely a general statement of omnipotence – something Job never denied during the debate – but should be read in the light of God's coming battle with Leviathan (41:8). If God can defeat even that evil, then truly no purpose of his can be thwarted by anything in creation – and more specifically, no purpose to do good to his saints can be stopped. 'You can do all things' means there is no tragedy God's unstoppable goodness cannot redeem. Formerly, Job was certain God's purposes for him were only sinister (10:13) and that all creation taught divine injustice (12:9; the verb *yd'*, 'to know', repeats in 10:13, 12:9 and 42:2). Now he is convinced of a better truth.

In verse 3, Job quotes YHWH's first question against himself (38:3), admitting he had no idea what he was talking about in his criticisms of God. (Note how YHWH's second speech prompts Job to respond more submissively to the first.) I have argued throughout this book that Job's mistaken conclusions about God are understandable, even though they miss the mark, because Job is never granted the larger perspective on his tragedy that the reader receives in chapters 1–2. Job remains ignorant of that larger perspective. He can, however, infer from YHWH's speeches how wrong he was to rail against God as an enemy when, all this time, God has stood as Job's champion against the chaos and darkness that invaded Job's life. The 'wonders' too great for Job (*niplā'ôt*) frequently elsewhere in the Old Testament speak of YHWH's great acts of salvation for his oppressed and needy people (Exod. 3:20; Josh. 3:5; Pss 72:18; 77:12; 86:10; 98:1; 131:1; 136:4; etc.). Job is mortified that he has been protesting against the only person both able and happy to save him – that he portrayed God as a sinister enemy when he is really Job's deepest friend.

In verses 4–5, Job moves on from God's claim about Job's ignorance to God's challenge for Job to respond. Job meets this challenge in an especially poignant and broken way. He confesses that all of his former knowledge of God – and it was not slight (1:1) – has become like vague hearsay and second-hand information ('the hearing of the ear') compared with what he now knows. But Job can express this new knowledge only with the phrase 'now my eye sees you'. Job is so taken up with God he can speak of nothing else but seeing him. In other words, the only response Job can make to God's rebuttal of his criticisms is to say, 'Now I see who you really are.' This obviously includes an admission that he has been wrong and God is right, but also far transcends it. Job is not merely intellectually convinced about some new idea having to do with God; he is entirely taken up with God himself. In fact, he repeats the word 'to hear' (*šm'*) twice at the beginning of verse 5, echoing its use at the start of verse 4, as if to say, 'You wanted me to listen to your speech and make an answer, Lord? All I can answer is: I see you.' Samuel Rutherford once wrote to another pastor from prison, '[A]ll was but children's play between Christ and me, till now. If one would have sworn unto me, I would not have believed what may be found in Christ.'[1] Job has reached the same blessed place.

---

[1] Rutherford 1818: 241.

Job's new vision of God is significant for another reason. The original terms of the ordeal in chapter 1 concerned whether Job loved God with any ulterior motive – for any reason other than God himself. Job is just about to be released from his suffering and return to the blessing of chapter 1, but almost the last thing he says exactly fulfils the conditions set up (without Job's knowledge) in the book's first chapter. To borrow Pauline language, Job is experiencing the all-surpassing worth of knowing YHWH, and is entirely content, even while still on the ash heap. Job never asked for the blessed life of chapter 1 back in any of the debates and does not do so now; he does not even know of the return to blessed normality about to meet him in verse 10. All Job gains from his suffering is God, and more of God; his restoration to blessing remains for ever secondary to this.

Job's final statement in verse 6 deepens the beauty and poignancy of his worship. I would translate it in the following way:

> Therefore I despise myself (*'al-kēn 'em'as*)
> and I am comforted about dust and ashes
>   (*wĕniḥamtî 'al-'āpār wā'ēper*).

I interpret this verse to advance upon Job's first response and withdrawal of his criticism in 40:3–5 in two ways. First, Job, going far beyond his prior admission that God is right, now expresses utter self-loathing over his former criticisms of God. The word he uses (*mā'as*) elsewhere speaks of a disgust close to nausea (Lev. 26:43–44; Judg. 9:38; Ps. 15:4).[2] This is quite a change from the appropriate but guarded statement in 40:3–5. Second, Job expresses his comfort in his suffering. For reasons discussed more fully below, I take 'dust and ashes' as a synecdoche for all of Job's suffering (see Job 30:19). This means that, without anything in his life improving, Job now says he is comforted over the same suffering that drove him to such desperate extremes before.

Taken in this way, verse 6 is a beautiful affirmation of trust and comfort in God while Job is still on the ash heap. This interpretation is not inevitable, however, for the verse's wording generates exegetical questions that are not easy to resolve and that lead to widely varying interpretations. Many verses in the book are similarly difficult to interpret, of course, but

---

[2] Curtis 1979: 503.

the climactic position of Job's final statement gives it a weight out of all proportion to its short length. In fact, some go so far as to read the verse as showing not repentance on Job's part, but further criticism of God, who allows extreme suffering. Doing so creates a significant domino effect that greatly influences how the divine speeches and even the entire book is read in a way that substantiates the 'anti-theodicy' interpretation discussed above. How one resolves the interpretation of Job's final statement in verse 6 depends in particular on three exegetical issues in the verse.

The first has to do with the lack of an explicit object for the first verb ('despise' or 'reject'). Job says only, 'Therefore I despise', leaving us to infer what he despises.[3] (The verb almost always takes a direct object elsewhere, even in Job; but strikingly, the only four exceptions to this in the Old Testament all occur in this book, in the present verse and in 7:16, 34:33 and 36:5.[4])

The second question has to do with the exact nuance of the niphal[5] of the verb *nḥm* with the preposition *'al*. In the niphal, this verb has three meanings: 'to regret/change one's mind', 'to be sorry' or 'to console oneself' (*HALOT* 688). The preposition *'al* is very flexible, with possible meanings including 'on', 'on top of', 'about', 'concerning', 'against', 'in accordance with', 'because', and so on (see further WOC 11.2.13). As a result, a wide variety of translations are hypothetically possible for this verb with this preposition.

The third question in this verse has to do with the exact nuance of the phrase 'dust and ashes', which occurs only two other times in the Old Testament: in Genesis 18:27 and Job 30:19. In the former, Abraham uses it to express humility as a mere mortal in his arbitration with the Almighty over Sodom's fate. The second usage is found in Job's mouth as a synecdoche for his suffering: 'God has cast me into the mire, and I have

---

[3] Some understand the verb according to *m's* II, 'flow, melt', a by-form of *mss*, perhaps in the sense of describing Job's new submission to God (see Clines 2011: 1207). But this would normally involve the niphal of the verb, not the qal (see *HALOT* 606, where qal *mss* is defined as 'to despair' and the niphal means 'to melt'; see also Morrow 1986: 215).

[4] Morrow 1986: 214.

[5] The niphal and piel of this doubly weak verb are indistinguishable in the perfect, being spelled in identical ways (see J-M 72f). There is also an overlap in meaning: although the niphal normally expresses the passive or reflexive of the qal, there are verbs for which the niphal acts as the passive/reflexive of the hiphil (the proper passive of which is normally the hophal) or the piel (circumventing the normal use of the pual as the passive intensive and hithpael as reflexive intensive). J-M 51c lists *nḥm* as one such example. This means that niphal *nḥm*, when it means 'to console oneself', is expressing the reflexive of the piel, 'to console'. As a result, it is allowable to turn to some examples of piel *nḥm* in the following discussion.

become like dust and ashes.' The ash heap Job sits on in 2:8 after being struck with sores should also be remembered when considering this phrase (the same word *'ēper* in 2:8, 'ash', is found also in 42:6).

These exegetical problems mean it is possible to translate this verse in multiple ways that, even if not all equally plausible in context, nevertheless do not violate the Hebrew.[6] Just with regard to the second verb, one could arguably translate as, 'I regret dust and ashes,' 'I am sorry for dust and ashes,' 'I console myself for dust and ashes,' 'I change my mind about dust and ashes,' 'I repent in dust and ashes' or 'I repent because of dust and ashes,' and so on. Furthermore, although most commentators plausibly assume the first verb refers to Job's rejection of his prior arguments against God or his very self, some understand Job to be rejecting God in this verse. Strange as this sounds to many Christian readers of the book, there is no direct object of the verb, and so this reading is not grammatically impossible. If one takes this option, the second clause could be taken as, 'I am sorry for dust and ashes,' understanding 'dust and ashes' to refer to humanity as a whole (in relation to Gen. 18:27). It is thus possible, without doing violence to the Hebrew, to understand Job to use his final speech to reject God and express sorrow for human beings, who have to put up with such an unfair deity: 'Therefore I despise you (God), and I feel sorry for dust and ashes (i.e., humanity in general).'[7] If this is correct, it colours everything that has come before: the wonders of verse 3 become ironic, as if Job is implying God is even more of a bully than Job thought;[8] God's unstoppable purposes (v. 2) are only sinister; the Leviathan speech either shows God's pride in the monster in a morally ugly way or reveals a dark side of God;[9] and the high point of the book becomes Job's protests, which turn out to be the truth about God.

As already stated, this rendering of Job's final statement does not violate the Hebrew of verse 6. What vitiates the cynical interpretation the translation generates is not the grammar or semantics of the verse itself but the context in which it is found. Job's restoration is soon to begin: he

---

[6] For exhaustive discussion of these and other possibilities, see Morrow 1986: 211–225; Krüger 2007: 217–229.

[7] First proposed by Curtis (1979: 497–511) and followed by Good (1990: 77, 375) and Greenstein (2009: 359–360).

[8] Good 1990: 371.

[9] Good dismisses chs. 40–41 as secondary because (according to him) they fail to advance the argument (1990: 497–498); this helps his cynical interpretation of 42:1–6 but is unconvincing on other grounds.

is just about to be vindicated in relation to his tormentors (vv. 7–9) and then restored in his family (vv. 10–17). If we interpret verse 6 as criticism of God, then God responds to continued criticism from Job by restoring him anyway – an act of kindness that contradicts Job's supposed characterization of God as unfair and bullying.[10] (If one argues that Job cloaked his criticism in the ambiguities of the verse such that God misunderstood him, one has the problem of the speaker of the beautiful and subtle poetry of chs. 38–41 missing a double entendre apparent to later critics.) The cynical reading of 42:6 also contradicts Job's custom elsewhere of openly and unambiguously protesting against God: Why would he cloak his putative criticism in ambiguous Hebrew when he was so unambiguous before?[11] And surely a rejection of God here would count as failing the Accuser's test from chapter 1 – a point the Accuser would not fail to bring to the Almighty's attention?

We are on firmer ground if we understand Job to be rejecting or despising his own words against God or his very self or both, in parallel with Job's first response. Furthermore, although the meaning of 'dust and ashes' is not immediately transparent, it is surely no great leap to see a reference in these two words to Job's tragedy from chapters 1–2. This fits perfectly with the phrase's other use in Job 30:19 and the reference to ashes in 2:8 as a kind of externalization of Job's inward grief.[12] The first and third exegetical issue are thus plausibly resolved. But what about the second? What is Job saying about dust and ashes?

Attention to the thirteen other examples of the verb *nhm* in combination with the preposition *'al* is helpful. Two main patterns emerge: niphal *nhm* with *'al* expresses either relenting from or repenting of some decision, or being comforted over some loss. The former occurs when God is asked either to relent from some promised disaster or does relent (see Exod. 32:12, 14; 1 Chr. 21:15; Ps. 90:13; Jer. 18:8, 10; Joel 2:13; Jon. 4:2) or when human beings repent of their sin (Jer. 8:6). The latter is seen when

---

[10] See Fox 2005: 366. Fox also justly comments that if this verse were found in a psalm, no-one would doubt it expressed repentance (2013: 18). Good himself seems to sense these problems as he struggles to explain Job's restoration, since this restoration is evidence of a fair world in which God restores people, but (according to Good) God's speeches reject any idea of a just universe (see Good's comments in 1990: 396–397).

[11] Fox 2013: 20.

[12] 'Dust and ashes' understood in relation to Gen. 18:27, as a way of referring to creaturely mortality, seems less likely, for it is not so much Job's status as a mortal that animates him during the debate as the overwhelming pain he experiences as one under God's hand, for no reason he can see.

David is comforted over Amnon's death (2 Sam. 13:39), Rachel refuses to be comforted over her children (Jer. 31:15), the survivors of exile are comforted over their losses (Ezek. 14:22) or Pharaoh is imagined to be comforted over his lost armies (Ezek. 32:31). There are no examples of the meaning 'to be sorry' (as in Gen. 6:6) occurring with niphal *nḥm* and the preposition *'al*; only the first and third definitions listed above are in evidence elsewhere in the Old Testament. It is also significant that the preposition *'al* is not elsewhere used spatially with niphal *nḥm*. It rather consistently shows the object in relation to which the relenting or comforting occurs.[13] This means that if Job is repenting 'on' dust and ashes (cf. ESV), he is using the phrase in an exceptional way in the Old Testament – which is possible in the subtle poetry of the book, but perhaps should not be our first exegetical choice.

We are left with two possibilities: consistent with the other uses of niphal *nḥm* with *'al*, Job is either relenting in the sense of changing his mind about dust and ashes, or he is being comforted about them. If 'dust and ashes' stand as a synecdoche for Job's suffering (consonant with 30:19), either sense fits so perfectly one suspects both are intended: Job is changing his mind about his suffering and what it means in such a way that he is comforted about it.[14] The scars and losses Job thought testified against him about God's irrational anger (16:8) no longer have that meaning.[15] Although Job still does not know why he suffered, he knows God is not angry with him and there is no sin that can explain his pain. The losses are still every bit as real, but his reconciliation with his divine friend means they do not pain him as they used to. Thus is Job comforted.

It is important to remember where Job is when he says this: still on the ash heap (2:8), the place of uncleanness, still missing his dead children, still alienated from his wife, still covered in loathsome sores, still close to death, all without any idea that all this suffering is about to end. The only hopeful change that has occurred so far is Job's relationship to God – but while Job's external circumstances remain just as miserable, he is comforted over all his losses in his new vision of God. Job's comfort has

---

[13] Krüger 2007: 224.

[14] Krüger points out that every other use of niphal or piel *nḥm* in Job has the sense of 'comfort' (see 2:10; 6:8–10; 7:13–14; 15:11; 16:2; 21:34; 29:25; 42:11) and so argues it should have that sense here (ibid. 223–224). Since Job's comfort over his suffering involves changing his mind about what suffering means, however, a double entendre in this verse should not be ruled out.

[15] Ibid. 227.

nothing to do with explanations or improved circumstances, but only in seeing and knowing God in a deeper way. Without understanding his own predicament any better, Job repents not of any sin, but only of not knowing God well enough.[16]

All in all, it is difficult to find words adequate to express how profound and moving Job's utter disgust with himself and ecstatic worship of God are.[17] At the same time, without lessening the happy resolution Job enjoys here, some questions inevitably surface. Is it necessary to keep Job in the dark about what caused his suffering in the first place? And why is the Accuser apparently absent from the end of the book when he plays so crucial a role in its beginning?

Why does Job never receive an explanation for his suffering?

We noted above how Job's trust and worship in continued suffering are even more moving because he remains completely ignorant of the cause of that suffering, or that it will very soon end. But at this point in the story, Job has proved beyond all doubt he serves and loves God simply for God's own sake, irrespective of any blessing he may gain or loss he may incur

---

[16] Carson 1992: 376.

[17] Given how important v. 6 is for both the resolution of Job's agony and the resolution of the entire book, it is worth asking why he does not express himself more clearly. Why not give a direct object for his rejection or disgust, for example? It could be that this is one more example of the unusually complex poetry of the book. But perhaps a deeper reason is at work. Part of the difficulty of reading Job is the lack of any commentary or evaluation or guidance from God or the narrator at key junctures where significant interpretative decisions must be made. This was noted in relation to YHWH's second speech, where Behemoth and Leviathan are described, but what we should infer from these descriptions is left unstated (explicitly, at least). The figure of Elihu is another example, for not a single word of praise or blame is registered about him in the book (Elihu is left out of the negative evaluation of the friends in 42:7). This lack of guidance has the effect of bringing readers' assumptions and presuppositions to the foreground; without help from the narrator, readers must rely on conclusions formed from the rest of the OT and their theology in general. This is especially noticeable with regard to the character of God: perhaps more than any other OT book, the book of Job brings to the surface what the reader already thinks about YHWH, in such a way that those suspicious of him will be much more so by the end of the book of Job, and those already trusting will find YHWH even more trustworthy by the end (this helps to explain the radically different comments about the character of God made by different interpreters of Job). One cannot help but wonder if this calculated ambiguity is meant to soften some and harden others (cf. Isa. 6:9–10): no readers remain neutral towards God as they work through the book. What Bruce Waltke wrote about OT theology in general seems especially appropriate to the interpretation of Job: '[s]piritual discernment is a prerequisite for doing Old Testament theology because, like a parable, it is a masterpiece of misdirection, yielding its wealth only to those with eyes to see and ears to hear' (2007: 36).

because of it. This was hardly in doubt in chapters 1–2 and is absolutely obvious by the end of the book, since Job finds comfort only in God himself (42:5), without saying anything about any possible return to the blessings of chapters 1–2. Whatever unwise and untrue things Job said about God during the debate, Job never cut off his relationship with God by cursing him; indeed, Job would not have agonized so deeply in those chapters if God had not meant so much to him.[18] Job has learned, of course, that his suffering was not due to some irrational and sinister change in God's character, nor because of any sin in himself. But what harm could there be in revealing to Job why God allowed this tragedy, now that the ordeal has been successfully passed? Two considerations suggest themselves.

First, if the machinations of the Accuser in the divine council were revealed to Job, the book would speak less directly to later readers who suffer without ever knowing why.[19] But, more importantly, there is a sense in which Job must remain for ever ignorant of what is revealed to the reader in chapters 1–2 or the validity of the outcome of the test might be jeopardized. Were Job to learn about the accusation that he really loves only the secondary blessings loyalty to God brings, it would be possible for the Accuser to renew his allegations in a slightly different form, claiming that Job endures suffering and says what he does in chapter 42 only in hope of being blessed as a result. As Christopher Seitz writes, 'if Job had known the gambit, the accuser could still argue that such love was mechanistic, based upon defense of God's honour in hope of ultimate reward'.[20] Job's continued ignorance is the only way to demonstrate beyond all doubt the purity of his motives in remaining faithful to God.

An analogy with human relationships is helpful at this point. If a human friend were to allow the death of one of my children by (say) failing to protect the child in some way, but never gave me an explanation or apologized, I would not stay friends with that person – I would break our relationship. But when God allows that kind of suffering, without explanation or apology, and the sufferer struggles, says foolish things of which

---

[18] Carson 1992: 377.

[19] Fox 2005: 355.

[20] Seitz 1989: 16–17; see also Sutherland 2004: 10. Sutherland also astutely points out how God never raises the subject with Job of loving God only for God's sake – which is exactly what makes Job's unconditional loyalty possible, for were God to raise it with Job, Job's trust and worship might be suspected of having ulterior motives (ibid.).

he or she later repents, but endures in a relationship with God, that sufferer proves the validity of the worship of God as God, and how different his or her relationship with him is from other human relationships that involve some give and take. This means that Job's perpetual ignorance proves he is relating to God *as God*, in a way far transcending every other relationship of Job's, and seals him in that God-honouring relationship. 'Now my eye sees you.'

At the same time, however, the fact that the narrator does reveal the larger circumstances surrounding Job's agony in chapters 1–2 to the reader is no ambiguous hint to us that when God allows inexplicable pain to ruin our lives, there are larger factors involved that we will never fully understand. We are assured, despite all appearances to the contrary, that God remains for ever our friend and defender, but are also warned that, like Job, we will never know why our suffering happened, even though there were reasons behind it. This is the only way the reality of our relationship with God can be proved – our faithful ignorance is the only means to demonstrate that we are relating to God as God and Lord and honouring him as such. As a result, Christopher Ash is surely correct when he writes that '[e]very morning we ought to wake up and say to ourselves, "There is a vicious, dark, spiritual battle being waged over me today,"'[21] one that we will sense dimly but never fully understand. In fact, faithful readers of the book of Job 'ought to expect that the normal Christian life will be full of unresolved waiting and yearning for God', such that we will often be asking, 'What is God doing? Where is he? Oh, that I might meet with him!'[22] This unresolved waiting is not at all a sign of failure in discipleship but 'the integrating arrow of hope that holds together the authentic Christian life'.[23] But just as the readers cannot expect some transcendent perspective that explains their own Joblike experiences of suffering, so the comforts Job receives become ours when we suffer without explanation and endure in our relationship with God anyway. Job is not the only one to receive a new vision of God that reduces all prior knowledge of him to child's play, mere rumours and hearsay. Nor is he the only saint to be utterly and infinitely comforted even while sitting on the ash heap.

---

[21] Ash 2014: 427.
[22] Ibid. 429.
[23] Ibid.

What about the Accuser?

But what about the Accuser? Does the supernatural opponent who caused so much trouble at the book's beginning ever receive his due?

Readers who follow the faith of Job but have the benefit of a completed canon can trace an implied answer to this question of which the book's characters would have been unaware. When John writes of 'the great dragon . . . that ancient serpent, who is called the devil and Satan', who is thrown out of heaven in Revelation 12:9, he helps his readers connect the serpent symbolism of the Old Testament with the Christian's great adversary in the New Testament. As a result, when we read of the coming defeat of the twisting serpent Leviathan in Job 41, we receive an implicit assurance that the accusations which brought such suffering on Job will one day be silenced for ever, for Leviathan's defeat is also Satan's.

This promise may, in fact, be hinted at in the text itself in 41:4:[24]

> I will not keep silence concerning his limbs (*lô' 'aḥărîš badāyw*),
> his mighty strength, or his goodly frame (*ûdĕbar gĕbûrôt
> wĕḥîn 'erkô*).

The initial clause 'I will not keep silence' is unambiguous. Every other word God uses, however, is susceptible to double meanings in such a way that one suspects a double entendre is intentional. To begin with, the use of the word *bad* in the first clause can mean 'parts' or 'limbs' (Job 18:13), but a homonym means 'foolish talk' or 'boasting' (as in Job 11:3; see also Isa. 16:6; Jer. 48:30; *HALOT* 109). It is thus perfectly defensible to translate the first clause as, 'Will I not silence his foolish talk?' The word *dābār* begins the second clause, which means either 'word' or 'thing'; as a result, one might easily translate the phrase as either 'the matter of his strength' or 'his strong word'. Finally, the last word in the verse means something like 'arrangement' (Exod. 40:4) or 'value' (Job 28:13). Since everything that follows 41:12 describes Leviathan's physical characteristics, it is plausible to understand Leviathan's physical 'arrangement' to be in view in this verse and translate as 'goodly frame' (ESV). At the same time, the verb from which the noun is derived is used elsewhere in the book to speak of arranging or preparing an argument (Job 13:18; 23:4;

---

[24] As noticed by Habel 1985: 555; Gibson 1992: 134; Fyall 2002: 161.

33:5).[25] A derived noun is also used one other time to refer to those musings before one speaks (Prov. 16:1). Additionally, the noun *ḥēn* can elsewhere describe speech (Ps. 45:3; Prov. 22:11; Eccl. 10:12). As a result, 'persuasive case' is defensible as a translation. Taken all together, this yields the following alternative translation: 'Will I not silence his boastings, his mighty word, or his persuasive case?'[26] If taken in this way, the verse is saying that whatever accusations the Satan brings against God's saints will be defeated. That the verb *'rk* can also refer to an army arranging itself for battle (Judg. 20:22)[27] helps to seal the overlap between this translation and that found in most modern versions, according to which Leviathan's physical prowess is being described.

Since none of the human characters in the book are aware of the Accuser's role in the story, this wordplay about Leviathan's speech would have remained undetectable to them. But readers with access to the completed biblical story can find in the double meanings of 41:12 yet one more promise when they find themselves in a situation similar to Job's: not only will the evil power at loose in God's world one day be destroyed, but also the accusations he brings against God's saints will be silenced.

Job's restoration (42:7–17)

Since Job has beyond all doubt proved the sincerity of his love for God, there is no reason for the suffering that would demonstrate and seal this sincerity to continue. Although he remains for ever ignorant of the larger theatre on which his story played out, God's normal policy of giving his saints both knowledge of himself and being generous in earthly things can be reinstated, so that Job returns to his blessed life. The book's final passage and denouement unfolds in two movements: having been restored spiritually (42:1–6), Job is restored socially by being vindicated in relation to his friends (vv. 7–9) and then being comforted by his family (vv. 10–17). As with verses 1–6, however, multiple exegetical difficulties meet us that will need some discussion as we read of Job's moving into his happy future.

---

[25] Habel 1985: 555; Gibson 1992: 134.
[26] Newsom 2003: 251.
[27] As pointed out by Habel 1985: 555.

'Job spoke rightly about me':[28] Job's vindication (vv. 7–9)

Job's restoration begins with one of the most shocking statements in the entire book: God's anger burns against Eliphaz, Bildad and Zophar, because they did not speak rightly about God – the way Job did (v. 7)! If the last phrase were not present, of course, the verse would be unremarkable, for the friends obviously completely misunderstood God's role in Job's agony. As the verse is written, however, God apparently prefers Job's speech to that of the friends – Job, who spoke of God as some vicious tyrant who destroys innocent lives for fun (9:22–24). Commentators naturally struggle to explain this shocking verse. A number of possible solutions immediately suggest themselves that, on further reflection, fail to explain the verse as it stands.[29] The central issue is found in the comparison between the friends' speech and Job's, for this suggests God is referring to the debate between them from chapter 3 onwards. For this reason, it will not do to turn to Job's beautiful confessions before the debate in 1:21 and 2:10 to explain this preference, for the friends were not present until 2:11. (Furthermore, Job's statements in 1:21 and 2:10 are already obviously right and already confirmed as such by the narrator in 1:22 and 2:10.) We cannot turn to 42:1–6 to explain God's approval of Job's speech for the same reason, for the friends are not addressed by God in that part of the book (38:2–3; 40:7–8). Job also speaks more about himself than God in his final speech, but God commends Job for his speech about God. Nor is it sufficient to point to the way Job continues to address God directly in the course of chapters 3–31 while the friends speak only about God, for then there would be no need to qualify Job's speech as 'right' or 'correct'; God need only say that Job spoke to him, unlike the friends.

At the same time, however, God's vindication of Job and his speech to the detriment of the friends need not be taken as an undiscriminating and total approval of every last thing Job said during the debate, for it is surely significant that God says this about Job only after Job repents of his criticisms of God's putative injustice.[30] As Rick Moore writes, 'Job says,

---

[28] This is my translation.

[29] Further exploration of these difficulties and a fuller exploration of Job's 'right speech' about God are given in Ortlund 2018: 350–358.

[30] This speaks against the sceptical readings of this verse, which take v. 7 to be an admission on God's part of his injustice in his treatment of Job and a vindication of Job's protest as containing the truth about God (e.g. as done by Greenstein 2009: 360; Clines 2011: 1231).

"I have been wrong," whereupon God says, "You have been right." '[31] Within the framework of this qualification, it is possible to find statements Job makes in the course of the debate that accurately reflect who God is – even if only in a negative form. It was stated above that what drives the vociferousness of Job's protests is just exactly how much he values God and a right relationship with him; if this did not matter so much to Job, it would not cause him such agony when he thought he had lost it for no reason. This love for God shows itself in specific passages in significant ways. For example, Job's curse on creation in chapter 3 implies that without God's smile and friendship, Job does not see any point to his existence, blessed or otherwise – indeed, without God's friendship, Job sees no point for creation itself to exist. And were Job to have lost God's friendship, this is a correct conclusion to draw; Job is wrong only about God's heart towards him, not the value of a relationship with God. The same kind of ironic valuation of God is seen in 9:21. As argued above, Job's confusion about himself ('I do not know myself', my tr.) reflects an accurate and admirable view of how God's moral judgment of a person is the most real thing about that person. Despite the fact that Job knows he has done nothing to deserve the 'punishment' of chapters 1–2, all self-generated certainty melts before the unassailable judgment of God. This is a true thing to say about God; Job has mistaken only what judgment God has made of him. Job also speaks rightly about God in the sense that, from Job's perspective during the debate, the friends are bowing to a bully only in order to get nice treatment from him; Job, by contrast, refuses to bow to a God in whom goodness is separate from power. Job refuses to accept something is right just because God did it – and in so doing, he is saying something true about God, for 'power separated from goodness is . . . just satanic'.[32] It is not for nothing that Job says God abhors special pleading on his behalf (13:7–9).[33]

Of course, these correct statements by Job during the debate are all in addition to his continued assertions of faith (such as in 19:25–27 and

---

[31] Moore 1983: 21.

[32] Stump 2013: 218; see 217–218 more generally.

[33] Kidner 1985: 62. The danger of special pleading on God's behalf is not an abstract issue in the book of Job. After all, the friends, in pressing Job to confess sins he knows he never committed, are unintentionally advancing the Accuser's agenda for Job. This is the case because if Job gives in to the friends and invents some confession of sin in order to escape his suffering, Job compromises integrity with God in order to have a nice life – which would prove the devil's accusation to be true (Carson 1992: 379; Walton 2012: 107).

ch. 26) and his admirable desire to meet with God and speak with him, exposing himself to God's scrutiny (13:20–24), all of which doubtless also falls under God's approval. Despite all this, however, verse 7 remains shocking and is probably intended to be so. But the surprise of this verse is comforting as well. God is being very gracious to Job, giving him as much credit as he can. He also calls Job his 'servant' (v. 7), a privileged role from 1:8 he has not lost.[34] Apparently YHWH would rather have someone struggle and endure in a relationship with him than take refuge in perfect theories that reduce God to more familiar dimensions.

In fact, to speak of YHWH's 'preferring' Job's imperfect but faithful speech is far too weak a term, for God is terribly angry with the friends. This is seen in the sevenfold sacrifice that must be offered for God's anger to be pacified (v. 8). Normally, only one animal is sufficient (Lev. 1:1 – 6:7), but in this case it takes no fewer than fourteen to appease God's wrath against these well-intentioned men (2:11), who tormented Job so egregiously (19:22). But in a sense, not even sacrifice is enough, for verse 8 implies that God's anger against the friends will be expiated only when Job himself intercedes on their behalf. This accomplishes several things at once. First of all, it breaks the theology of the friends. This is seen in the simple fact that God treats the friends here better than they deserve, restoring them to his own favour not on the basis of their prior repentance but because of the intercession of their better.[35] In fact, the exact wording of verse 8 implies a profound rejection of the friends' retribution theology: while most modern translations have God saying he will not treat the friends 'according to their folly', the Hebrew has only 'folly': 'so as not to commit some folly'. Although the reading of modern translations may be correct, God may in fact be saying that treating the friends according to their own theology would be deeply foolish of him! It is also striking that God, despite being angry, takes the initiative in the friends' restoration before it even occurs to them to repent. God wants the friends to be restored along with Job. But they are clearly being demoted and Job

---

[34] Other encounters between God and human beings show a similar graciousness in taking statements or actions by the human partner in the most generous and gracious way possible. E.g. in Gen 32:28, God approves of Jacob's striving because it shows some faith in God as the source of blessing even in the midst of much mistrust and deception; also, in John 4:16–17 the Samaritan woman's denial of a husband is accepted on the technicality she married none of the five lovers she had taken.

[35] Janzen 2009: 107. Waltke points out the ironic fulfilment of Eliphaz's promise in 22:26–27 in this verse (2007: 945).

vindicated in this process. Bruce Waltke rightly points out that '[t]he restoration of the community demands public confession of the public wrong done to one of its members'.[36] Since part of Job's pain was the 'help' offered by his friends, his restoration involves his vindication in relation to them. At the same time, Job's intercession prevents any further anger or criticism from Job against them in the future. After all, lingering resentment on Job's part towards his friends would have spoiled God's renewed goodness to him. In fact, the wording of verse 10 (perfect verb with an infinitive construct) implies that God's restoration of Job and Job's intercession for his friends are concomitant actions; that is, the restoration of verse 10 will not happen until Job intercedes.

Yhwh restores the fortunes of Job (vv. 10–17)

The book of Job is frightening to read and tiring to finish, but Job's ordeal does not last for ever. The book's final passage shows the nightmare at last ending and Job's re-entering that blessing and fullness God intends as the normal course of things for his children. This is consistent with the rest of the Old Testament, which elsewhere teaches our journeys through the 'valley of the shadow of death' are journeys, not our destination. Overwhelming as these experiences sometimes are, they are always temporary. Job's was as well (v. 10). This is significant in ways that go beyond simply giving a literary resolution to the story.

First, we see that the book of Job nuances the law of retribution without rejecting it. Only the friends' shallow and mechanistic articulation of retribution is denied. It still holds true, by the book's end, that obedience is rewarded with blessing and that God's world is ultimately a fair and just place. Indeed, Michael Fox insightfully points out that when the Accuser complains of how God has 'put a hedge around' Job's life so that everything he touches prospers (1:10), Satan assumes that the normal course of events in God's world is for obedience and loyalty to be rewarded; while exceptions or 'local disturbances' are possible, they are only exceptions to God's standard policy.[37] Perhaps we might say the book of Job relativizes the law of retribution around God himself, subordinating it to his own prerogative to administer his creation according to his own will and not according to mechanistic principles, thereby reserving God's right to

---

[36] Waltke 2007: 945.
[37] Fox 2005: 359–360.

interrupt blessing when necessary. This nuancing of retribution is not in disagreement with other parts of the Old Testament. For example, both 1 Kings 21 and 2 Kings 14:24–27 show neither righteous Naboth nor sinful Israel getting what each deserves in an immediate or obvious way. Proverbs similarly understands that the best lives are sometimes the most difficult and repeatedly encourages the son that such difficulty is by no means too high a price to pay in loyalty to God (see e.g. Prov. 15:16–17; 16:8, 19; 17:1; 22:1). In other words, the theology of Job's friends is at variance with the rest of the Old Testament. But this nuancing of the Old Testament's theology of retribution that occurs in Job and elsewhere is not really surprising, for if the law of retribution worked mechanically and quickly, with an always clear connection between good behaviour and reward, a relationship with God himself would become impossible. Love of God for his own sake would be reduced to a kind of transaction, hardly different from pulling the lever on a slot machine.[38] Michael Fox gets to the heart of the issue: '[i]nexplicable suffering has a role in the divine economy, for it makes true piety possible.'[39] The contribution of the book of Job is to explore more fully these tragic interruptions in such a way that faith in the God who allows them is not shattered but deepened.

The book of Job's last passage is significant in a second way that its unadorned and unemphatic expression may hide. These last verses enact and, in a sense, enflesh the victory over chaos and evil hinted at in chapter 41. If the book were to end with Job's beautiful confession in 42:1–6, the book would remain tragic to some extent, for although the most important issue of the rift between Job and God would have been healed, nothing else in Job's life has been restored at this point. By analogy, when Lear holds his beloved Cordelia in his arms as she dies and then dies himself, his kingdom in ruins and his friends scattered, the dramatic impact of the play as a tragedy is sealed, but it remains for ever a tragedy. God has something better for Job. Although Leviathan has not been finally defeated, Job's return to comfort and joy stands as a token and sign of God's promise of that final victory.[40] The book's epilogue shows God making good on his claims in chapters 38–41 in a provisional but real way that shows the normal course of creation is to be safety and blessing.[41]

---

[38] McCann 1997: 21.
[39] Fox 2005: 362–363.
[40] Waltke 2007: 944.
[41] Dumbrell 2000: 96.

Job experiences this safety and blessing at multiple levels, both directly from God (as he confirms in vv. 5–6) and from his family and friends (v. 11). No part of Job's tragedy is left untouched: his family succeeds in the comfort his three friends intended but completely failed to deliver (2:11). The contrast between Job's family and friends in this verse and the earlier debate is sharpened as we notice that no words are recorded spoken to Job, only sympathy and comfort, as well as gifts. These gifts might have been a sign of honour to one formerly shamed (30:1) and might also have been intended to help Job rebuild his ruined estate.[42]

> When a member of the covenant community is in trouble, his family gives him 'practical gifts' to help rebuild him, not head-shaking advice. In this way too they restrain evil, including eliminating the evil of words harshly spoken to one another.[43]

It gets better: God not only gives Job a return to the blessed life of chapter 1, but makes his life better than ever (vv. 12–15). One significant detail in Job's restoration deserves special attention. In Pentateuchal legislation, wives normally received whatever inheritance waited for them in their husbands' families; they were economically 'disinherited' from their family of origin. This naturally made widows terribly vulnerable, prompting exceptions to be made in their favour (e.g. Num. 27:1–11; 36:1–12). Without any outside prompting, however, Job sets aside funds for his three daughters in case they are widowed. This small detail reveals how profoundly Job has been reconciled to God's present administration of creation, in which the normal order of things is safety and blessing, but not every tragedy is prevented ahead of time. Job, knowing his own daughters may suffer widowhood, has turned from protesting against a God who allows such things to doing what he can to care for those who may suffer. And surely the readers are being nudged at this point to ask themselves how they can imitate Job's concern and action for vulnerable people in God's good but still sometimes dangerous world. In other words, the revelation of Leviathan as a force humans can barely comprehend,

---

[42] Hartley 1988: 541.

[43] Waltke 2007: 945. Job's wife is, of course, conspicuous by her absence; although she enjoys the new family of v. 13, nothing is said about whether she receives the comfort of v. 11 along with her husband. Is this silence significant? Having failed the ordeal (2:9), is she unable to participate fully in the comfort of its resolution?

much less contain, leads the readers of Job not to quietism or despair but to renewed action on behalf of those suffering. As Bruce Waltke writes, the book of Job teaches that God's people 'establish God's rule with a chastened humility that only God rules the whole, that they cannot impose God's rule as kings themselves, and with a chastened confession that only God is sovereign'.[44] Only with 'a chastened awareness of [our] own limitations and dependence on the God who allows wickedness'[45] do we 'become wise and persevere in spite of the inexplicable chaotic energy that threatens' human life.[46]

God has even further joys waiting for Job. Given the tragically high infant mortality rates in the ANE and low life expectancy, Job's enjoyment not just of his grandchildren but his great-grandchildren (v. 16) would have been a joy very few in that time and place received. The ending to Job's story is like a fairy tale in its perfection. This ending does not erase Job's former tragedy, of course; Job's first ten children still lie in their graves. But God gives his faithful servant every blessing a saint can receive within this present age.

'And Job died, an old man, and full of days' (v. 17). And so the book that bears his name ends. The straightforward narration belies the great poignancy of this profound saint dying in faith, not having received the things promised, but (as it were) greeting them only from afar (Heb. 11:13). The vivid poetry of Leviathan's prowess and danger lingers in the imagination as the reader transitions to the brief and matter-of-fact narration of Job's end, with the promise of the monster's defeat still in the future.

The book of Job and the question of theodicy

We have finished our journey through the book of Job and I have made reference at many points to what implications the book has for thinking about theodicy and the problem of evil. It is time to draw these references together in order to articulate the book's unique contribution to these questions within the Old Testament. As we will see, the book of Job distinguishes itself from other responses in the Old Testament to evil in

---

44 Ibid. 927.
45 Ibid. 943.
46 Ibid. 927.

several important ways. Perhaps most importantly, the book of Job counts as a theodicy only in a very qualified sense. This is because a justification or explanation of God's tolerance of and providential guidance of evil is found in the book only in a restricted and ironic form – that is to say, only in relation to the reader and not the characters of the book. At the same time, I believe the book of Job nourishes, in a way that is exceptional in the Old Testament, a radically cheerful and joyful faith in a God whose rule allows and sometimes calls for unimaginable suffering. Without at all denigrating the fact that other Old Testament books strengthen faith that is both rugged and realistic, the book of Job has something unique to teach us.

In order to appreciate the paradoxical way in which the book of Job for the most part fails as a theodicy but can produce in readers a 'gay and mocking courage', let me sketch the contours of theodicy in the Old Testament in a more general sense as a larger context within which to appreciate the unique contribution of the book of Job. We begin with a distinction between 'strong' and 'weak' theodicies. Laato and de Moor helpfully distinguish between Old Testament texts that count as 'strong' theodicies in the sense of providing an explicit justification as to why it is right for God to allow or cause suffering, and 'weak' theodicies that, lacking this, nevertheless attempt to make suffering intelligible in the world God rules.[47] With this distinction in mind, Laato and de Moor summarize both 'strong' and 'weak' theodicies found in the Old Testament according to the following categories:[48]

1 A retributive theodicy: God allows or inflicts suffering because he is meting out justice for sin.
2 An educative theodicy: God allows or inflicts suffering so that we grow spiritually and learn how to live more wisely.
3 An eschatological theodicy: whatever God's people suffer in the here and now, the inbreaking of the new age will rebalance all losses and abundantly reward faithfulness.
4 Mystery: God's ways are so much higher than ours, and there is so much we do not know, that God cannot be blamed when tragedy occurs.

---

[47] Laato and de Moor 2003: x.
[48] Ibid. xxx–liv.

5 A theodicy of communion: suffering prompts an intimacy with
   God that could otherwise not occur, especially in the sense
   of experiencing divine pathos in which God partakes in our
   sufferings.
6 Determinism: although not a comfort, some Old Testament
   texts explain suffering as determined and inescapable.

This typology is helpful and examples from the Old Testament of each
of these categories readily come to mind. A retributive theodicy that
justifies suffering as a just and necessary response to sin is clearly at work
when (for instance) David laments the wounds that fester and stink
because of his own foolishness (Ps. 38:5). One also thinks of the exile of
the people of the northern kingdom in 2 Kings 17:7–18 because of their
chronic and ingrained idolatry, committed heedless of every warning and
all God's goodness in the past. Even though the exile leads to the greatest
and most-lamented example of suffering in the Old Testament, it is
entirely justified (cf. Jer. 5:19). An educative theodicy is perhaps easiest to
see in the New Testament (Rom. 5:3; Jas 1:2–3), but is present in the Old
Testament as well, such as when Joseph's sufferings transform him from
the insecure and arrogant young man boasting to his brothers (Gen.
37:1–11) to one happy to reconcile with them and use his God-given
position to their benefit (50:15–21); note as well how Joseph grows from
bearing tales about his brothers (37:2) to remaining silent when falsely
accused (39:11–20). Daniel 7 forms an obvious Old Testament example of
an eschatological theodicy, especially in its vision of the glory of the
coming kingdom (v. 27) after the destruction of the rebellious powers of
this age (v. 26). Some of the Preacher's statements support both the fourth
and sixth categories listed above as he acknowledges both our inability to
understand God's work in the world and our inability to change the way
God has structured the human condition (life 'under the sun') with its
varied joys and pains (see Eccl. 3:14–15; 6:10–12; 7:13–14; 8:17). While not
counting as a theodicy in the strong sense of the word, Ecclesiastes still
makes sense of evil and suffering with reference to human ignorance over
God's unassailable and unchangeable work in all things.

Finally, with regard to a 'communion' theodicy, Laato and de Moor
unsurprisingly cite Job's confession from 42:5: 'Now my eye sees you.'[49]

---

[49] Ibid. xlviii.

Certain psalms of lament are also cited, in which David experiences an intimacy with God in the midst of adversity and anguish (e.g. Pss 3:5–6; 4:7–8); even if these texts do not explicitly explain evil in relation to knowing God more intimately, the association of suffering with trust implies as much. Laato and de Moor give more attention, however, to defining this category of theodicy specifically as an intimacy with God in which he suffers with humanity. Isaiah 63:9 is quoted in this connection ('In all their affliction, he was afflicted') as well as the substitutionary suffering of the Servant in Isaiah 53:4.[50]

More Old Testament examples could be given of Laato and de Moor's typology in ways that suggest it is an accurate and helpful way of summarizing various Old Testament responses to the presence of evil and suffering in the world God rules. But we could perhaps question the extent to which the book of Job sits comfortably within their category of a 'communion' theodicy or any of the others they offer. The formulation Laato and de Moor give to this category of theodicy would seem to exclude the book of Job, for although God's tone towards Job in his speech is sympathetic and gentle, no hint is given in the text that God suffers along with Job. Nor is Job's confession of a new vision of God in 42:5, beautiful and moving as it is, presented in such a way that would count as a justification for or explanation of his prior suffering: Job speaks only of being comforted in God in the midst of his suffering (v. 6), before his miserable circumstances are changed for the better (vv. 7–17). Job does not claim that this new vision was made possible by the agonies of chapters 1–2 in such a way that explains why or justifies God's decision to allow them. No claim is made that this new vision of God is a greater good than the evil Job suffered (a greater good which would not be possible without that suffering) in such a way as to justify or explain that evil. Job speaks only of comfort in God in the midst of suffering. This is not to deny outright that certain greater goods can be gained only by allowing some evil; I think this claim is entirely defensible on biblical and more general philosophical grounds. Nor am I denying absolutely any connection between Job's sufferings and his final vision of God: doubtless it is true both that the new vision Job receives in 42:5 would not have been possible without the nightmare of chapters 1–2 and that this new vision outweighed all the pain of those former chapters. The only point here is that

---

[50] Ibid. xlix–liii.

Job himself does not explicitly make these connections; I am trying to follow as closely as possible what Job does and does not say. A contrast with the Joseph story is instructive at this point. At more than one juncture in the story, Joseph makes insightful connections between his sufferings and the greater good God accomplishes through them, such as when he says that it was not his brothers and slave traders who sent him to Egypt, but God himself, to save many lives – a salvation that would have been impossible without Joseph's suffering a great deal (Gen. 45:7; cf. Gen. 50:20). Job does not draw these connections. With this in mind, it is hard to call the book of Job a theodicy in a straightforward way.

There are other reasons why the book of Job qualifies as a 'communion' theodicy in only a limited way. It was noted above that God does defend his justice and goodness to Job in the face of the chaotic elements he allows to remain present and active in his creation, whether the churning sea of 38:8–11, or the unclean animals of chapter 39, or the more sinister powers represented by Behemoth and Leviathan. The discussion of the last chapter showed, however, that God's argument was a 'minimal' one in the sense that it rebuts Job's claim that his suffering demonstrates God's lack of concern for what is just and counts as evidence against God's goodness. God demonstrates to Job that his decision to allow certain elements of chaos in his world (thus making suffering an ever-present possibility) does not contradict his concern for treating people fairly or his goodness to everything he has made. But nothing in God's speeches suggests that his decision to administer creation in this way is made because it is the only way to achieve certain kinds of good that would otherwise not be possible (e.g. punishing sin, or creating spiritual maturity in his people). This seems especially to be the case in YHWH's second speech. God does not defend Leviathan's dangerous presence in the world God rules with reference to the ways God brings good out of evil that would otherwise be unachievable. Once again, it is true to say, biblically and theologically, that God does bring good out of evil that would otherwise be impossible. But this forms no part of God's speeches to Job. God only assures Job he sees Leviathan far more clearly than Job does – that is, he is far more keenly aware of the evil at loose in his world than Job is – and will one day eradicate all chaos and evil from his world. Divine justice and goodness are defended against Job's protests to the contrary, but God does not invoke some external calculus that would demonstrate the rightness of God's decision to allow

Leviathan some agency in his world, such that Job could independently agree with God that this is, on balance, the right decision. Job is assured only of God's attention to the problem and his coming victory over it. For Job, that is enough.

All this is to say that Job as a character in the book does not receive a theodicy from God in the sense of an explanation or defence. As a result, to the extent that YHWH's speeches to Job speak to later readers, the reader does not receive an explanation in chapters 38–41 either. This is true with regard to both the strong and weak sense of the idea of theodicy; God does not justify his decision to allow evil in his administration of creation or reveal something that renders suffering intelligible to Job or to later readers. However, the book of Job does give the reader greater knowledge of Job's predicament than Job has. We are allowed to see the greater conflict occurring in the divine council that explains God's decision to allow Job's nightmare – and from this perspective the book of Job does count as a theodicy, because it explains why God sometimes allows terrible evil. Once again, Michael Fox's pithy summary, quoted above, of the moral issue of chapters 1–2 is worth remembering: '[i]nexplicable suffering has a role in the divine moral economy, for it makes true piety possible.'[51] We saw above how God sometimes must interrupt his normal policy of generosity in both spiritual and earthly blessings by taking away the latter to prove the sincerity of the relationship. Job did not know about this, but the reader does. In this way, the reader receives an explanation for God's toleration of evil and suffering that Job never did. This is, I believe, the only sense in which the book of Job counts as a theodicy, probably best characterized as a 'communion' theodicy – but not in the sense of an experience of God's pathos in human suffering (an idea never expressed in the book of Job), but only in the more general sense of knowing God more intimately through suffering and because of it. Much later in the biblical story Peter will speak of that inexpressible faith and joy that count as 'obtaining the outcome of your faith, the salvation of your souls' (1 Pet. 1:9). Although the language is different, the same truth applies to readers of Job 1 – 2 and 42:5, for when God takes away any reason to remain in a relationship with him outside God himself, we see him as God in a new way. Our affirmations of faith and love for God for his own sake, no longer hypothetical but gaining a terrible significance in suffering and loss, grant

---

[51] Fox 2005: 363.

us the outcome of our faith as we receive and relate to him in ways otherwise impossible.[52]

Even here, however, the explanation of Joblike suffering for the reader is somewhat ironic, for the readers are granted this explanation only in relation to Job's ordeal, not their own. No readers finish the book of Job expecting to be granted their own version of Job 1 – 2 when that 'dark, vicious spiritual battle'[53] being fought over God's people touches them directly. We can apply the truths learned there to our own situation, of course. We know that we should not automatically attribute suffering to some irrational change in God's character or some hidden sin in ourselves, and we know that sometimes God confirms and seals us in a saving faith by forcing us to hold on to him when we have every earthly reason to give up on him (cf. Job 2:9). But simultaneously it is implied to the reader that we will never receive an explanation from God for our own times of suffering, even though such larger factors are involved. The reader knows more about Job's predicament than Job did and more about the reason behind God's policies in his rule over all things, but the reader joins Job in faithful ignorance otherwise.

The larger perspective given in chapters 1–2 of the book of Job forms the only element in the book that could be described as a theodicy. Otherwise, the book cannot be described that way, especially in relation to YHWH's speeches to Job that so comfort Job at the end. This generates a further irony in that it positions the argument of this present book (in one sense) surprisingly close to the sceptical and cynical interpretations of Job put forward by Newsom, Crenshaw, Clines, Greenstein and others that have been previously discussed.[54] These scholars would not describe Job as a theodicy either, but in the different sense of being an 'anti-theodicy' because the book (according to their reading) positively demonstrates

---

[52] Robert Sutherland argues this point with particular finesse, writing of how 'gratuitous suffering is morally necessary' without God's being morally responsible for it, because it is the only way selfless love to God becomes possible. (Joblike suffering is 'gratuitous' in the sense that it serves no purpose – such as 'punishment or character development' – other than creating love for God. Since such selfless love is the highest good for creatures that outweighs the suffering involved, and since such love can come about in no other way, God is right to allow this suffering and the book of Job counts as a theodicy in this sense (2004: 11, 139). I am less confident than Sutherland that this makes Job a theodicy in a straightforward and unqualified sense, but I appreciate the way he articulates the issues involved in the book.

[53] Ash 2014: 427.

[54] See the sections on the significant rival interpretation of YHWH's first speech in ch. 3 of this book, possible interpretations of Behemoth and Leviathan in ch. 4, and the cynical interpretation of 42:6 discussed earlier in this chapter.

God's amorality and injustice. Enough has already been said about why this reading is unconvincing. But in arguing that the book of Job is a theodicy only in the minimal sense that the readers are granted insight into God's reasons for allowing inexplicable suffering in Job's case and not their own, it is, I hope, clear that I distinguish myself sharply from others who deny the book of Job is a theodicy on very different grounds.

This may seem like an anticlimactic conclusion to draw about a book that is so long and difficult: all that work to get through Job's 42 chapters, only to learn that no 'justification of the ways of God to man' is given? Fortunately, however, this does not at all mean that the book is silent or unhelpful with regard to the issue of inexplicable suffering. Tracing the shape of the answer given to Job in YHWH's speeches, together with Job's second response, all against the background of the Accuser's question in 1:9, sets the context for appreciating the unique contribution of the book of Job and that especially moving way in which the book can cultivate that happy and cheerful courage for God's people living in a world ruled by a supremely good King, but in which Leviathan is still active.

The unique contribution of the book of Job to suffering and the problem of evil

In order to appreciate fully the unique way in which the book of Job speaks to suffering, perhaps the best place to start is by considering how Job complicates our usual explanations of suffering. The typology of different theodicies given by Laato and de Moor was recommended above, but my sense is that most English-speaking evangelicals work with an even simpler set of explanations for suffering: God is either punishing us or making us grow (Laato and de Moor's first two categories). I remember an undergraduate class on Job in which a student put up his hand at one point and said, 'My mother is a Job. The story we are reading about inexplicable suffering is her story.' I asked him how other Christians had responded: 'How often did your mother's friends at church tell her she was doing something wrong and that as soon as she stopped, the pain would stop? Or that God was trying to teach her something? Or make her more like Jesus?' My student confirmed that his mother had been told this repeatedly. I asked if any of these explanations sufficed: Was there some sin she needed to stop? Some lesson she needed to learn? The student thought for a moment and said, 'No. That wasn't it.' The student understood the usual explanations for pain available to him were not helpful, but did not quite know how to articulate an alternative. My sense is that this kind of confusion is widespread.

Our common explanations for suffering are, of course, exactly those of Job's friends. (We resemble Eliphaz, Bildad and Zophar more than we realize.) But the book of Job helps us at just this point, for we have seen how Job is not suffering for any sin on his part, nor because God is trying to make him grow spiritually. As already argued, Job is already a mature saint (1:1), and Job cannot benefit from his ordeal in any way outside deeper intimacy with God without the Accuser's allegation regaining its force. Strange as it may sound, the spiritual benefits listed elsewhere as the happy results of suffering (such as in Rom. 5:3–5) cannot come into play in Job's ordeal, or the Accuser may suggest Job loves God for some reason other than God himself.[55] Even if the benefits are spiritual and not material, the same issue of love for God purely for God's sake remains. And it is significant that Job does not claim any personal benefit from his suffering: he speaks of God and God only when he comes to terms with his losses (42:5–6).

It appears we need a third category of suffering: 'useless' suffering, in which all that is gained from suffering is that God gives himself to us more deeply. The book of Job warns us that God will sometimes appear as if he were an enemy, as if his heart towards us had mysteriously changed. Gerard Manley Hopkins captures this perfectly in his poem 'Thou Art Indeed Just, Lord':

Wert thou my enemy, O thou my friend,
How wouldst thou worse, I wonder, than thou dost
Defeat, thwart me?

---

[55] Once again, anecdotal experience bears this out. I remember hearing in a seminary class of a missionary couple who lost a child while on the field. When asked what he learned from the experience, the husband replied, 'Nothing.' So far as he could tell, he did not grow as a result of that profound loss. Without at all denying that God often does introduce pain into our lives in order to guide it for his own good ends and give us the very precious gifts of endurance, character and hope (Rom. 5:3–5), his ways with his people are subtler than we sometimes realize.

Job earlier asked the very same question (13:24). But the book of Job helps us when we find ourselves suffering and unable to think of any sin that would explain our pain, or wondering what God is trying to teach us and are unable to come up with anything. Rather than torturing ourselves or our friends with these questions, we learn that sometimes God allows us to suffer, not because he is angry, not in order to cause us to grow into deeper Christlikeness, but only as a means of giving himself to us more deeply. He is, in fact, about the business of saving our souls and fitting us for eternity in so doing, for a relationship with God in which God is loved for his own sake and not as a means to some other end is the only kind of relationship that will save us. After all, every secondary blessing will be lost in death, and our worship in the eschaton will be a worship of God when he is 'all in all' (1 Cor. 15:28). The book of Job also teaches us that God's requirements of his saints when undergoing a kind of Joblike suffering are surprisingly minimal: like Job, all we have to do is hold on to our relationship with God and not 'curse' him. Like Job, we will doubtless say foolish things about God of which we are later deeply ashamed; but although God does confront these criticisms, he does so in an extraordinarily gentle way. God's standard is not perfect performance in pain but faithfulness.

So far as I am aware, the book of Job is the only place in the canon where 'useless' suffering that issues only in a new vision of God is explored. But times of Joblike suffering (suffering that is both extreme and inexplicable) are so common that this is a deeply valuable exploration. Note further that if the book of Job could be categorized more neatly as a theodicy, it would fail to be helpful in this way, for the quality of suffering it addresses is one that makes no sense and seems to produce no tangible benefits. Although it does not necessarily lessen the sharpness of the pain itself, knowing that God's heart has not changed towards you and that there is no mysterious lesson you are supposed to learn is no small comfort. It also prevents those horrible conversations in which well-intended Christians essentially blame their friends for their suffering. Even more comforting is the book's assurance that, even if you do not see a whirlwind (38:1), God is able to draw near as no-one else can in order to console you with his own person, so that you are completely at peace and can bless his name whether he takes or gives (1:21), without depending on a change in your circumstances. As stated already, the book of Job is about the all-surpassing worth of knowing God (Phil. 3:8). Job was, after all, vindicated for persevering in his relationship with God, despite what it cost him; Job is not a loser by the end of the book. (The only loser is the Accuser!) Nor are those who suffer like him and endure (imperfectly but genuinely) as he did. This is perhaps the biggest flaw of the sceptical interpretations of Job surveyed in this book: their criticisms of God gain traction only to the extent that they value earthly and secondary blessings above God and the knowledge of him.[56]

A second unique contribution of the book of Job to the problem of evil has to do with God's joy in his speeches. It was mentioned above how the proportions of God's second speech seem to be skewed: whereas every other poetic description in the Old Testament of God's warfare with chaos focuses solely on the defeat of the fleeing serpent, Job 41 hints at that defeat while focusing more on the creature's dangerous prowess and sinister habitat, and does so in a surprisingly positive way (41:12). While recognizing the difficulty of detecting tone in written texts (especially ancient ones), I cannot help but hear the description of Leviathan as happy, and even cheerful: 'What teeth! What scales! The glittering eyes, the fiery breath! Not a single weapon could even touch him!' Were any human to speak in this way of the evil Leviathan symbolizes, it would be inexcusably flippant and glib; but the very length of the description assures us that God sees clearly and in detail the evil at loose in his creation that would utterly overwhelm us. After hearing God's joy in that terrifying monster that we could not even touch, much less contain, it is impossible to see God or his world in quite the same way (remember how vv. 10–11 explicitly make this connection). If the one person who most clearly sees what is wrong with the world is simultaneously the happiest that the world should continue before it is made new, those in the service of this God can surely do the same.

This is the sort of thing easier to write about than to do. It must, however, be possible to look squarely at the brokenness of the world – human trafficking and cancer and labour camps and parents burying their children and sexual abuse – without at all diminishing in the slightest the horror of these evils, and nevertheless rejoice in God's creation along with its creator. In fact, the momentum of the poetry of

---

[56] As Eleonore Stump writes, commentators who insist that 'no effect on Job could justify what God allows Job to suffer' assume 'a scale of values for a human life' that should be questioned (2013: 218).

Job 41 suggests that clarity about the world's evil and awestruck worship of God go hand in hand: we will gain an ever humbler and more hushed reverence for God only as we see Leviathan more clearly. Paradoxically, it is only as we look without flinching at the monster thrashing about in the waters that we are able to say, 'Who then is he who can stand before [God]?' (v. 10). Perhaps only then can we fully appreciate him as the mighty saviour and defender and friend he really is. I know of no other book in the canon that engages with us in quite this way.

6

Summary and conclusion

This book has explored what contribution the book of Job makes to biblical theodicies and how it speaks to the problem of evil. A central burden has been (1) to understand correctly YHWH's speeches to Job in such a way that helps us move past the generalities given in some scholarly works, as if Job is reminded only of divine power and wisdom, and (2) to answer sceptical interpretations that see Job as an 'anti-theodicy' that demonstrates God's injustice. The key juncture in the argument has been the status of Behemoth and Leviathan as symbols of cosmic chaos and supernatural evil. We have considered at length the implied defeat of these monsters (40:19; 41:8) and the joy with which God speaks of them. At the same time, I have argued that the book of Job qualifies as a theodicy in only a very limited sense. The way in which the reader learns the larger purpose of God in allowing unbearable and inexplicable pain in Job's life in chapters 1–2 does count as a theodicy in the sense of an explanation for evil in God's world. Job, however, never receives this explanation, and the readers receive it only in relation to Job, not themselves. Although readers leave the book wiser about interpreting suffering that may seem to blacken God's character when God's deeper intent is that we will be sealed in a saving relationship with him, the kind of suffering the book of Job explores is one in which no direct explanation is given to the sufferer.

Even while arguing against the book of Job as a successful theodicy in the strict sense of the term, however, I have been at pains to articulate the ways in which the book nourishes cheerful and faithful obedience in the midst of suffering. The unique way in which 'useless' suffering is presented in the book as one dimension of God's relationship with his people has occupied us at length. This suffering is 'useless' in the sense that it is not explicable according to any normal category, such as punishment for sin or as a stimulus for spiritual growth, but terminates only in a deeper vision of God. The word 'useless' has been kept in quotes because, although it describes how, in one sense, nothing seems to come of these Joblike experiences, in another sense these times are very much not useless, because they seal us in the only kind of relationship with God that can save us – a relationship in which he is loved and worshipped purely for his own sake, irrespective of what external benefits we gain or lose because of our loyalty to him. The joy of God in his description of Leviathan is also very striking, and, so far as I can tell, unique in the canon. Confusing as it can be to read of God's apparent happiness in describing a dangerous monster, we have seen how God's joy in Leviathan reveals something profound about God himself. If God can rejoice in his world even when Leviathan is still loose, then it must be possible for those who trust in God to be utterly realistic about the sufferings of this present age and utterly joyful in the lives God has given us before the resurrection.

I have also tried to highlight the graciousness of God in the book of Job. God's initial question to Job in 38:2 is an extraordinarily gentle way to confront a man who has accused God of such terrible crimes, as if the Almighty were saying, 'Did you really know what you were talking about when you said all those things about me, Job?' His vindication of Job's speech about himself in contrast to that of the friends in 42:7 is similarly gracious. While not validating every claim Job has made, it shows that God takes Job's agonized cries in the best sense possible, and that he values highly someone holding on to a relationship with God even when many foolish things are said. Even God's statement to the Accuser in 2:3, difficult as it is to interpret, can be taken as a gracious defence of Job. Job is utterly unworthy of the accusations brought against him, and God is the first to say so. The consistent portrayal of God in the book of Job is completely different from Job's darkest fears about him, or the friends' reductive certainties.

But these reflections take on greater traction when reading the book with an eye to the New Testament. God allowed Job to suffer terribly – but allowed his Son to suffer even more terribly, and in a similar way, such that Job's agonies clearly prefigure those of that later Israelite who would innocently suffer the wrath of God to rebut the accusations of the devil. Where Job only *thought* he was under God's undeserved wrath, Jesus suffered that wrath to the fullest extent, without in any way deserving it. This means that God never allows one of his children to go through a Joblike ordeal without knowing, in the most intimate way possible, exactly what he is inflicting on his son or daughter. Furthermore, if it is moving to read of God's joy in creation together with his clear-sighted view of what is wrong with it, it is even more moving when we consider how much it cost God to redeem his creation. If God can still look on his sinful world with joy, knowing it will cost the death of his precious Son to redeem it – what then? What lives of courage and faith are appropriate for us, who take refuge in and trust such a God, knowing our smaller losses are swallowed up in his greater sacrifice, and his greater joy?

Bibliography

Albrektson, B. (1967), *History and the Gods: An Essay on the Idea of Historical Events as Divine Manifestations in the Ancient Near East and in Israel*, ConBNT 1, Lund: CWK Gleerup.

Alden, R. (1993), *Job*, NAC 11, Nashville: B&H.

Alter, R. (2011), *The Art of Biblical Poetry*, New York: Basic.

Andersen, F. (1976), *Job: An Introduction and Commentary*, TOTC, Leicester: Inter-Varsity Press; Downers Grove: InterVarsity Press.

Andersen, R. (2015), 'The Elihu Speeches: Their Place and Sense in the Book of Job', *TynBul* 66: 75–94.

Anderson, B. (1994), 'The Slaying of the Fleeing, Twisting Serpent: Isaiah 27:1 in Context', in L. Hopfe (ed.), *Uncovering Ancient Stones*, Winona Lake: Eisenbrauns, 3–15.

Angel, A. (2014), *Playing with Dragons: Living with Suffering and God*, Eugene: Cascade.

Ash, C. (2014), *Job: The Wisdom of the Cross*, Preaching the Word, Wheaton: Crossway.

Atkinson, D. (1991), *The Message of Job*, Leicester: Inter-Varsity Press; Downers Grove: InterVarsity Press.

Baldwin, S. (2018), 'Miserable but Not Monochrome: The Distinctive Characteristics and Perspectives of Job's Three Comforters', *Them* 43: 359–375.

Balentine, S. (1998), '"What Are Human Beings, That You Make So Much of Them?" Divine Disclosure from the Whirlwind: "Look at Behemoth"', in T. Linafelt and T. K. Beal (eds.), *God in the Fray: A Tribute to Walter Brueggemann*, Minneapolis: Fortress, 259–278.

—— (2002), 'My Servant Job Shall Pray for You', *ThTo* 58: 502–518.

—— (2006), *Job*, SHBC, Macon: Smyth & Helwys.

Bartholomew, C. (2014), *When You Want to Yell at God*, Bellingham: Lexham.

Batto, B. (1992), *Slaying the Dragon*, Louisville: Westminster.

—— (1999), 'Behemoth', in K. van der Toorn, B. Becking and P. van der Horst (eds.), *Dictionary of Deities and Demons in the Bible*, 2nd edn, Leiden: Brill, 165–169.

Belcher, R. (2017), *Job: The Mystery of Suffering and God's Sovereignty*, Focus on the Bible, Fearn: Christian Focus.

Brenner, A. (1981), 'God's Answer to Job', *VT* 31: 129–137.

Brown, W. (2014), *Wisdom's Wonder: Character, Creation, and Crisis in the Bible's Wisdom Literature*, Grand Rapids: Eerdmans.

Brueggemann, W. (1997), *Theology of the Old Testament: Testimony, Dispute, Advocacy*, Minneapolis: Fortress.

Burrell, D. (2008), *Deconstructing Theodicy: Why Job Has Nothing to Say to the Puzzle of Suffering*, Grand Rapids: Brazos.

Caquot, A. (1992), 'Le Léviathan de Job 40:25–41:26', *RB* 99: 40–69.

Carpenter, E., and M. Grisanti (1997), '*rš*'', in *NIDOTTE* 3: 1201–1204.

Carson, D. A. (1992), 'Mystery and Faith in Job 38:1–42:16', in Roy Zuck (ed.), *Sitting with Job: Selected Studies in the Book of Job*, Grand Rapids: Baker Book House, 373–380.

Clines, D. J. A. (1989), *Job 1–20*, WBC 17, Nashville: Thomas Nelson.

—— (1998), 'Quarter Days Gone: Job 24 and the Absence of God', in T. Linafelt and T. K. Beal (eds.), *God in the Fray: A Tribute to Walter Brueggemann*, Minneapolis: Fortress, 242–258.

—— (2004), 'Job's Fifth Friend: An Ethical Critique of the Book of Job', *BibInt* 12: 232–250.

—— (2006), *Job 21–37*, WBC 18A, Waco: Word.

—— (2011), *Job 38–42*, WBC 18B, Nashville: Thomas Nelson.

Cohen, M. (1996), *Miqra'ot Gedolot: HaKeter: Isaiah*, Jerusalem: Keter.

Cook, S. L., C. L. Patton and J. W. Watts (eds.) (2001), *The Whirlwind: Essays on Job, Hermeneutics and Theology in Memory of Jane Morse*, JSOTSup 336, Sheffield: Sheffield Academic Press.

Cornelius, I. (1990), 'The Sun Epiphany in Job 38:12–15', *JNSL* 16: 25–43.

Crenshaw, J. (1993), 'The Concept of God in OT Wisdom', in L. G. Perdue, B. B. Scott and W. J. Wiseman (eds.), *In Search of Wisdom: Essays in Memory of John G. Gammie*, Louisville: Westminster John Knox, 1–18.

—— (1995), *Urgent Advice and Probing Questions: Collected Writings on Old Testament Wisdom*, Macon: Mercer University Press.

—— (1998), *Old Testament Wisdom: An Introduction*, Louisville: Westminster John Knox.

—— (2005), *Defending God: Biblical Responses to the Problem of Evil*, Oxford: Oxford University Press.

—— (2011), *Reading Job: A Literary and Theological Commentary*, Macon: Smyth & Helwys.

Csapo, E. (2005), *Theories of Mythology*, Oxford: Blackwell.

Curtis, J. (1979), 'On Job's Response to Yahweh', *JBL* 98: 497–511.

Day, J. (1985), *God's Conflict with the Dragon and the Sea*, Cambridge: Cambridge University Press.

Delitzsch, F. (1949), *Biblical Commentary on the Book of Job*, tr. F. Bolton, Grand Rapids: Eerdmans.

Dell, K. (1991), *The Book of Job as Skeptical Literature*, BZAW 197, Berlin: de Gruyter.

Dempster, S. (2005), 'Review of *The Book of Job: The Contest of Moral Imaginations*', *PRSt* 32: 349–351.

Dhorme, E. (1984), *A Commentary on the Book of Job*, tr. H. Knight, Nashville: Thomas Nelson.

Dick, M. (1992), 'The Legal Metaphor in Job 31', in R. Zuck (ed.), *Sitting with Job: Selected Studies in the Book of Job*, Grand Rapids: Baker Book House, 321–334.

—— (2006), 'The Neo-Assyrian Royal Lion Hunt and Yahweh's Answer to Job', *JBL* 125: 243–270.

Dietrich, M., O. Loretz and J. Sanmartin (2013), *The Cuneiform Alphabetic Texts from Ugarit, Ras Ibn Hani and Other Places*, ALASPM 8, Münster: Ugarit-Verlag.

Doty, W. (1986), *Mythography: The Study of Myths and Rituals*, Alabama: University of Alabama Press.

Dumbrell, W. (2000), 'The Purpose of the Book of Job', in J. I. Packer and S. K. Soderlund (eds.), *The Way of Wisdom: Essays in Honor of Bruce K. Waltke*, Grand Rapids: Zondervan, 91–105.

Emerton, J. (1982), 'Leviathan and *ltn*: The Vocalization of the Ugaritic Word for the Dragon', *VT* 32: 327–331.

Estes, D. (2005), *Handbook on the Wisdom Books and Psalms*, Grand Rapids: Baker Academic.

Fishbane, M. (1971), 'Jeremiah IV 23–26 and Job III 3–13: A Recovered Use of the Creation Pattern', *VT* 21: 151–167.

—— (2003), *Biblical Myth and Rabbinic Mythmaking*, Oxford: Oxford University Press.

Forsyth, N. (1987), *The Old Enemy: Satan and the Combat Myth*, Princeton: Princeton University Press.

Fox, M. (1981), 'Job 38 and God's Rhetoric', *Semeia* 18: 53–61.

—— (1999), *A Time to Tear Down and a Time to Build Up: A Rereading of Ecclesiastes*, Grand Rapids: Eerdmans.

—— (2000), *Proverbs 1–9*, AB 18a, New Haven: Yale University Press.

—— (2005), 'Job the Pious', *ZAW* 117: 351–366.

—— (2009), *Proverbs 10–31*, AB 18b, New Haven: Yale University Press.

—— (2012), 'Behemoth and Leviathan', *Bib* 93: 261–267.

—— (2013), 'God's Answer and Job's Response', *Bib* 94: 1–23.

—— (2018), 'The Meanings of the Book of Job', *JBL* 137: 7–18.

Fyall, R. (2002), *Now My Eyes Have Seen You: Images of Creation and Evil in the Book of Job*, NSBT 12, Leicester: Apollos; Downers Grove: InterVarsity Press.

Gammie, J. (1978), 'Behemoth and Leviathan: On the Didactic and Theological Significance of Job 40:25–26', in J. Gammie, W. Brueggemann, W. L. Humphreys and J. M. Ward (eds.), *Israelite Wisdom*, Missoula: Scholars Press, 217–231.

George, A. (1999), *The Epic of Gilgamesh*, London: Penguin.

Gibson, D. (2016), *Destiny: Learning to Live by Preparing to Die*, London: Inter-Varsity Press.

Gibson, J. C. L. (1978), *Canaanite Myths and Legends*, Edinburgh: T&T Clark.

—— (1988), 'On Evil in the Book of Job', in L. Eslingler (ed.), *Ascribe to the Lord: Biblical and Other Studies in Memory of Peter C. Craigie*, JSOTSup 67, Sheffield, JSOT Press, 399–419.

—— (1992), 'A New Look at Job 41.1–4 (English 41.9–12)', in R. Carroll (ed.), *Text as Pretext: Essays in Honour of Robert Davidson*, JSOTSup 138, Sheffield: Sheffield Academic Press, 129–139.

Glatzner, N. (ed.) (1969), *The Dimensions of Job: A Study and Selected Readings*, New York: Schocken.

Glazov, G. (2002), 'The Significance of the "Hand on the Mouth" Gesture in Job XL 4', *VT* 52: 30–41.

Goldingay, J. (2007), *Psalms 51–100*, BCOTWP, Grand Rapids: Baker Academic.

Good, E. (1990), *In Turns of Tempest: A Reading of Job*, Stanford: Stanford University Press.

Gordis, R. (1965), *The Book of God and Man: A Study of Job*, Chicago: University of Chicago Press.

—— (1978), *The Book of Job: Commentary, New Translation and Special Studies*, New York: Jewish Theological Seminary of America.

Gowan, D. (1986), 'God's Answer to Job: How Is It an Answer?', *HBT* 8: 85–102.

Greenstein, E. (1999), 'In Job's Face/Facing Job', in F. Black, R. Boer and E. Runions (eds.), *The Labour of Reading: Desire, Alienation, and Biblical Interpretation*, Atlanta: Society of Biblical Literature, 301–317.

—— (2009), 'The Problem of Evil in the Book of Job', in N. Fox, D. Glatt-Gilad and M. Williams (eds.), *Mishneh Todah: Studies in Deuteronomy and Its Cultural Environment in Honor of Jeffrey H. Tigay*, Winona Lake: Eisenbrauns, 333–362.

Habel, N. (1985), *The Book of Job*, OTL, Philadelphia: Westminster.

—— (1992), 'In Defense of God the Sage', in L. Perdue (ed.), *The Voice from the Whirlwind: Interpreting the Book of Job*, Nashville: Abingdon, 21–38.

Ham, T. C. (2013), 'The Gentle Voice of God in Job 38', *JBL* 132: 527–541.

Hart, G. (1988), *Dictionary of Ancient Egyptian Gods and Goddesses*, London: Routledge.

Hartley, J. (1988), *The Book of Job*, NICOT, Grand Rapids: Eerdmans.

—— (1997), 'Job, Theology of', in *NIDOTTE* 4: 780–796.

Hossfeld, F.-L., and E. Zenger (2005), *Psalms 2: A Commentary on Psalms 51–100*, Hermeneia, tr. L. Maloney, Minneapolis: Fortress.

Jacobsen, T. (1968), 'The Battle between Marduk and Tiamat', *JAOS* 1: 104–108.

Janzen, J. G. (1986), *Job*, Interpretation, Louisville: Westminster John Knox.

—— (2009), *At the Scent of Water: The Ground of Hope in the Book of Job*, Grand Rapids: Eerdmans.

Johnston, P. (2002), *Shades of Sheol: Death and Afterlife in the Old Testament*, Leicester: Apollos; Downers Grove: InterVarsity Press.

Kang, C.-G. (2017), *Behemot und Leviathan: Studien zur Komposition und Theologie von Hiob 38,1–42,6*, WMANT 149, Göttingen: Vandenhoeck & Ruprecht.

Keel, O. (1978a), *Jahwes Entgegnung an Ijob*, Göttingen: Vandenhoeck & Ruprecht.

—— (1978b), *The Symbolism of the Biblical World*, tr. T. Hallet, New York: Seabury.

Kidner, D. (1985), *The Wisdom of Proverbs, Job, and Ecclesiastes: An Introduction to Wisdom Literature*, Downers Grove: InterVarsity Press.

Kitchen, K. A. (2003), *On the Reliability of the Old Testament*, Grand Rapids: Eerdmans.

Krüger, T. (2007), 'Did Job Repent?', in T. Krüger (ed.), *Das Buch Hiob und seine Interpretationen: Beiträge zum Hiob-Symposium auf dem Monte Verità vom 14.–19. August 2005*, ATANT 88, Zürich: Theologischer Verlag Zürich, 217–229.

Laato, A., and J. C. de Moor (eds.) (2003), *Theodicy in the World of the Bible*, Leiden: Brill.

Lévêque, J. (1994), 'L'Interprétation des discours de YHWH (Job 38, 1–42,6)', in W. A. M. van Beuken (ed.), *The Book of Job*, BETL 114, Leuven: Peeters, 203–222.

Lewis, C. S. (1946), *George MacDonald: An Anthology*, London: Geoffrey Bles.

—— (1972), *God in the Dock: Essays in Theology and Ethics*, Grand Rapids: Eerdmans.

—— (1976), *A Grief Observed*, New York: Bantam.

Lloyd, A. (ed.) (2014), *Gods, Priests, and Men: Studies in the Religion of Pharaonic Egypt by Aylward M. Blackman*, Studies in Egyptology, London: Routledge.

Longman, T. (2016), *Job*, BCOTWP, Grand Rapids: Baker Academic.

López, R. (2016), 'The Meaning of "Behemoth" and "Leviathan" in Job', *BSac* 173: 401–424.

Luc, A. (2000), 'Storm and the Message of Job', *JSOT* 87: 111–123.

Luckenbill, D. (1968), *Ancient Records of Assyria and Babylonia*, New York: Greenwood.

Mabie, F. (2008), 'Chaos and Death', in *DOTWPW*, 41–54.

McCann, J. C. (1997), 'Wisdom's Dilemma: The Book of Job, the Final Form of the Book of Psalms, and the Entire Bible', in M. Barré (ed.), *Wisdom, You Are My Sister*, Washington, D.C.: Catholic Biblical Association, 18–30.

Bibliography

McKenna, D. (1992), 'God's Revelation and Job's Repentance', in
R. Zuck (ed.), *Sitting with Job: Selected Studies in the Book of Job*,
Grand Rapids: Baker Book House, 381–410.

Merton, T. (1983), *No Man Is an Island*, San Diego: Harvest.

Mettinger, T. N. D. (1992), 'The God of Job: Avenger, Tyrant, or Victor?',
in L. Perdue (ed.), *The Voice from the Whirlwind: Interpreting the
Book of Job*, Nashville: Abingdon, 39–49.

—— (2005), *In Search of God: The Meaning and Message of the
Everlasting Names*, Minneapolis: Augsburg Fortress.

Miller, P. (2000), 'Cosmology and World Order in the Old Testament:
The Divine Council as Cosmic-Political Symbol', in P. Miller (ed.),
Israelite Religion and Biblical Theology, JSOTSup 267, Sheffield:
Sheffield Academic Press, 422–444.

Moore, R. (1983), 'The Integrity of Job', *CBQ* 45: 17–31.

Morenz, S. (1992), *Egyptian Religion*, tr. A. Keep, Ithaca: Cornell
University Press.

Morrow, W. (1986), 'Consolation, Rejection, and Repentance in Job
42:6', *JBL* 105: 211–225.

Murphy, R. (1996), *The Tree of Life: An Exploration of Biblical Wisdom
Literature*, Grand Rapids: Eerdmans.

Nam, D.-W. (2003), *Talking About God: Job 42: 7–9 and the Nature
of God in the Book of Job*, SBL, New York: Peter Lang.

Naselli, A. (2012), *From Typology to Doxology: Paul's Use of Isaiah and
Job in Romans 11:34–35*, Eugene: Wipf & Stock.

Newell, L. B. (1984), 'Job: Repentant or Rebellious?', *WTJ* 46.2: 298–316.

Newsom, C. (1996), 'Job', in L. Keck (ed.), *NIB* 4: 317–637.

—— (2003), *The Book of Job: The Contest of Moral Imaginations*,
New York: Oxford University Press.

Niehaus, J. (1995), *God at Sinai: Covenant and Theophany in the Bible
and the Ancient Near East*, SOTBT, Grand Rapids: Zondervan.

O'Connor, K. (2003), 'Wild Raging Creativity: The Scene in the
Whirlwind (Job 38–41)', in B. Strawn and N. Bowen (eds.), *A God
So Near: Essays on Old Testament Theology in Honor of Patrick
D. Miller*, Winona Lake: Eisenbrauns, 171–179.

Ollenberger, B. (1987), 'Isaiah's Creation Theology', *ExAud* 3: 54–71.

Ortlund, E. (2010), *Theophany and* Chaoskampf: *The Interpretation of
Theophanic Imagery in the Baal Epic, Isaiah, and the Twelve*, GUS 5,
Piscataway: Gorgias.

—— (2013), 'The Identity of Leviathan and the Meaning of the Book of Job', *TJ* 34: 17–30.

—— (2018), 'How Did Job Speak Rightly about God?' *Them* 43: 350–358.

Parsons, G. (1992), 'Literary Features of the Book of Job', in R. Zuck (ed.), *Sitting with Job: Selected Studies in the Book of Job*, Grand Rapids: Baker Book House, 35–50.

Patton, C. L. (2001), 'The Beauty of the Beast: Leviathan and Behemoth in Light of Catholic Theology', in S. L. Cook, C. L. Patton and J. W. Watts (eds.), *The Whirlwind: Essays on Job, Hermeneutics and Theology in Memory of Jane Morse*, JSOTSup 336, Sheffield: Sheffield Academic Press, 142–167.

Paul, M. (1997), 'Leviathan', in *NIDOTTE* 2: 778–780.

Perdue, L. (1991), *Wisdom in Revolt: Metaphorical Theology in the Book of Job*, JSOTSup 29, Sheffield: Almond.

Polzin, R. (1977), *Biblical Structuralism: Method and Subjectivity in the Study of Ancient Texts*, Minneapolis: Fortress.

Pope, M. (1973), *Job*, AB 15, New York: Doubleday.

Rendtorff, R. (1986), *The Old Testament: An Introduction*, tr. John Bowden, Minneapolis: Fortress.

Rowley, H. H. (1983), *The Book of Job*, NCB, Grand Rapids: Eerdmans.

Rowold, H. (1986), 'Leviathan and Job in Job 41.2–3', *JBL* 105: 104–109.

Ruprecht, E. (1971), 'Das Nilpferd im Hiobbuch', *VT* 21: 209–231.

Rutherford, S. (1818), *Three Hundred and Fifty-Two Religious Letters*, Glasgow: Thomas Lochhead.

Scholnick, S. (1982), 'The Meaning of Mishpat in the Book of Job', *JBL* 101: 521–529.

Seitz, C. (1989), 'Job: Full-Structure, Movement, and Interpretation', *Int* 43: 5–17.

Seow, C.-L. (1997), *Ecclesiastes*, AB 18c, New Haven: Yale University Press.

—— (2011), 'Elihu's Revelation', *ThTo* 68: 253–271.

—— (2013), *Job 1–21: Interpretation and Commentary*, Illuminations, Grand Rapids: Eerdmans.

Shields, M. (2010), 'Malevolent or Mysterious? God's Character in the Prologue of Job', *TynBul* 61: 255–270.

Stump, E. (2013), *Wandering in Darkness: Narrative and the Problem of Suffering*, Oxford: Oxford University Press.

Sutherland, R. (2004), *Putting God on Trial: The Biblical Book of Job*, Victoria, B.C.: Trafford.

Terrien, S. (2005), *Job*, CAT, Geneva: Labor et Fides.

Timmer, D. (2009a), 'Character Formed in the Crucible: Job's Relationship with God and Joban Character Ethics', *JTI* 3: 1–16.

—— (2009b), 'God's Speeches, Job's Responses, and the Problem of Coherence in the Book of Job: Sapiential Pedagogy Revisited', *CBQ* 71: 286–305.

Tsevat, M. (1980), 'The Meaning of the Book of Job', in *The Meaning of the Book of Job and Other Biblical Studies*, New York: Ktav, 1–39.

Uehlinger, C. (1995), 'Leviathan', in K. van der Toorn, B. Becking and P. W. van der Horst (eds.), *Dictionary of Deities and Demons in the Bible*, 2nd edn, Leiden: Brill, 511–515.

Viberg, A. (2000), 'Job', in *NDBT*, 200–203.

Waltke, B. (2004), *The Book of Proverbs: Chapters 1–15*, NICOT, Grand Rapids: Eerdmans.

—— (2005), *The Book of Proverbs: Chapters 15–31*, NICOT, Grand Rapids: Eerdmans.

—— (2007), *An Old Testament Theology: An Exegetical, Canonical, and Thematic Approach*, Grand Rapids: Zondervan.

Walton, J. (2008), 'Job 1: Book of', in *DOTWPW*, 333–346.

—— (2009), *The Lost World of Genesis 1*, Downers Grove: InterVarsity Press.

—— (2012), *Job*, NIVAC, Grand Rapids: Eerdmans.

Watson, R. (2005), *Chaos Uncreated: A Reassessment of the Theme of 'Chaos' in the Hebrew Bible*, BZAW 341, Berlin: de Gruyter.

Westermann, C. (1981), *The Structure of the Book of Job: A Form-Critical Analysis*, Minneapolis: Augsburg.

Wharton, J. (1999), *Job*, Westminster Bible Companion, Louisville: Westminster John Knox.

Whybray, R. (1998), *Job*, Sheffield: Sheffield Academic Press.

Williams, J. (1992), 'The Theophany of Job', in R. Zuck (ed.), *Sitting with Job: Selected Studies in the Book of Job*, Grand Rapids: Baker Book House, 359–372.

Williamson, P. (2017), *Death and the Afterlife: Biblical Perspectives on Ultimate Questions*, NSBT 44, London: Apollos; Downers Grove: InterVarsity Press.

Wilson, G. (2007), *Job*, NABC, Carlisle: Paternoster.

Wilson, K. (1975), 'Return to the Problems of Behemoth and Leviathan', *VT* 25: 1–14.

Wilson, L. (2015), *Job*, THC, Grand Rapids: Eerdmans.

Wolfers, D. (1990), 'The Lord's Second Speech in the Book of Job', *VT* 40: 474–499.

—— (1995), *Deep Things Out of Darkness: The Book of Job, Essays and a New English Translation*, Grand Rapids: Eerdmans.

Young, E. (1969), *The Book of Isaiah*, NICOT, Grand Rapids: Eerdmans.

Index of authors

Index of authors

Index of Scripture references

Titles in this series:

An index of Scripture references for all the volumes may be found at
http://www.thegospelcoalition.org/resources/nsbt.